Cracking the IT Architect Interview

The ultimate guide to successful interviews for Enterprise, Business, Domain, Solution, and Technical Architect roles as well as IT Advisory Consultant and Software Designer roles

Sameer Paradkar

BIRMINGHAM - MUMBAI

Cracking the IT Architect Interview

First published: November 2016

Production reference: 1251116

Published by Packt Publishing Ltd.
Livery Place
35 Livery Street
Birmingham
B3 2PB, UK.
ISBN 978-1-78712-169-0

www.packtpub.com

Credits

Author
Sameer Paradkar

Reviewer
James D Miller

Commissioning Editor
Veena Pagare

Acquisition Editor
Lester Frias

Content Development Editor
Amrita Noronha

Technical Editor
Deepti Tuscano

Copy Editor
Safis Editing

Project Coordinator
Shweta H Birwatkar

Proofreader
Safis Editing

Indexer
Aishwarya Gangawane

Graphics
Disha Haria

Production Coordinator
Nilesh Mohite

About the Author

Sameer Paradkar is an enterprise architect with 15+ years of solid experience in the ICT industry which spans across consulting, systems integration, and product development. He is an Open Group TOGAF, Oracle Master Java EA, TMForum NGOSS, IBM SOA Solutions, IBM Cloud Solutions, IBM MobileFirst, ITIL Foundation V3 and COBIT 5 certified enterprise architect. He serves as an advisory architect on enterprise architecture programs and continues to work as a subject matter expert. He has worked on multiple architecture transformations and modernization engagements in the USA, UK, Europe, Asia Pacific and the Middle East Regions that presented a phased roadmap to the transformation that maximized the business value while minimizing risks and costs.

Sameer is part of IT Strategy and Transformation Practice in AtoS. Prior to AtoS, he has worked in organizations such as EY - IT Advisory, IBM GBS, Wipro Consulting Services, TechMahindra, and Infosys Technologies and specializes in IT strategies and enterprise transformation engagements.

I would like to dedicate this book to my wife, family members and friends for their encouragement, support and love.

Many people throughout my career have directly and indirectly contributed to this book. I would like to take this opportunity to acknowledge their contribution, influence, and inspiration. I believe I am lucky to have found opportunities to work with extremely talented and exceptions individuals who extended their wholehearted support throughout my career. My eternal thanks to them for believing in me and providing exciting opportunities. I would like to thank my team members, chief and lead architects, mentors, discussion partners, reviewers, and supporters, whose valuable comments and feedback have significantly contributed to this book. I look forward to your comments and valuable inputs on an on-going basis. I would like to recognize and thank my current and former colleagues who made my corporate journey exciting, enriching and fulfilling.

About the Reviewer

James D Miller is an IBM certified expert, creative innovator and accomplished director, senior project leader and application/system architect with more than 35 years of extensive applications and system design and development experience across multiple platforms and technologies. Experiences include introducing customers to new and sometimes disruptive technologies and platforms, integrating with IBM Watson Analytics, Cognos BI, TM1 and Web architecture design, systems analysis, GUI design and testing, database modelling and systems analysis, design, and development of OLAP, Client/Server, web and mainframe applications and systems utilizing: IBM Watson Analytics, IBM Cognos BI and TM1 (TM1 rules, TI, TM1Web and planning manager), Cognos Framework Manager, dynaSight - ArcPlan, ASP, DHTML, XML, IIS, MS Visual Basic and VBA, Visual Studio, PERL, SPLUNK, WebSuite, MS SQL Server, ORACLE, SYBASE Server, and so on.

Responsibilities have also included all aspects of Windows and SQL solution development and design including: analysis; GUI (and website) design; data modelling; table, screen/form and script development; SQL (and remote stored procedures and triggers) development/testing; test preparation and management and training of programming staff. Other experience includes development of ETL infrastructure such as data transfer automation between mainframe (DB2, Lawson, Great Plains, and so on.) systems and client/server SQL server and web-based applications and integration of enterprise applications and data sources.

Mr. Miller has acted as Internet Applications Development manager responsible for the design, development, QA and delivery of multiple wesites including online trading applications, warehouse process control and scheduling systems, administrative and control applications. Mr. Miller also was responsible for the design, development and administration of a web-based financial reporting system for a 450 million dollar organization, reporting directly to the CFO and his executive team.

Mr. Miller has also been responsible for managing and directing multiple resources in various management roles including project and team leader, lead developer and applications development director.

Jim has authored *Cognos TM1 Developers Certification Guide, Mastering Splunk, Learning IBM Watson Analytics,* and a number of whitepapers on best practices such as *Establishing a Center of Excellence* and continues to post blogs on a number of relevant topics based upon personal experiences and industry best practices.

Jim is a perpetual learner continuing to pursue experiences and certifications, currently holding the following current technical certifications:

IBM Certified Business Analyst - Cognos TM1

IBM Cognos TM1 Master 385 Certification (perfect score 100% on exam)

IBM Certified Advanced Solution Expert - Cognos TM1

IBM Cognos TM1 10.1 Administrator Certification C2020-703 (perfect score 100% on exam)

IBM OpenPages Developer Fundamentals C2020-001-ENU (98% on exam)

IBM Cognos 10 BI Administrator C2020-622 (98% on exam)

IBM Cognos 10 BI Professional C2020-180

He has the following specialties, the evaluation and introduction of innovative and disruptive technologies, Cloud migration, IBM Watson Analytics, Big Data, Data Visualizations, Cognos BI and TM1 application Design and Development, OLAP, Visual Basic, SQL Server, Forecasting and Planning; International Application Development, Business Intelligence, Project Development & Delivery and process improvement.

I would like to thank Nanette L. Miller: "...who is always on my mind and always in my heart..."

www.PacktPub.com

For support files and downloads related to your book, please visit www.PacktPub.com.

Did you know that Packt offers eBook versions of every book published, with PDF and ePub files available? You can upgrade to the eBook version at www.PacktPub.com and as a print book customer, you are entitled to a discount on the eBook copy. Get in touch with us at service@packtpub.com for more details.

At www.PacktPub.com, you can also read a collection of free technical articles, sign up for a range of free newsletters and receive exclusive discounts and offers on Packt books and eBooks.

https://www.packtpub.com/mapt

Get the most in-demand software skills with Mapt. Mapt gives you full access to all Packt books and video courses, as well as industry-leading tools to help you plan your personal development and advance your career.

Why subscribe?

- Fully searchable across every book published by Packt
- Copy and paste, print, and bookmark content
- On demand and accessible via a web browser

Table of Contents

Preface

An architect typically attends several interviews and discussions for jobs or projects during his or her entire career. There is always a dire need to look up and read multiple books and references before these interviews/discussions so that you stay on top of things. I have had instances of archiving multiple sets of core references just for these interview discussions. I have worked for MNCs and big 4 consulting organizations in the past and have done tons of projects which required me to take up discussions with customers on an ongoing basis. It's not easy to know beforehand which areas should one focus to for the preparations. In terms of the scope, this books gives a clear and concise picture of what to expect in such interviews and how to prepare for this critical juncture in your career.

From an architect's perspective, it is not possible to revise or learn all these key areas without a good reference artifact. The goal of this title is to cover all the core architectural domains. This artifact will assist the solution, domain and enterprise architects to perform well in their interview discussions and to launch a successful career. This book also tackles the NFR domain which is the key aspect to be addressed while architecting applications.

The interviewers will also be able to leverage this book to make sure they hire a candidate with the right competencies depending on the job requirements. This book contains a broad range of topics relating to design and architecture and is written in a concise way supplemented with diagrams and tables.

This book will also assist all solution and enterprise architects to become competent in their respective areas. Usually, it takes years to understand the core concepts, fundamentals, patterns and principles related to architecture and designs but this artifact is a gold mine that typically discussed during an interview. There will always be a need to work on architecture engagements where an architect may have limited or no expertise, but this book tackles all the critical domain to provide the right guidance for architects be in solution architecture or non-functional requirements or SOA. The best way to fast track this is to read relevant domain and proactively practice these on live projects. It has worked for me, and it will work for you as well.

This will be like one of those books you will have to retain in your library so that every time there is a discussion coming up you can quickly spend time reading and revisiting the key sections or domains.

The book also includes a probability indicator for each of the question to indicate the likelihood of this being asked during your discussion. The book has close to 14 domains and around 350+ questions covering these domains. Based on my past experience I can only say that you will have more than 80 % of the topics addressed in this book to be coming up in your next interview discussion.

The book is an honest attempt to share with a practitioner, SMEs and aspirants our experiences, learning, insights and proven methodologies that will benefit them in the long run.

All the best

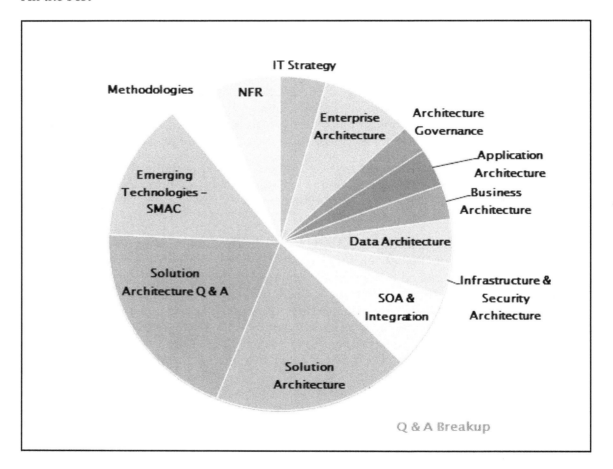

Q & A breakup

Coverage of the book (expertise gained):

- This book is a:
    - Is a reference guide for architecture practitioners to help them on various architecture & strategy engagements
    - Is a reference guide for seasoned and aspiring practitioners to guide them for their interview discussions
    - Is a reference guide for interview panels for selecting architects for their practice/units while bringing in standardization in the selection process.
- More than 350+ questions in 12 domains including a chapter on social, mobile, analytics and cloud (SMAC).
- Covers all architecture domains including EA (business, data, infrastructure and application), SA, integration, NFRs and security and SOA.
- Extended coverage from IT Strategy to NFRs domains.
- The book covers a section on non-functional requirements among other domains.
- Based on our experience the assurance is that as least 80% of contents will be discussed during a typical architect's interview.
- There is a section on advisory domain which is not very easy to find and is generally a product of years of extensive experience.
- The questions have a probability indicator for all questions. Probability indicator depicts the likely hood of the questions or topic coming up in the discussion may be directly or through' reference of the work done based on industry maturity, trends, criticality.
- The book can be selectively read based on the relevant domains

- The coverage is extensive in terms of depth and breadth of a domains addressed in the title
- The title has more than 60+ diagrams depicting various scenarios, models and methodologies.

Key concepts that will be covered in the book are:

- IT strategy and NFR, methodologies, best practices and frameworks
- Best practices architecting, KPI and success factors
- Concepts, principles and guidelines for various domains
- Leadership and architecture governance
- Enterprise architects IT strategy and NFR, methodologies, best practices and frameworks
- Common pitfalls to be avoided and patterns to leverage
- Emerging technologies--social, mobile, analytics and cloud (SMAC)
- Techniques related to analysis, NFRs and solutioning
- SOA and integration
- Techniques, best practices, and patterns for web and enterprise topologies
- Frameworks and methodologies to evangelize web and enterprise applications
- Solution architecture Q&A scenarios
- Techniques, models and case studies
- Tools, best practices, techniques, and processes
- Design guidelines used for architecting applications & systems
- Understand various best practices, principles and patterns
- Get a holistic view of key concepts, design principles, and patterns related to evangelizing web and enterprise applications
- Use the book as a reference guide for adopting best practices, standards and design guidelines
- Concepts, principles, KPI and success factors for various domains

What this book covers

Chapter 1, *Architects Role and Growth Path*, this chapter will describes core architecture skills and competencies, architects role in ICT and consulting industries, architects growth -paths and competency framework.

Chapter 2, *IT Strategy and Advisory*, this chapter covers the Q&A for IT strategy and advisory domain. Meeting customer needs and demands and creating technology adoption roadmaps is the primary goal/objective for IT strategy engagements. By going through the type of questions asked related to vision, strategy and roadmaps of a company, you'll be able to describe the key aspects such as best practices and frameworks, Concepts, principles and guidelines

Chapter 3, *Enterprise Architecture and Modernization*, this chapter covers the Q&A for enterprise architecture and modernization domain. Enterprise architecture is a collection of strategic information that describes business, application, data and infrastructure to operate the business. This also includes mission and goals, business processes, roles, organizational structures, information, applications and systems. The section includes Q&A for the enterprise architecture, application architecture, business architecture, and data architecture, infrastructure and security and architecture governance.

Chapter 4, *SOA and Integration*, this chapter covers the Q&A for SOA and integration domain. SOA is a set of design principles for building a suite of interoperable, flexible and reusable services based architecture. This section include Q&A for SOA key capabilities, SOA ROI, SOA modernization approaches, SOA entry points, ESB, BPEL, BPM, SOA and security, SOA KPIs, OSIMM, top-down and bottom-up approach, SOA patterns.

Chapter 5, *Solution Architecture and Design*, this chapter covers the Q&A for solution architecture and design domain. The Q&A covers the following areas JEE framework, OOAD-UML, session management, distributed DB, replication, performance issues, Spring framework, Hibernate, Agile model, MVC and design patterns

Chapter 6, *Emerging Technology*, this chapter covers the Q&A for emerging technologies which includes big data, cloud, Amazon Web Services (AWS), analytics, social media, and enterprise mobility.

Chapter 7, *Methodologies, Frameworks and NFRs*, this chapter covers the Q&A for frameworks and non functional requirements domain. An architecture framework provides principles and practices for creating and using the architecture description of a system. It structures architects' thinking by dividing the architecture description into domains, layers or views, and offers models--typically metrics and diagrams for documenting each view.

This chapter also covers the solutioning of NFRs providing insights into how they will be addressed in the solutioning phase. This section covers key NFRs that are most critical for any project and for each NFR provides the various alternatives pertaining to the solution, the design principle that needs to be applied to achieve the desired outcome for e.g. high availability or scalability or reliability as covered.

Chapter 8, *Interview Preparations*, this chapter covers interview preparations, competencies and case studies and summary.

Domains/Roles	Interview Panels	IT Strategy Consultants	Technical Architect/Designers	Solution Architect	Domain Architect	Enterprise/Lead Architect	Business Architect
IT Strategy	▓	▓			▓	▓	▓
Enterprise Architecture	▓	▓			▓	▓	▓
Architecture Governance	▓	▓			▓	▓	▓
Application Architecture	▓		▓	▓	▓	▓	
Business Architecture	▓				▓	▓	▓
Data Architecture	▓				▓	▓	▓
Infrastructure & Security Architecture	▓		▓	▓	▓	▓	▓
SOA & Integration	▓		▓	▓		▓	▓
Solution Architecture	▓		▓	▓		▓	
Solution Architecture Scenario Q & A	▓		▓	▓		▓	
Emerging Technologies – SMAC	▓		▓	▓	▓	▓	▓
Methodologies & Frameworks	▓		▓	▓	▓	▓	▓
NFR	▓		▓	▓		▓	▓

Competency Heat-map

Who this book is for

The primary audiences for this title are the gamut of roles starting from IT consultant to chief architect who are responsible to lead and deliver strategic, tactical and operational engagements for fortune 100 customers worldwide. This title is for SMEs with background and competencies in IT advisory, designing and architecture and would like to gain advance and next level skills. The audiences for this book include:

- Chief and lead architects
- Enterprise architects
- Business architects
- IT strategy and advisory consultants

- Domains architects (infrastructure, data, application, business and security)
- Solution architects
- Technical architects/designers
- Students--IT and computer science streams
- Interview panels

 Warnings or important notes appear in a box like this.

 Tips and tricks appear like this.

Reader feedback

Feedback from our readers is always welcome. Let us know what you think about this book-what you liked or disliked. Reader feedback is important for us as it helps us develop titles that you will really get the most out of. To send us general feedback, simply e-mail feedback@packtpub.com, and mention the book's title in the subject of your message. If there is a topic that you have expertise in and you are interested in either writing or contributing to a book, see our author guide at www.packtpub.com/authors.

Customer support

Now that you are the proud owner of a Packt book, we have a number of things to help you to get the most from your purchase.

Downloading the color images of this book

We also provide you with a PDF file that has color images of the screenshots/diagrams used in this book. The color images will help you better understand the changes in the output. You can download this file from https://www.packtpub.com/sites/default/files/downloads/CrackingtheITArchitectInterview.pdf.

Errata

Although we have taken every care to ensure the accuracy of our content, mistakes do happen. If you find a mistake in one of our books-maybe a mistake in the text or the code-we would be grateful if you could report this to us. By doing so, you can save other readers from frustration and help us improve subsequent versions of this book. If you find any errata, please report them by visiting http://www.packtpub.com/submit-errata, selecting your book, clicking on the **Errata Submission Form** link, and entering the details of your errata. Once your errata are verified, your submission will be accepted and the errata will be uploaded to our website or added to any list of existing errata under the Errata section of that title.

To view the previously submitted errata, go to https://www.packtpub.com/books/content/support and enter the name of the book in the search field. The required information will appear under the **Errata** section.

Piracy

Piracy of copyrighted material on the Internet is an ongoing problem across all media. At Packt, we take the protection of our copyright and licenses very seriously. If you come across any illegal copies of our works in any form on the Internet, please provide us with the location address or website name immediately so that we can pursue a remedy.

Please contact us at copyright@packtpub.com with a link to the suspected pirated material.

We appreciate your help in protecting our authors and our ability to bring you valuable content.

Questions

If you have a problem with any aspect of this book, you can contact us at questions@packtpub.com, and we will do our best to address the problem.

1
Architect Roles and Growth Paths

A good architect is one who leads by example, and without a good understanding of the technology stack and business domain, an architect is not equipped to deliver the pre-requisite outcomes for the enterprise. The team members typically have deep-dive expertise in the specific technology areas but will lack confidence in the architect if he is not competent with in the domain or technology.

The architect is the bridge between the technology and the business team, and hence he/she must understand all aspects of the technology stack to be able to liaise with the business team. The architect must be conversant in the business domain in order to drive the team and all the stakeholders toward a common organizational goal. An architect might not be busy all the time, but he/she leverages decades of expertise to solve and monitor the organizational IT landscape, making quick decisions during various stages of the SDLC. The project manager handles the people management aspects, freeing the architect of the hassles of operational tasks.

An excellent architect is pretty much a hands-on person and should be able to mentor members of the design and implementation teams. He/she should be knowledgeable and competent to handle any complex situation.

An architect's success in interviews does not come easily. One has to spend hours prior to each interview, wading through various books and references for preparation. The motivation for this book was to consolidate all this information into a single reference guide that will save time prior to interviews and can be a ready reference for important topics that need to be revised before the interviews.

An architect's critical competencies

Architecture competencies are the ability to effectively carry out the functions and activities necessary to produce architectures that are aligned with organization's business goals. A competent software architect is one who produces high-quality software architectures with acceptable cost. The following paragraphs explain the critical qualities for an software architect:

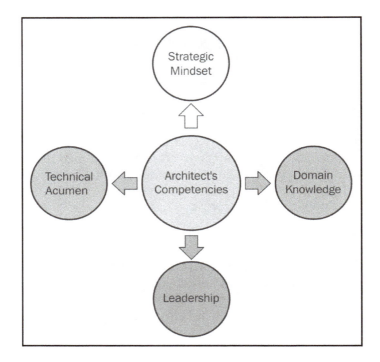

Figure 1: Architects Compentencies

- **Leadership**: The architect has to make decisions and take ownership, and a lot of times, the right choice is not simple. The architect needs to find a solution that works, and it may not always be the best alternative on technical merits but it should work best in the given situation. To take such decisions, the architect must have an excellent understanding of the cultural and political environments within the organizations and should have the ability to generate buy-in from the key stakeholders.

- **Strategic Mindset**: This is the ability of an architect to look at things from a 10,000-foot elevation, at a strategic level, isolating the operational nuances. This requires creating an organizational vision and then dividing it into achievable objectives to make it simpler for all the stakeholders to achieve these results. For example, making the product a market leader Architects are often tasked with finding an alternative solution that provides the best ROI to the organization and creating a business case for getting sponsorship. Architects often work with top-level executives such as CEO, CTO, and CIO, where it is necessary to create and present strategic architectures and roadmaps for organizations.

- **Domain Knowledge**: It is a critical aspect to understand the problem domain before creating and defining a solution. It is also a mandatory requirement to be knowledgeable about the domain-specific requirements, such as legal and regulatory requirements. A sound domain understanding is not only essential for understanding the requirements and evangelizing the target state but also helps in articulating the right decisions. The architect must be able speak the business vocabulary and draw experiences from the domain to be able to have meaningful discussions with the business stakeholders.

- **Technical Acumen**: This is a key competency as architects are hired for their technical expertise and acumen. The architect should have a breadth of expertise in technologies and platforms to understand their strengths and weaknesses and make the right decisions. Even for technical architect roles, it is mandatory to have skills in multiple technology stacks and frameworks and to be knowledgeable about technology trends.

Architects' growth paths

Software architecture discipline has matured since its inception. This architecture practice is no longer reserved for the veteran practitioners. The core concepts and principles of this discipline can now be acquired in training programs, books and college curriculum. The discipline is turning from an art into a competency accessible through training and experience. A significant number of methodologies, frameworks and processes have been developed to support various perspectives of the architectural practice. A software architect is responsible for creating the most appropriate architecture for the enterprise or system to suit the business goals, fulfill user requirements, and achieve the desired business outcome.

A software architect's career starts with a rigorous education in computer science. An architect is liable for making the hardest decisions on software architecture and design. Hence he/she must have a sound understanding of the concepts, patterns, and principles independent of any programming languages.

There are a number of flavors of architect that exist: enterprise architect, business architect, business strategy architect, solution architect, infrastructure architect, security architect, integration architect, technical architect, systems architect and software designer.

There are other variations as well, but this section describes the previously mentioned flavors in more detail. Finally, for an architect, learning must never stop. Continuous participation in the communities and learning about new technologies, methodologies, and frameworks are mandatory for value creation and to stay ahead of the demand curve.

The following paragraphs describe various roles basis the role definition, artifacts and the competencies:

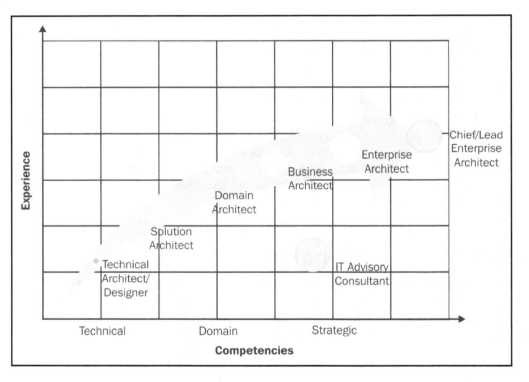

Figure 2: Architects Competencies

Enterprise architect/chief architect/lead architect

Enterprise architects create the CxO's vision and strategy for organizations. This includes defining strategic roadmaps, selecting appropriate technology stacks and providing guidance to the design and builds teams:

Artifacts: IT strategies, capability maps, city plans, integration strategies, as-is/to-be analysis, architectural principles, gap analysis, life cycle analysis, and application portfolio strategy.

Description: EAs help the chief technology officer/chief information officer/chief executive officer/chief marketing officer to ensure that the IT budgets are aligned with the organization's business strategy and that it will provide a competitive advantage for the enterprise. EAs are also responsible for establishing standards and frameworks and setting up a governance structure to align all the programs with the defined standards and frameworks. In some enterprises, this role may be merged with the CxO and has the title *Chief Architect*.

Competencies: Deep-dive competencies in IT and business, negotiation and leadership skills, experience in program management, governance, knowledge in enterprise architecture and modeling techniques.

Business architect

Business architects work with the business to thoroughly articulate the businesses operating model. They are competent in business architecture, capability modelling and business processes modeling. They also support solution architects with analysis of existing or new solutions.

Artifacts: Business process maps, use scenarios, information modeling.

Description: They are skilled to know how the IT application support the business needs and recommends capability or process improvements along with enterprise architects. Business architects also support ongoing engagements in the organization using their authority to ensure that projects deliver value to the business. Business architects drive the critical areas related to business process improvements. The business architect is also a critical resource in every organization.

Competencies: Deep knowledge in the business, process modeling, requirement analysis, and workshop leadership skills.

Domain architects

Domain architects focus on a specific domain and have deep expertise in that area.

Artifacts: Domain diagrams, domain maps, interfaces, technical interfaces, integration strategies.

Description: Typically these architects only concentrate on specific areas, for example, security architect, information architect, integration architect, infrastructure architect, data architect, business architect, and so on.

Competencies: Broad technical competencies, deep competencies in infrastructure, data models, service orientation, and a good understanding of enterprise architecture.

Solution architect

A solution architect is responsible for implementing strategic IT architecture.

Artifacts: Application diagrams, system maps, service interfaces, technical interfaces, integration strategies.

Description: Solution architects define the architectural solution, finalize the technology stack in adherence to principles and guidelines, handle stakeholder communications, and make critical decisions specific to technology options. The solution architect mediates between technology and business team members and various other stakeholders. The solution architect is the go to **Subject Matter Expert (SME)** for any technology decisions, challenges and conflicts.

Competencies: Broad technical knowledge, deep competencies in infrastructure and data models, service orientation, and good understanding of enterprise architecture.

Technical architect/designer

The technical architect is a SME in a specific technology or framework.

Artifacts: Frameworks, class models, patterns, and aspects.

Description: Technical architect have expertise in the underlying platform, its components, and are able to articulate the strengths and weakness of the technology platform. The TA is liable for creating and defining the best architecture leveraging this specific technology platform, and also mentoring the implementation teams. Technology architect are competent in different tools, the latest trends, and different architectural alternatives for implementing the solution.

Competencies: Deep knowledge in programming, frameworks, standards, and technical modeling.

Qualities of an architect

This describes the skills, knowledge, qualification, experience, or capability:

- Visual thinking is the ability to communicate with diagrams and illustrations.
- The ability to communicate complex ideas to wide audience and well as excellent written communication skills.
- A solid foundation of process engineering, lean or six sigma.
- A solid expertise in the capability modeling, processes modelling, and application-to-capability mapping and service oriented modelling.
- The skill to drive architectural review discussion using the various methods of architectural evaluation.
- Expertise in software development methodologies such as waterfall, RUP, agile and spiral.
- Expertise in infrastructure domain, including servers, load balancers, storage, networking, firewalls and routing.
- Understanding of the security domain including authentication, encryption, authorization, security mechanisms and PKI.
- Expertise in the data management, RDBMS, extract-translate-load, business intelligence data management, data integration, data distribution and caching strategies.
- The ability to address the system quality attribute that should be paramount to the system, and provide alternatives in the solution.
- Architects must be able to inspire and motivate the team members. A large part of the job is to evangelize and influence a set of ideals in the organization.
- There will be times when an architect will have to negotiate with the stakeholders to get the final node. Architects are in an individual contributor's role and do not get into people management.
- Critical thinking, that is, being able to think swiftly, is often required.
- Architects often have to work with a set of complex and unique problems and challenges, and be able to articulate and provide solutions.
- Big thinking is the ability to analyze at a problem from 360-degree perspective than a tunnel vision effect.

- Business acumen. Understanding the domain in which one works is essential, to help you understand how the technology can affect the business. Being in sync with the business gives architect's much-needed credibility.
- Process orientation is the ability of thinking in terms of process which includes process modelling, capability modelling and service modelling.
- People skills is the ability to interacting with various stakeholders on an ongoing basis.

An architect's competency framework

The purpose of the architecture competency framework is to help architects understand the competencies for required different architect roles within the industry. To address this challenge, the architecture competency framework provides a standard set of guidelines for the architecting skills and proficiency levels for SMEs to perform the various roles defined within the framework.

The framework defines the following roles for a team undertaking the development of enterprise architecture:

- Architecture sponsor
- Architecture board members
- Chief/lead architects
- Enterprise architect, business strategy architect, business architect, data architect, application architect, technology architect, integration and security architect
- Program and project managers
- Software designer

The framework also includes a number of tables matching roles with skills and proficiency levels within each skill category. A single table shows the definition of enterprise architecture skills by role.

Benefits of competency framework

The advantages of using the architecture skills framework are summarized as follows:

- Reduced time, cost, and risk for the overall solution development
- Reduced time and cost to set up architecture teams
- Reduced time, cost, and risk in training hiring and managing architecture SMEs

Roles	Architecture Sponsor	EA Manager	Program Manager	IT Advisory Consultant	Designer	Technical Architect	Solution Architect	Domain Architect	Business Architect	Enterprise Architect	Chief Architect
Leadership	1	2	2	2	1	1	2	2	3	3	3
Stakeholder Management	3	2	2	1	1	2	2	2	3	3	3
Risk Management	2	2	2	2	1	2	2	2	3	3	3
Business Process	1	1	1	2	2	2	2	3	3	3	2
Organization Design	1	1	1	2	1	1	2	3	3	3	2
Data Design	1	1	1	2	2	2	2	3	2	2	2
Application Design	1	1	1	2	2	2	2	3	2	2	2
System Integration	1	1	1	2	2	2	2	3	2	2	2
Service Design	1	1	1	1	2	2	2	2	2	2	2
Architecture Principles	2	2	2	2	1	2	2	3	3	3	3
Solution Modelling	1	1	1	2	2	2	2	3	2	3	2
Benefit Analysis	1	1	1	2	1	1	2	3	3	3	2
Project Management	1	2	2	1	1	2	2	2	2	2	3

Figure 3: Architecture competency framework

Summary

Individual passion is the primary driving factor that determines the growth path of an architect. For instance, a security architect who is passionate about the domain of IT security and must have developed an immensely valuable body of knowledge over time should ideally not be coerced into making a shift to a solution architect and eventually a governance role. There are at least three layers of architects:

- **Technologist:** These roles have broad and narrow competencies in a specific technology or framework and are at the start of the value chain, for example, network architect, security architect, application architect, process architect, web architect, data architect.
- **T-shape**: These roles have broad and deep competencies and are in the middle of the chain, for example, information architect, infrastructure architect, business architect or solution architect.
- **Governance:** These roles on the top of value chain for, for example, lead architect, chief architect, enterprise architect or CTO

This progression is not for everyone, and importantly does not define the success or growth of an architect. This would be optimal for organizations to get creative about fostering career growth paths for each of these role buckets. At the end of the day, SMEs from across these pools need to work together effectively to define solutions. Well rounded individuals from these pools collaborating effectively are the recipe for success in an architecture focused solutions delivery organization. Instating creative and vertical growth paths within each of these pools would stand to benefit both the individuals and the organization.

Architects should be passionate about the work, whether it is being broad and deep in a specific technology area, or developing cross technology/functional breadth. The key is an architect understands the personal tradeoffs of each choice, for instance, a database architect considering a shift to a broader solutions architect role should be aware of the fact that developing a broader knowledge base of technology will become a higher priority to succeed in the role than continuing to go deep into architecting database solutions. The key consideration is to follow ones heart and passion, opportunities to grow and succeed in the domain will materialize over time.

2
IT Strategy and Advisory

This is one of the key sections of the title and deals with IT strategy and advisory domain. This section and the following sections have been written in a Q&A format and are well supported by elaborate diagrams where applicable. This chapter is structured in a way that starts with the strategy and advisory domain and ends with non-functional requirements. You can choose to go through this sequentially from the first to the last or pick and choose the sections relevant to your competencies. The following six domains are covered in the following chapters of the book:

IT Strategy and Advisory	Enterprise Architecture and Modernization	SOA and Integration
Solution Architecture and Design	Emerging Technologies-SMAC	Methodologies, Frameworks, and NFRs

IT strategy

This section covers the Q & A for IT strategy and advisory domain. Meeting customer needs and demands and creating technology adoption roadmaps is the primary goal/objective for IT strategy engagements. By answering these types of questions related to vision, strategy and roadmaps of a company, one will be able to understand the key aspects such as vision, IT strategy and roadmap, guiding principles and frameworks and tools.

What is architectural vision and what information does it contain?

Architecture vision is created and defined during the engagement initiation phase. The purpose of architecture vision is to agree with the key organizational stakeholders the requisite outcome for the IT architecture. Architecture vision emphasizes the benefits of the proposed architecture to the decision-makers and is like the elevator pitch for senior executives and CxOs. It also shows how the target architecture supports business strategy, business objectives, and stakeholder concerns.

Architecture vision artifact contents:

- Organizational problem definition
- Stakeholders' goals and objectives
- Business process definition
- Actors and roles
- Organizational restraints
- IT principles and standards
- Architecture strategy
- Mapping the proposed architecture to business processes and requirements

Phase	Description
Vision (the dream to be achieved)	Created by consensus. This forms a mental image of a future to which people can align. It describes something possible, not necessarily predictable. It provides direction and focus, for example, offering a patented product for the retail domain.
Mission (the statement of business)	This establishes the business reason for the organization's existence and defines current and future business in terms of product, services, customer, and price. For example, we strive to expedite improvements in education by creating software products.
Goals (the results to be achieved)	This explains an ideal state to be realized by organization in future. It is defined with and related directly to organization vision and mission. It guides everyday decisions making and events. For example, reduce overall budget costs by 10% by 20xx.
Objective (plans to reach the desired results)	This emphasizes on organizational concerns and milestones. It establish tasks to be accomplished to achieve desired goals. It is measurable in terms of whether or not they are achieved.

Table 1: Architecture Roadmap

Probability indicator:

Why do enterprises need to undergo transformation or modernization?

Today's IT organizations are carrying a heavy burden of applications that are not delivering value to the business. Transformation or modernization is needed to simplify the functionality of existing applications, reduce the amount of old technology, remove inefficiencies, and introduce new capabilities. Companies have more applications than the business needs and are forced to spend valuable IT resources on supporting obsolete systems, hence the need to go through a transformation. The key business and technology drivers for transformation include:

Business priorities	Technology priorities
Increasing enterprise growth	Analytics and business intelligence
Delivering operational results	Mobile technologies
Reducing enterprise costs	Cloud computing (SaaS, IaaS, and PaaS)
Attracting and retaining new customers	Collaboration technologies (workflow)
Improving IT applications and infrastructure	Legacy modernization
Creating new products and services (innovation)	IT management
Improving efficiency	CRM
Attracting and retaining the workforce	Virtualization
Implementing analytics and big data	Security
Expanding into new markets and geographies	ERP applications

Table 2: Business and technology priorities – Gartner 2014

Probability indicator:

What are the enterprise transformation challenges?

The following is a list of typical challenges for enterprise transformation initiatives:

- Budgets are restricted and the focus of the application strategy shifts from innovation to cost cutting
- The resources to support growth and new development are not available and must be found from within the IT organization
- Cost is a key barrier for all transformation and modernization initiatives
- It is difficult to demonstrate fast **Return on Investment** (**ROI**) to get the business buy-in

Probability indicator:

What are the guiding principles for enterprise transformation?

The following is a list of guiding principles for enterprise architecture transformation:

- Scalable and maintainable IT landscape while ensuring standardized infrastructure
- Treating application retirement as an essential step in the lifecycle
- Adoption of new methodologies and frameworks for transforming and modernizing applications
- Establishing clear transformational governance
- Simplifying business processes
- Leveraging SMAC (social, mobile, analytics, and cloud) is a key to digital transforming the enterprise

The following diagram shows the value quadrants for transformation and depicts the business benefits for transformation:

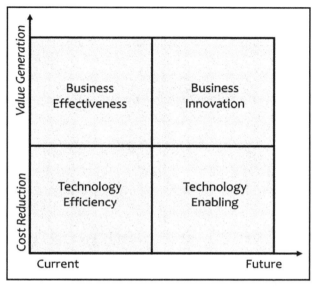

Figure 1: EA value quadrant

Probability indicator: 🐞🐞🐞

What is the overall architecture transformation approach and what are the benefits?

The top architecture transformation strategies involve standardizing the application portfolio by reducing the number of custom-built IT applications and moving towards a common set of applications, technologies, and infrastructure.

There are multiple strategies for transforming the applications, including but not limited to **standardization, consolidation, replacement, migration, clouding, renewal, decommission, retention,** and **simplification.**

Architecture transformation is comparable to open-heart surgery. A top-down and bottom-up approach are leveraged to envision the future state. A combination of these techniques and architecture frameworks will facilitate building the future end state architecture. An excellent option is always a robust and simple one against an unstable and complex one.

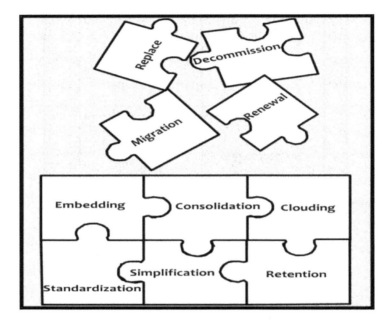

Figure 2: Modernization strategies

The following are the key benefits of any EA transformation:

- Creating value for the business, for example, business IT alignment
- Cut overall cost for the business, for example, decommissioning, data archiving, and cloud computing
- Increase productivity, for example, removing inefficiencies, removing Excel-sheets-based reporting, and incorporating service management, that is, ITIL processes
- Innovate new applications and services, for example, leveraging the competitive advantage of social business, cloud, or analytics
- Increase quality of application, for example, standardization and simplification, usage of frameworks

- Improve flexibility of IT systems, for example, IT can deliver more value to business

- Create better IT and business alignment
- Improve efficiency of IT systems, for example, automating processes or removing manual intervention

Probability indicator: 👍👍👍

What is the typical road map for engagement (emphasis is on the architectural phases)?

The following table illustrates the architecture of a **Software Development Life Cycle (SDLC)**:

Phase	Description
IT strategy	Typically we engage with the customers to build an IT strategy or work with the customer to build IT strategy in a specific area, for example, supply chain management strategy, cloud strategy or SOA strategy. This phase also leverages accelerators or frameworks that may be organizations intellectual property (IPs).
Architecture transformation	EA transformation focuses on the solution definition. This is the next phase after the IT strategy. The team works with the customers to understand their challenges, gaps and pain areas by running workshops or through discussions. The next phase is envisioning future state architecture for the enterprise. The transformation engagement can be an end-to-end enterprise architecture engagement or specific to a business area like customer relationship management, SOA or SMAC. The transformation engagement includes current state, future state, gap and impact analysis and IT Roadmap, solution definition, planning, costing and road map preparations. For example, CRM solution architecture, SOA.
Architecture governance	Compliance reviews, managing risks, and guiding implementations. This is predominately applicable during the design, build, and operate phases.

Table 3: Architecture Phases

The following image illustrates the components in detail:

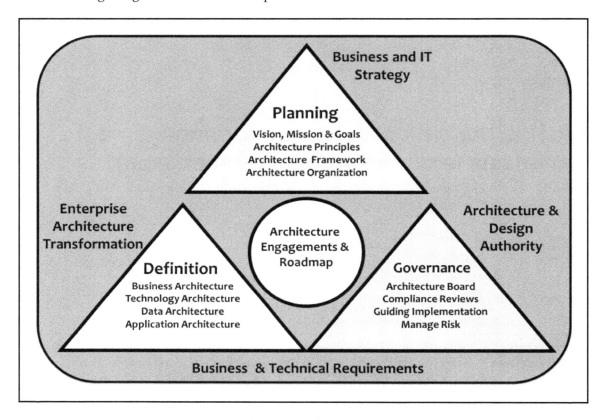

Figure 3: Various EA SDLC phases

Probability indicator:

What are the different frameworks/tools that are leveraged during strategy/advisory engagements? How do strategy frameworks help customers?

Various frameworks and tools are leveraged during advisory and strategy engagement, and most of them would be specific to an organization. These frameworks have focused questions that are asked to the customers/senior executive to identify gaps in capabilities for an organization or to get a sense of the maturity level of a certain function. This gives them a clearer picture of the weak areas and where IT could support improving the efficiencies. Please see this list of common frameworks:

- EA maturity assessment
- SOA maturity assessment
- Multi-channel assessment
- TCO-Cloud
- ROI-EA
- SOA ROI

Frameworks are recommended when there is a general guidance required for knowing the capability gaps in the landscape or the level of maturity for a certain function. These may also help identify quick wins. Workshops are planned with key customer personnel to determine how well you currently implement each best practice for a given domain. The frameworks assist in the following areas:

- Detailed assessment, providing the current and target maturity levels
- Identify go to market opportunities
- Capture pain points and opportunities for investments
- Identifying quick wins
- Enables client to determine the roadmap on how to embark on larger transformation journeys

These are four to six weeks of engagement with a price point between 150-200K, used as an investment, partially funded or in a fully funded model.

Probability indicator:

What are the benefits of IT strategy engagements?

Meeting customer needs and demands is the primary goal/objective for strategy engagements. The strategy engagements provide benefits in one or more of the following areas:

- Increase revenue
- Reduce cost of operations by enabling new capabilities, for example, self-service portals
- Increase sales through new revenue streams
- Identify new areas of growth, for example, new Geo
- Improves customer experience, for example, multi-channel
- Deliver more predictable outcomes to customers
- Differentiate in a commoditized market, for example, product innovations
- Comply with regulations and laws, for example, Sarbanes-Oxley

Probability indicator: 👌👌👌

How do you engage with a senior executive in the organization, for example, CxO or IT director?

This is done via a set of focused discussions with the senior executives/CxO to understand the pain areas/challenges in the application landscape/business landscape. The latest trends in social, mobile, analytics and cloud SMAC are taken into considerations during this phase and are the key to devising the plan of action. The outcome of these discussions is typically an IT strategy engagement undertaken for the areas that would have inefficiencies, for example, APR or CRM or where new capabilities are required to be built SMAC or/and maturity has to be accessed for a certain function for example, SOA. Strategy or advisory frameworks play a key role in this phase and are key talking points during such discussions. The outcome of these discussions may also result in the initiation of the transformation initiative like end-to-end EA transformation, but it is the IT strategy work that kick-starts the overall process (please refer to question architectural phases).

Probability indicator: 👌👌👌

What is competitive analysis (aka market scan) and what are the benefits?

Competitive analysis is the process of analyzing the competitive landscape in the business domain, including strengths and weaknesses of your organization and your competitors. It involves identifying the strategies that can improvise your market position and weaknesses that prevent the organization from entering into new markets. The process also includes the barriers that the organization needs to erect to prevent others from eroding the market position.

Competitive analysis is a basis for the competitive strategy for multinational corporations. Business experts note that competitive analysis transcends industry areas and the practice is deeply relevant to all industries. Competitive analysis is a methodology of comparing your company, products, and services against market competitors in your industry. This is a key part of organizational planning, which is used to establish company strategies, goals, and tactics. Top management normally conduct strategic planning meetings at least once a year but may review competitors more often if competition is high.

Benefits of competitive analysis:

- Improve offering
- Planning market entry/product development
- Market gaps
- Market trends
- Marketing

Probability indicator:

What is Decision Matrix Analysis or Pugh Matrix Analysis?

Decision Matrix Analysis or Pugh Matrix Analysis is a key technique leveraged for making critical decisions. It is powerful where you have a number of alternatives to choose from, and many different factors to take into consideration. This is an excellent technique to leverage in any important decision making where there isn't a clear-cut and obvious preferred option. Leveraging Decision Matrix Analysis means that you can take decisions rationally, at a time when other people might be struggling to make decisions.

A simple decision matrix consists of establishing different options that are scored and added to obtain a final score. Importantly, these option are not weighted in the process.

A weighted decision matrix operates in very similar to the simple decision matrix but introduces the concept of weighting the criteria in order of importance, that is, the more critical the criteria, the higher the weight. All these options are scored and multiplied by the weight in order to produce a final result. The advantage of the decision matrix is that subjective opinions are made more objective.

The decision matrix analysis is leveraged in the following areas:

- RFP evaluation matrix
- Cost/benefit analysis matrix
- Solutions prioritization matrix
- Vendor selection matrix
- Criteria/alternatives matrix
- Supplier selection matrix

Probability indicator:

How would you engage with CxO to sell SMAC offering?

SMAC technologies are the capabilities that give enterprises a competitive edge over its market competition. When deployed in the IT landscape, these capabilities provide synergetic solutions for digitally transforming an organization to enable it for the future. Emphasize the fundamentals, the processes, and the methodologies for SMAC during the conversation. Be prepared to mention the lists of top vendors in this space, the key user scenarios (the journey) and the benefits to the enterprise. Be ready with the reference architecture or the fundamental building block for each of SMAC components. The examples of SMAC implementations for the competitors will be a critical point to include in the discussion. The following list provides the key benefits of SMAC that are typically the selling points for these capabilities.

Domain	Description
Social	Social media allows sharing and creation of knowledge via social networks, which enhances collaboration and information exchange. To drive business goals and objectives social media helps unlock the knowledge from individuals and facilitate propagation of this knowledge.
Mobile	The advancements in smart devices are bringing in an era of ubiquitous connectivity. Mobile technologies are evolving and transforming the IT landscape. End users are now able to access information anywhere and on the go through these smart devices.
Analytics	Big data analytics allows companies to analyze new forms of data in the cloud, which generates unprecedented insight to enable real-time, critical decision making. Analytics enables supply chains, facilitates marketing, and optimizes CRM processes.
Cloud	Cloud technology is becoming the new foundation of the IT ecosystem and is the fulcrum of the SMAC stack. The cloud computing lends businesses agility, cutting the costs associated with physical server maintenance and breaking down the barriers of geography. Cloud provides limitless scalability and powers the transformative combination of analytic, mobile and social capabilities.

Table 4: Emerging Technologies

Probability indicator: 👆👆👆

How are projects prioritized as part of the IT roadmap?

Projects are prioritized by ascertaining the business value delivered against the cost of delivering them. The approach is first to determine, the net benefit of all of the solution building blocks/increments delivered by the projects, and then verify that the risks have been effectively mitigated. Afterward, the intent is to gain the requisite consensus at the enterprise level to create a prioritized list of projects based upon solution building blocks. The net benefit and the risk will provide the basis for planning and resource allocation. It is important to articulate all costs to ensure that executives understand the net benefit in terms of the cost savings over time.

- Buy versus build options are evaluated and target architectures are created
- Strategic parameters for change are articulated
- Transition work projects and packages are identified, that is, moving from current to target state
- Benefits, costs and dependencies of the projects are weighed
- Quick wins are identified
- High-value, long-term projects are ranked and prioritized

This includes work products such as an architecture requirements specification, a roadmap, capability assessment, and an implementation with migration plan and transition architecture.

Probability indicator:

What does the company need to execute a business strategy?

The approach to execution of business strategy:

- Business architecture is the initial stage in EA transformation initiative Subsequent phases will align capabilities to applications and establish the data flows between those applications
- Defining reference models, capability models, and logical building blocks for the enterprise

- Logical building blocks need to be identified and information gathered and compared for levels of maturity in each capability
- Capabilities, people, processes, and technology need to be identified to deliver business strategy
- Establishing capability maps, information maps, value streams, and business processes
- The relationship between components from appropriate perspectives (that is, risk, compliance technical, acceptability, and so on) needs to be established

Probability indicator:

Summary

The goal of IT strategy is to gain a competitive advantage to be able to achieve the organization's objectives. Strategic direction is decided by a thoughtful eye on the business horizon. The foundation of competitive strategy is matching up an organization's strategic capabilities with the present and future needs and wants of customers. The fit between organizations strategic capabilities and the customers' needs and wants determines the strategic portfolio of products and services for the organization. The key to establishing this strategic direction are the four key areas:

- Competitive advantage in markets that gives an edge over rivals
- Customers and their current and future needs
- Products and services to develop and support
- Sales and services for the customers

3
Enterprise Architecture and Modernization

An **enterprise architecture** (EA) is a conceptual blueprint that defines the structure and operation of an organization. The intent of an is to determine how an organization can most effectively achieve its current and future objectives. EA is a well-defined practice for conducting enterprise analysis, design, planning, and implementation, using a holistic approach at all times, for the successful development and execution of strategy. Enterprise architecture applies architecture principles and practices to guide organizations through the business, information, process, and technology changes necessary to execute their strategies.

Practitioners of enterprise architecture, enterprise architects, are responsible for performing the analysis of business structure and processes and are often called upon to draw conclusions from the information collected to address the goals of enterprise architecture: effectiveness, efficiency, agility, and durability.

Enterprise architecture

EA definition

An EA is a collation of strategic assets describing business and the technologies essential to enable the business functions. This includes business goals, business processes, applications, information, organizational structures and roles. An enterprise architecture summarizes the assets required to implement technology solutions to cater to future business goals. The EA predominately consist of four domains: application, data, business, and infrastructure. The following diagram depicts these domains:

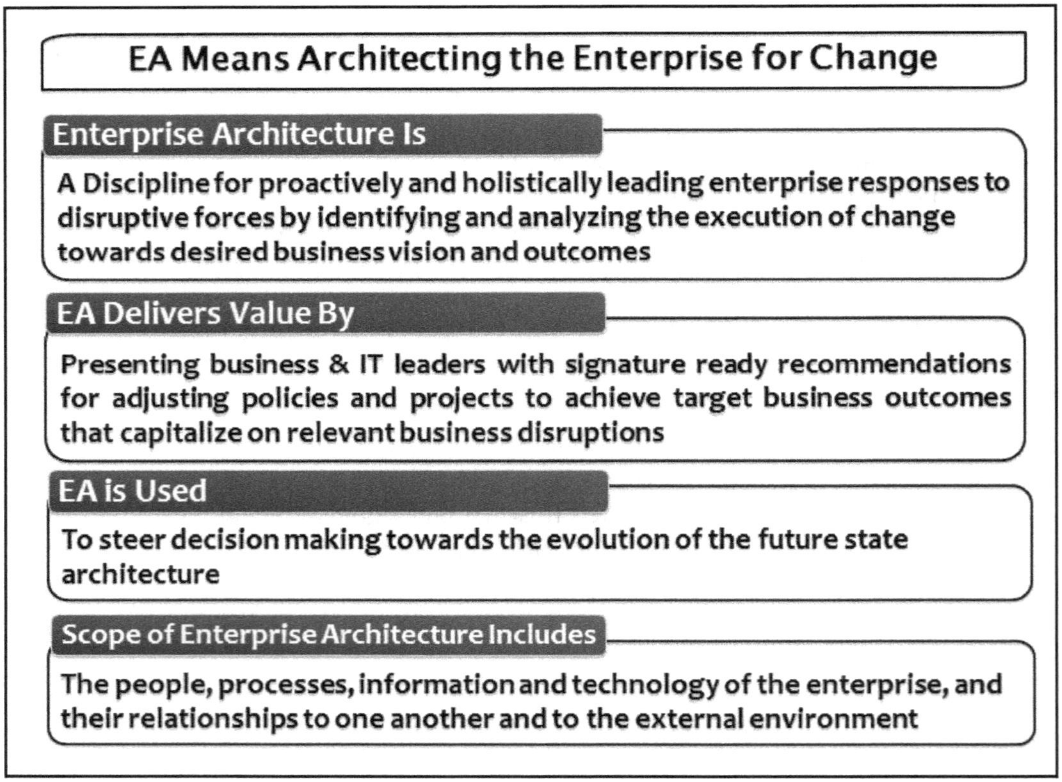

EA Means Architecting the Enterprise for Change

Enterprise Architecture Is

A Discipline for proactively and holistically leading enterprise responses to disruptive forces by identifying and analyzing the execution of change towards desired business vision and outcomes

EA Delivers Value By

Presenting business & IT leaders with signature ready recommendations for adjusting policies and projects to achieve target business outcomes that capitalize on relevant business disruptions

EA is Used

To steer decision making towards the evolution of the future state architecture

Scope of Enterprise Architecture Includes

The people, processes, information and technology of the enterprise, and their relationships to one another and to the external environment

Figure 1: EA definition

EA value proposition

EA is a strategic asset leveraged to shape the organization and is key to aligning the current IT investments and efficient planning of future investments. EA is a strategic tool for classifying opportunities to improve key metrics such as IT costs, operational efficiencies, and customer experience. EA helps to achieve business-IT alignment, reduce time-to-market, and manage change and risk. Elevator pitch expounds the value of EA. The benefits of EA are as follows:

- EA is the key to cost reduction, innovation, flexibility, and revenue generation
- EA enables transparency for all business stakeholders
- EA facilitates pragmatic cost effective options for IT initiatives
- EA is the bridge between IT and business strategy and goals
- EA enables IT budgets on strategic engagements rather than operational ones
- EA ensures alignment of IT spending with business strategy
- EA breaks down IT silos, enabling solutions that reduce time to market and engagement risk
- EA provides business value for the organization through various IT initiatives
- EA enables competitive advantage by ensuring IT budgets are aligned with strategic assets
- EA drives cross-silo technology initiatives to resolve challenges in business
- EA enables opportunities and improves IT alignment to business goals

EA roadmap

The EA roadmap summarizes the current target state incremental transitioning to the end state architecture. The EA roadmap includes the application, business, data, and infrastructure domains. This roadmap outlines the projects to implement the target architecture in an incremental manner. This includes risks and issues, prioritization, migration strategy, success factors and estimated costs.

Probability indicator: &&&

What is the starting point for building enterprise architecture?

EA approach

This is usually done by understanding the business model/business architecture of the enterprise, namely the value chain processes. Porter's value chain is the right place to start putting the puzzle together for the business capability maps. Reference architectures, such as TMForum NGOSS in telecom, Energetics in oil and gas, DoDAF in defense, BIAN in banking, and ACORD in insurance, are vital during the architecture definition phase. The business strategy and goals are critical to decide the scope of EA when the final solution is pieced together.

EA roadmap

The EA roadmap outlines a plan to enable the transitioning from the current to the target state. The EA roadmap includes all the four EA domains: the business, application, data, and infrastructure components. This roadmap outlines the incremental initiatives needed to implement the target state. This includes risks and issues, prioritization, migration strategy, success factors, and estimated costs.

This roadmap consists of initiatives that are prioritized based on the business value against the cost of delivery. The technique is to arrive at the net benefit increments delivered by these initiatives, verifying that the risks are minimized, and then gain the requisite consensus at the enterprise level to create a prioritized list of projects based on solution building blocks and net benefit and risk. This will be the basis for resource allocation in the projects. It is important to estimate costs and to ensure that senior executives understand the benefits in terms of the cost savings over a period of time.

EA trends

The IT trends important to EA are SMAC: social, mobile, analytics, cloud and IoT. Refer to the following table which depicts the business and technology priorities for 2014.

Probability indicator: 👍👍

Which stakeholders would participate in the enterprise architecture life cycle?

EA stakeholders

Enterprise architects are leaders and are at the top of the value chain in an organization. As leaders, EAs guide and mentor team members during various SDLCs of engagement and thus add value. The following table provides the list of stakeholders involved in the EA life cycle:

Role	Description
Chief architect	The enterprise architect reports to the chief architect. He/she is likely to tell you exactly how they expect you to help them.
CIO	The CIO drives the alignment of IT spending with business strategies, ensuring IT transparency.
CEO	The CEO is often keen about the IT metrics, IT strategy, IT cost control, and innovations. The CEO is responsible for the day-to-day management decisions and for implementing short and long term plans.
COO	The COO drives the operational efficiencies through automations and tools. The COO may also be keen about trends in the architectural domain.
Business CXO	The business CXO is keen about virtually all aspects of EA. One thing that is of special interest is the business strategy and it's mapping to IT initiatives.
CTO	The CTO oversees current technology and creates policy, identifying opportunities and risks for the business, managing R&D, and monitoring technology and social trends that could impact the organization.
IT directors	IT directors are part of the architectural decision-making process and may drive enterprise-wide architectural initiatives.
IT managers	IT managers are involved in the EA process of strategy development and blueprinting. They ensure their projects get through the governance without hiccups and arrange risk and mitigations
Business architects	Business architecture SMEs define business capabilities in line with the strategy and contribute to the business strategy and plans.
Data architects	SMEs of data architecture design and create the organization's data architecture. They define how the data will be stored and consumed and integrate different entities and IT systems.

Business analysts	SMEs who analyze the business domain and articulate its business or processes, assessing the business model or its integration with technology.
Solution architects	An SME of solution architecture typically is part of the development team. SAs translate requirements created by business analysts into the architecture and articulate it through design artifacts.

Table 1: EA Stakeholders

Probability indicator: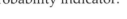

What are architecture principles?

Architecture principles guide all technology decisions and support the strategic direction of the business. Principles are guidelines and rules, intended to be enduring and seldom revised, that support the way an organization fulfills its goals. Architecture principles are the guidelines for the deployment of IT assets across the organization and form the basis for future IT decisions. Each principle is related back to the business objectives and key architecture drivers. The architecture principles may be established at one or all of these levels:

- Enterprise principles provide the reference for decision making in an enterprise and guides the organization in fulfilling its mission. They are found in governmental and not-for-profit organizations and also in commercial organizations as a means of facilitating decision making across an enterprise. They are a key to a successful architecture governance mechanism.
- Information technology principles provide guidelines on the deployment of IT assets across the organization. They are articulated to ensure the IT landscape is efficient and cost-effective.
- Architecture principles are a sub-set of IT principles. They can be either governing principles for the architecture process, affecting the development and use of the EA or principles that govern the implementation of the architecture, establishing guidance for designing and developing IT applications.

The following diagram depicts the architecture principles:

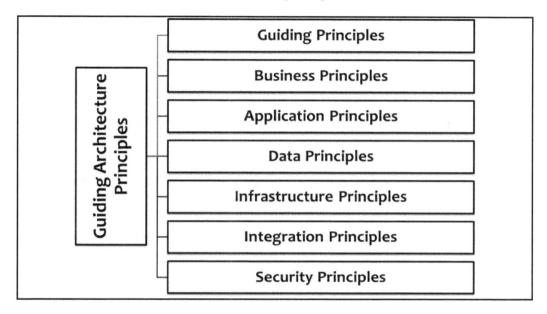

Figure 2: Architectural principles

Probability indicator:

Why do you need architecture principles?

Architecture principles are derived from the organization's core values. Principles are a collection of statements used to assist in decision making and are not hard-and-fast rules. They are timeless in nature and change infrequently. The benefits of architecture principles

- Establish criteria for new systems being introduced into the technical environment
- Steer technology planning and investment activities
- Decision making and are leveraged as a guideline

Architectural principles are mandatory to any successful EA practice for several reasons:

Role	Description
Principles are easy to socialize	Politics is one of the key inefficiencies in the architectural roadmap. Principles can breakdown such barriers and get stakeholders aligned with an architectural roadmap.
Principles stabilize	Principles are enduring and are difficult to change, hence they protects the EA from wild swings based on politics and culture.
Principles make you smarter	Principles are the guidelines to drive architectural decision making and the core values and direction for EA initiatives.
Principles make governance efficient	Publishing the EA principles and IT roadmap earlier are the best practices for governance processes and guide exactly where the architecture is heading.
Principles drive metrics	Evaluating initiatives against a set of principles is a source of EA metrics.

Table 2: Architecture Principles

Probability indicator: 👍

What are the most important artifacts of an enterprise architecture engagement?

As part of typical transformation projects there are various phases, and for each phase, there will be different artifacts that are produced. The key artifacts are:

Artifact	Description
As-is assessment report	This current state assessment report takes elaborate stock of the current state of the enterprise in ways to assess where each business unit stands.
To-be architecture	The goal of to-be architecture is to define critical IT applications necessary to process the data and enable business goals. The end state architecture is based on open standards and frameworks. For example, **The Open Group Architecture Framework** (**TOGAF**) or TMForum NGOSS (eTOM, TAM, and SID) framework.
Gap and impact analysis	As a part of the transformation, the objective of this artifact is to identify and define gaps and impacts on the IT landscape.

IT roadmap	This artifact outlines the transitioning of the architecture from the current to the target state.
Architecture principle	Principles are guidelines and rules, intended to be enduring and seldom revised , that support the way an organization sets about fulfilling its goal.
Reference architecture	Reference architecture is a reusable-asset and stakeholders can refer to it for best practices. Reference architecture can be leveraged to choose the best solution for a particular domain from an offering catalog.

Table 3: EA Artifacts

Probability indicator: 👍👍

How does enterprise architecture support strategy and business goals?

The enterprise architecture enables the understanding of information assets, business processes, target operating models, and IT infrastructure as a means to designing businesses for future. In the long term, the objective for business is to leverage the enterprise architecture to enable business agility and alignment. The top priority of EA is to align with business objectives and hence the journey of adoption focuses on key business areas.

Enterprise architecture requires strong governance to establish business and IT compliance with business goals and objectives. The architecture governance enables continuous assessment and enforcement of compliance for the entire roadmap.

Probability indicator: 👍👍

Explain a complex engagement in which you were the EA and the challenges you faced

Approach

Provide emphasis on how it helped the business address their existing and potential issues and challenges. For example, you and your team were able to analyze the problem areas in the business and technology landscape and recommended a roadmap to resolve these challenges and issues. This includes opportunities to leverage the innovation by using, for example, SMAC capabilities. Emphasize how it improved the KPI and KRAs by removing inefficiencies in the business processes. Please describe the business context and how your recommendation helped to solve those challenges and benefits.

Challenges

The following table lists the typical challenges you will face while working on complex projects:

Type of challenges	Description
Critical	• Managing interdependencies within and between business and IT units • Determining interdependencies and the impact of changes in IT and business • Bringing the EA into compliance with standards, processes, and frameworks • Making visible the contribution of IT to the business success of the enterprise • Analyzing and appraising the potential impact of organizational restructuring
Common	• Building EA that supports the organizational vision and addresses the IT strategy for next three to five years. • Business and IT alignment • Regulatory and compliance • Budget optimizations • Steering future development of EA • Identifying the potential for IT systems optimizations

Table 4: EA Challenges

How would you mediate opposing views ?

There are various ways to support opposition architectural viewpoints:

- The best way is to support it through best practices, standards, and reference architectures for the given domain
- Similar work that you did in the past that relates to the business domain/sub-domain
- Justify it against the associated cost, effort, and risks
- Create a business case of pros and cons with respect to the different viewpoints (pain areas, challenges, issues), decision matrix technique

Probability indicator: 👍 👍

Explain where you applied strategic thinking to impact business results

Approach

As an architect, we do this all the time when developing roadmaps for customers. In one of my past engagements, a typical top down and a bottom up approach for solution, development was leveraged. Be prepared with the details of your project in terms of the requirement/problem statement. The methodology followed the solution recommendations and the benefits provided to the customer. The interviewer will be keen to know the key findings and the recommendations made on such an EA program.

Recommendations and key finding of strategic engagements examples include:

- Consolidation of multiple CRM-like functionalities into a single application to reduce TCO.
- Leveraging SOA reference architecture as the starting point for building the integration solutions for the enterprise. Recommend SOA stack to remove point-to-point integration and manual operations in the enterprise, thus removing inefficiencies.
- Leveraging SDLC processes as part of the life cycle processes to ensure that software is maintainable, manageable, and governed.

- Leveraging application monitoring solutions for the enterprise which includes support for release management, change management, deployment of software to monitoring, and management of applications and infrastructure in the landscape.
- SOA Technology stacks consisting of BPM, ESB, adapters, SDK, BAM, BPA, B2B, and so on
- Establishing an EA or SOA governance framework and organization to drive EA/SOA adoption across the enterprise.
- Leveraging of frameworks, methodologies, and tools such as SOMA, COBIT, TOGAF, eTOM, and so on.

Probability indicator: 👍

Can you provide an example where you drove a business initiative by promoting cross-organizational participation?

In one of my past projects for a Telco operator, there was a need to call various stakeholders from different BUs for a brainstorming session for one of the important business requirement which was about building convergence as part of the Telco network. Since it cut across various domains/BUs pertaining to OSS, BSS, architecture, operations, and business analysis, all these stakeholders had to be called for a joined discussion to brainstorm and decide the way forward for these critical requirements that were part of the future state architecture phase.

Probability indicator: 👍 👍

How did you introduced a new standard and ensured its adoption?

I have in my past engagements introduced a new standard based on the assessment finding. This was related to an SOA initiative for a large Telco operator. Once the gaps were identified, it ensured that the impact of the gaps on the business and the steps required to overcome them through leveraging IT solutions were devised.

Recommendations examples followed with the figure:

- SOA Technology stacks consisting of BPM, ESB, Adapters, SDK, BAM, BPA, B2B, and so on
- Establishing an SOA governance framework and organization to drive adoption across the enterprise
- SOA SDLC processes, such as service identification and requirements, among others, were suggested as part of the SOA adoption journey
- Alignment to best practices and standards for SOA; for example, WS*

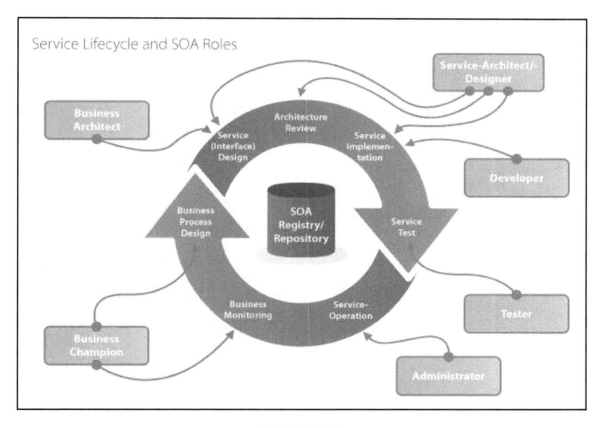

Figure 3: SOA life cycle

Probability indicator: 👍👍

How to managed change in a complex environment for EA?

Methodology

The architecture change management process is very closely related to the architecture governance processes and to the management of the architecture contract between the architecture function and the business users. The change process establishes how changes will be managed, the techniques to be applied, and the methodologies to be leveraged. The process introduces filtering and determines which phases of the architecture processes are impacted.

There are many techniques to change management; for example, frameworks such as PRINCE, ITIL; and so on. An organization that already has a change management methodology in place may as well customize it for architecture. The following table describes an approach to architecture change management, aimed particularly at dynamic enterprise architecture. The approach is based on classifying architectural changes into three categories:

Type	Description
Simplification change	This is typically handled via a change mechanism and is driven by the necessity to reduce cost.
Incremental change	This is also capable of being handled via change methodology, or may need limited re-architecting, depending on the scope. This is driven by the necessity to derive additional value from existing IT investment.
Re-architecting change	This requires executing the full architecture through the architecture development life cycle. This is driven by the factor to increase investment in order to create new business value.

Table 5: Managing Changes in EA

Probability indicator: 👍 👍

How is EA ROI calculated? What are critical success factors for EA?

Methodology

The ROI for EA is difficult to calculate and successful EA bears fruit over a period of time, even taking 5 years or more. It is possible to measure aspects of ROI, and one can start with what can be improved as is obvious from the as-is EA. Measure the cost of IT, for example, or the stability of your platform and technology. Then measure them again to see if they have improved as one progresses along the EA. Review the business case to understand the benefits it is expected to deliver. Identify tangible and intangible benefits and convert intangible benefits to tangible factors. All intangible benefits can be converted to tangible factors with a clear understanding of the gain.

Cost	Amount spent on EA phase
Benefits	Amount gained from EA
Benefits to cost ratio	Ratio of EA benefits to cost
ROI %	Ratio of adjusted EA benefits to cost
Net present value	Discounted cash flows of EA
Break even point	Point where benefits exceed cost for EA

Table 6: EA ROI

Critical success factors for EA

The following lists the CSFs for EA initiatives:

- Secure the entire management commitment and the scope for EA
- Customize methodologies and enterprise processes to fit EA frameworks
- Use tools and products to support software developments
- Use training and coaching to ensure that knowledge and commitment is within specified limits
- Use metrics to monitor the impact of enterprise architecture
- Create a set oriented fractal meta-model
- Use SMEs for risk and governance management

Probability indicator:

What are the benefits of EA? What are the benefits of EA for existing IT versus greenfield initiatives?

Benefits of EA

The benefits of EA are as follows:

- EA is the key to cost optimization, innovation, flexibility, and organization revenue generation
- EA reduces technology costs and accelerates time to market by facilitating common approaches
- EA provides IT transparency for business stakeholders
- EA facilitates pragmatic, cost-effective approaches to IT projects
- EA is the bridge between business strategy and IT execution
- EA shifts IT spending to strategic initiatives rather than temporary stop-gap engagements
- EA flags redundant, non-strategic and high-risk projects before they get funding
- EA ensures alignment of IT spending with business strategy
- EA breaks down IT silos, finding common solutions that reduce time to market and risk
- EA provides IT transparency required to design solutions that provide business value for the organization as a whole
- EA develops a competitive advantage by ensuring that IT spending is focused on strategic core competencies
- EA drives the cross-silo technology initiatives to resolve challenges in business
- EA develops opportunities that dramatically improve IT responsiveness to business needs

Benefits comparison – greenfield versus existing IT implementation

Let's look at the comparison:

- For existing large setups, the potential benefits are cost reductions in the IT operations, streamlining the solution set. If the EA is run efficiently, it can play a crucial role in making the enterprise agile, that is, its ability to adapt to changes. Large organizations, in particular, cannot always adapt easily, but if they have a handle on their EA they have a much better chance.

- With greenfield implementations, the organization has the opportunity to define EA principles, standards, guidelines, and views from scratch, and the ability to apply an architecture method such as TOGAF from scratch. Following a standard methodology means a higher rate of success for the project, as all aspects will be considered in the architecture. Greenfield organizations don't have a legacy of bad technology, troublesome solutions, and historical bad decisions to accommodate-their focus can be on the present and the future.

Probability indicator:

Why do you need a current state architectural blueprint?

The rational is for this as follows.

Current state EA represents the organization's as-is architecture. This is the critical asset of the IT organization. There are many reasons why the current state artifacts are so valuable:

Pain points	Description
Project architecture	It's not feasible to successfully modify a complex landscape one does not understand. Current state architecture artifacts are the basis for solution architecture and IT architects can't change a system without a current state artifact. Modifying an undocumented architecture is expensive and risky.
Knowledge retention	If you don't have a current state blueprint, you probably depend on the knowledge in your architects' heads. When the old timers leave the organization that knowledge is lost. The next architect will likely recommend replacing systems they don't understand. It's common for IT systems to be replaced simply because no one understands them.
Impact assessments	Current state architecture is mandatory for architectural impact assessments and without artifacts, one needs to do extensive research to know the impact and will be risky
IT transparency	Assets will facilitate IT transparency and are indispensable resources. Assets are critical and support the strategic decision process.

Duplication of effort	When assets don't exist, programs, stakeholders, and business departments need to conduct research when they need to modify the current state architecture. This is duplication of effort and is expensive for the enterprises.
Architectural governance	Without a current state blueprint it will be impossible for IT governance to function correctly. Stakeholders in governance need to thoroughly know the current state architecture so as to judge the impact of proposed changes.
Business strategy and IT strategy	Business strategy leverages capabilities and capital investments. Business strategy planners need to understand the current state of the technology platforms and business and hence current state architecture is a critical input for IT strategic planning.
Reference and training	Current state architecture artifacts are critical references for the entire IT organization including operations, support, and training processes.

Probability indicator: 👍

What are the common current state architectural blueprint mistakes?

Current state assets are essential for the success of an IT organization as one can't effectively manage a complex undocumented landscape. Despite the criticality of the current state, many enterprises get it incorrect. Common mistakes include:

Mistakes	Description
Stale architecture	Stale architecture is ambiguous and unusable. Updating current state assets should be a mandatory governance process or else a process needs to be in place to ensure that no changes happen without being reflected in the artifact.
Centralized architecture	A single member must not be responsible for creating and maintaining architecture assets and EAs should update the assets. The EA team should be accountable for updates.
Duplication of effort	When artifacts become troublesome, stakeholders will find ways to derail initiatives. The current state asset should not duplicate engagement artifacts.

Too detailed	Artifact templates should be flexible at the high level and there is a tendency to add to templates until they become too large and complex to maintain.
Architecture tools	EA tools simplify the management of current state assets and facilitate architecture views so that changes need to be entered once. EA tools also allow you to generate more value from your assets

Table 7: Blueprinting Mistakes

Probability indicator:

Describe typical TOC for an end state EA document created for your earlier engagement

The EA document's typical contents are as follows:

Item	Description
Introduction	Consisting of document objective, scope and audience, stakeholder, and communication protocol and/or charter
Company vision and objective	Company vision and objective and how that will be realized by the EA
Target audiences	Summary of target audiences for the artifact
Document positioning	Describes where the document is positioned with respect to the roadmap phases.
Architectural assumptions	These are a set of architectural assumptions captured for the engagement
Architectural decisions	The set of technical decisions that summarize these decisions.
Risk and mitigation	These are the identified risks and potential mitigation actions for the entire engagement.
Architectural principles	The set of architecture principle that are laid out as part of the EA program.
Approach methodology	Approach and methodology that is followed to arrive at the target EA state

Application views	UML package, class, sequence and component diagrams. Documentation on functionality and the large scale structure of major components.
Technology views	UML deployment diagrams showing servers, databases, storage, load balancers, firewalls, and DMZ, with a commentary on these illustrations.
Business views	Target operating models, business processes, business capabilities, business services, and user scenarios. Interaction views illustrating the processes of the application and documentation.
Use case views	Summary of architecturally significant use case scenarios. Interaction diagrams for architecture significant use-cases
Reference architect and domain frameworks	Reference architecture and domain frameworks as applicable to the domain, for example, eTOM, SID, ITIL
Architecture governance	A guidance on how future and current architecture would be governed and managed as part of the program
Product recommendations for various domains	This section lists the products/solutions for various areas of EA with its solution architecture along with a comparative analysis

Table 8: EA TOC

Critical sections of an EA artifact

The EA document should include three key sections which are:

- Architecture decisions
- Architecture assumptions ·
- Risk and mitigation

The risk and mitigation section is one of the key sections of the document. The following table provides an example of the risk and mitigation section:

Identified risk	Mitigation
Interacting with a merchant bank may result in sensitive data getting compromised	Architecture must provide encryption and decryption while interacting with the bank interface
Interacting with the auctioning market place may result in sensitive data getting compromised	Architecture must provide encryption and decryption while interacting with the auctioning market place

Application unavailability for the merchant bank may result in the decrease of customer satisfaction and loss of revenues	Merchant bank should provide high availability architecture
Application unavailability for the auctioning market place may result in the decrease of customer satisfaction and loss of revenues	Auctioning market place should provide high availability architecture

Table 9: Risk and Mitigation

EA tools

These tools are leveraged by EA stakeholders for their strategic planning through to execution. Strategic decision making is provided through capturing key enterprise context, along with content development and analysis capabilities across the technology, information, business, and application architectures domains. Effectively share your EA assets with technical and non-technical stakeholders across your organization and invite them to view, analyze, and provide input. There are gamut of tools available for architectural artifacts, but the usage is predominately driven by the customer organization. The following are the widely leveraged tools for architectural assets:

MS Visio	MS Word	MS PowerPoint
IBM rational systems architect (EA modeling tool)	Troux (complete life cycle management)	Archi-Mate (UML modeling)
ARIS (BPM modeling tool)		

Probability indicator: 👍👍

How do you evaluate architecture conforms to the enterprise architecture?

It is key to align EA initiatives during the initiation phase to ensure architecture compliance processes are included in the planning phase. Once the architecture has been defined, a compliance assessment should be carried out. The compliance assessment ensures architecture conforms to the defined organizational EA. This enables engaging team members and giving feedback on the target EA. The compliance assessment includes checklists for information, applications, infrastructure, security, management, monitoring, frameworks, and products.

Probability indicator: 👍 👍

What is an architecture vision and what are the stakeholder concerns?

An architecture vision is created and defined during the engagement initiation phase. The purpose of the vision is to build consensus with key stakeholders of the plan's requisite outcome for the IT architecture. The vision emphasizes the benefits of the proposed architecture to decision makers and is like the elevator pitch for senior executives and CXOs. The architecture vision also shows how the target architecture supports business strategy, business objectives, and stakeholder concerns.

The architecture vision artifact contents include:

- Organizational problem definition
- Stakeholders' goals and objectives
- Business process definition
- Actors and roles
- Organizational restraints
- IT principles and standards
- Architecture strategy
- Mapping the proposed architecture to business processes and requirements

Stakeholder concerns

A stakeholder is an individual, team, or organization having an interest in the realization of the EA. Many initiatives have representatives from various stakeholder groups, but their importance will differ. However, if you do not include each class, you will have a problem. One has to prioritize and balance the needs of different stakeholder groups, so that when conflicts occur, well informed decisions are done. Each group of individuals will have their own interests, requirements, and needs to be met.

- Work with different units of the organization to drive value from its IT assets
- Leverage a matrix structure for software architects
- Provide thought leadership in governance, strategy, innovation, cost optimization, and efficiency
- Work together with senior leadership to execute EA strategy
- Form a team consisting of EA, TA, infrastructure specialists, and application developers
- Guide the IT team in the usage and development of IT applications and infrastructure

Probability indicator:

What are business capability maps ?

The business capability map is the key asset in business architecture. The business capability map is the business architecture defining the business' ability to execute. It is standard practice to provide, from level 1 to 3, deep dive view capability maps. Ideally, business capability maps are maintained in a business process management or EA tool. Business architects maintain current and target states in the capability maps. The target states are based on business strategy and goals and are referred to as **Target Operating Models (TOM)**.

Level 1

The level 1 capability map defines high-level capabilities of the business and is often segregated by the location, product, and department. For example, the following figure illustrates the level 1 capabilities of a software sales department:

Figure 4: Business capability map (level 1)

Level 2

The level 2 capability map is another level in detail and answers questions without getting into the *why"* or *"how:*

Figure 5: Business capability map (level 2)

Level 3

The level 3 capability map is a high-level process diagram that begins to answer the *how*:

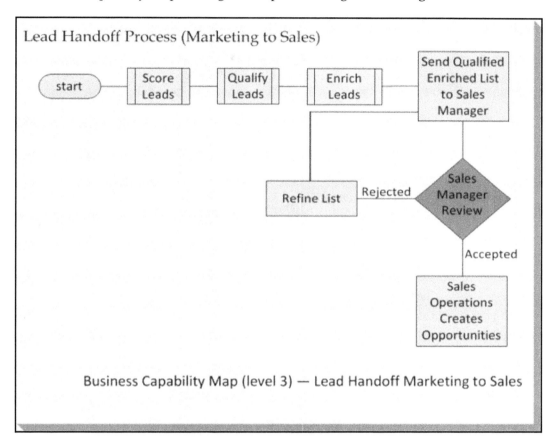

Figure 6: Business capability map (level 3)

Business capability driven enterprise architecture

Everything about the business can be inter-locked with capabilities and they are the keys that integrate the business architecture to the IT application and data domains. They are the taxonomy for business execution. Business capabilities are simply descriptions of business functionality. They are usually broken down into a hierarchy of two-three levels. Capabilities are business vocabulary that establishes what the business does. Business strategy can also be defined in terms of capabilities and KPIs and can be defined at the capability level. There are several benefits to business capability driven EA:

- Business capabilities can establish business requirements in a structured model
- Top down planning defines the "why" and "what" before "how"
- Business capabilities can be standardized across industries
- Business capabilities are represented in visual models to articulate easily
- Defining metrics at the capability level is a great way to align business and IT

Business, PMO, and EA is often mapped to business capabilities. For example:

- Business strategy–business capabilities
- Data–business capabilities
- Products–business capabilities
- Projects–business capabilities
- Applications–business capabilities

Probability indicator:

How to build an enterprise taxonomy

These are vocabularies leveraged to describe an organization. Any patterns from your operations, business, or technology can potentially be described in taxonomies. Taxonomies are hierarchical and are defined at levels which means progressively in further detail. A good taxonomy is valuable and easy to sell. Enterprise taxonomies fit your capabilities, models, and strategies into neat boxes. In other words, they have the power to impose order on complex enterprises. Common examples include:

- Organizational roles
- Product catalogues

- Customer types
- Order types
- Operational capabilities
- Technology platforms
- Business capabilities

Value of enterprise taxonomies

Taxonomies impose order and hence can easily be perceived as rigid or dictatorial. The key to selling a taxonomy in the organization is stakeholder collaboration. Stakeholders who are consulted are less likely to resist adoption. They will ensure that information is interpreted consistently. There are several valuable uses for taxonomies, for example, drive reporting and metrics, clarifying communication, and improving business processes and documentation.

Probability indicator:

What are the secrets of successful enterprise architecture?

EAs should be aware of the issues facing key executives such as CXO. This means keeping a pulse on key engagements, KPIs, and initiatives. Rules of thumb for succeeding with EA are:

Mistakes	Description
Clear vision	Establish simple and clear vision. Religiously follow the vision and publish it so that all the stakeholders are aware. Integrate the mission, goals, and objective back to the vision.
Keep it lean	EA practice should be lean and highly focused SMEs. An army of enterprise architects is not required for the organization.
Measurable objectives	KPIs for efficiency, costs, and customer experience have to be monitored. Integrate the vision and EA initiatives to these metrics.
Governance	Aligning projects with EA will require support from senior management. It is the key to enabling relationships with architects and key decision makers for governance to succeed.
Stay consistent	Inconsistent EA is risky and all may be lost. EA artifacts should be consistent, and should tie back with the vision.

| Stick to enterprise architecture | Often enterprise architects get pulled into the finer details of engagements but successful architects understand the scope of EA and stick to it. EA templates and style guides should be established and rolled out. EA is all about communication and an effective style is the key to a successful EA. |
| Quick wins | EA is inherently a long journey and it is important to show value to the business stakeholders on a regular basis. EA is not an endless process that is impossible to tie to quarterly results. |

Table 10: Secrets of Successful EA

Probability indicator: 👍 👍

What are the things your CIO can do to ensure enterprise architecture success?

The best practices to ensure EA success are as follows.

EA programs often fail due to lack of support and insight from top management. Here are key things a CIO can do to ensure the EA investment achieves the significant payback:

Best Practices	Description
Set a clear EA mandate	As the EA team struggles to define and achieve recognition, give the team the support it deserves with an achievable mandate. Communicate clearly the mandate to the IT organization. If the EA team's mandate includes business architecture, it needs to be communicated to the business in a joint statement that includes support from CEOs and CXOs.
Get EA in front of the business	Streamline architectural communication to your business through EA and ensure the chief architect is in front of the business.
Give EA a governance role	EA involvement significantly increases engagement success rates, reduces costs, and effectively aligns IT with business strategy. EAs are effective when they are part of the architectural decision-making process for critical initiatives.
Learn about EA	EA is critical to your success as a CIO. Ask the EA team for an overview of the EA and a good place to start is the TOGAF framework.

Table 11: CIO EA Success

Probability indicator:

Why enterprise architecture engagements do not succeed

EA was conceived to address the complexity of IT applications and their misalignment with business strategy. Similar issues still exist, augmented by the increasing pace of technology change. Here are the failure areas, followed by recommendations on how to avoid them:

Root cause	Description
Lack of sponsorship	Sponsored EA are able to build trust by consistently delivering value for the business. Lack of sponsorship will lead to the failure of the best of breed architects.
Hiring or promoting the wrong person	Often technical people get promoted when they lack other important aspects. The SMEs should be interested in the domain, the ability to translate technology into business outcomes, and the ability to communicate and present.
Building an ivory tower	Programs hire a bunch of brilliant EAs who re-treat for a long time and return with high-end frameworks. They present to the leadership, who have no idea about the contents. Ivory towers tend to increase the complexity and derail these engagements.
Maintaining the EA artifact factory	Few EA teams are busy documenting as-is architecture. They have a significant number of assets at their disposal and instead these teams should focus on producing measurable outcomes.
Clinging to a particular framework	There are significant numbers of EA frameworks, and there is no silver bullet among them. The best method is to study the key frameworks, customize the key 10% to fit the organization's requirements and business strategy.
Thinking enterprise architecture equals technology architecture	Most EA programs are initiated by IT and never progress beyond the technology domain although technology standards, roadmaps, and engineering practices will produce cheaper, simpler, and reusable solutions they won't align your IT investments with business goals.

Table 12: EA Failure Reasons

Probability indicator:

What are the common mistakes made by enterprise architects?

The common mistakes made by enterprise architects are as follows:

Mistakes	Description
Focusing on one domain	The scope of EA includes the data, application, infrastructure and business domain but on many occasions EAs focus on one domain and few architects are business-oriented, lacking insight into technical details.
Long and complex	EA needs to be clearly and precisely understood and this is difficult if it is overly complex, thus EA should be short and simple.
Working in a bubble	EA is about breaking the silos in favor of common solutions. The key role of enterprise architects is to drive the EA process and define the EA with support from business.
Governance	Governance is the most challenging aspect of EA and is also the most neglected area but is critical to be enabled for all engagements and initiatives.
Silver bullets	A few EAs prefer solutions that they tend to apply to all situations and often take the shape of a trendy concept such as SOA or big data.
Jargon	Standardized terms such as TOGAF and ITIL are great if you are discussing with peers but an enterprise architect has to be a great communicator, and part of this is leveraging the vocabulary that the all stakeholders can understand.

Table 13: Common Mistake by Enterprise Architects

Probability indicator: 👍 👍

Is enterprise architecture dead?

There may be significant gaps between business and IT due to legacy system, culture and politics. EA is supposed to fix these gaps with a unified and standardize approach to application, business, data, and infrastructure architecture:

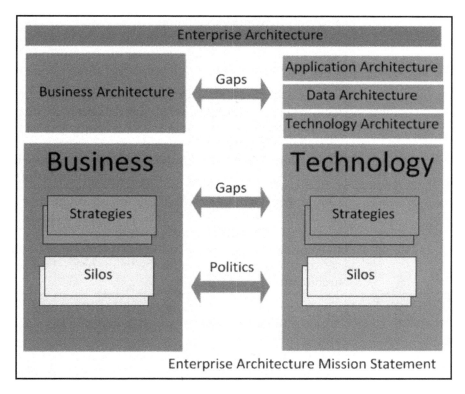

Figure 7: Dead enterprise architecture

The representation of EA pitfalls is as follows:

Pitfall	Description
Wrong lead architect	Challenge: The biggest EA problem as a chief architect is an ineffective leader. He may understand EA well but has ineffective leadership skills that even a good team structure and staffing cannot overcome. Resolution: Such an architect should be replaced by an SME with strong soft skills such as communication and presentation and being well respected and strategically aligned.
Insufficient stakeholder support	Challenge: This happens when key stakeholders outside the EA team don't participate in the EA engagements and top management questions its value. Resolution: Make EA initiative a top priority across the organization and secure executive-team sponsorship.
Not engaging business stakeholders	Challenge: When business and IT are not aligned, issues include non-technical SMEs trying to make technical decisions and EAs become too tactical in response. Resolution: EAs get involved in the development of business strategy and collaborate with the team for the business architecture.
Doing only technical domain-level architecture	Challenge: This dated EA approach is still in use in organizations and is narrower in scope than technical architecture. Resolution: Holistic EA best-practice is an added value as it includes business, data, application, and infrastructure domains.
Not measuring and not communicating the impact	Challenge: The value of EA is indirect, so it may not be obvious in the engagement and hence exposes the program to risk of failure. Resolution: EAs create a slide to demonstrate each success story of EA or the business outcomes incrementally. They should include measurements of EA in the roadmap.

Not establishing effective EA governance	Challenge: Enterprise architects have to avoid the temptation to wait for more architecture content before setting governance processes. Resolution: Development of EA and governance goes hand-in-hand.

Table 14: EA Pitfalls

Probability indicator:

How do IT support new business initiatives?

EA must be able to visualize the big picture, the forest as opposed to the trees. This will also circle back to the need of having an extensible architecture where building blocks can be plugged into the landscape with the minimum effort and risk.

Businesses should not view IT as a key component to their overall business plans. IT can shape the business strategy of an organization. Businesses can leverage IT capabilities to mold their future plans. The key is to ensure that IT is aligned with the business. This is done through building the end-to-end picture of the business landscape or the business architecture and see where IT can support areas. Organizations that leverage new technologies in production, marketing, and other business processes stand a better chance of beating their market competitors. Companies choose the best IT components for their businesses when business and IT strategy head in the same directions. This results in happier employees and customers, which will increase the production and customer consumption of products.

Probability indicator:

Architecture governance

Architecture governance is the methodology by which EAs are managed and controlled at an enterprise level. It includes the following:

- Establishing a system of controls for creation and management of architectural assets and ensuring the efficient introduction and evolution of architecture standards and best practices
- Establishing methodology for compliance with regulatory frameworks and industry standards

- Defining methodologies supporting effective management of governance processes with agreed parameters
- Establishing framework to ensure accountability to the stakeholder community, both external and internal to enterprises

Probability indicator: 👍 👍

What value does enterprise architecture governance create?

Governance is a framework consisting of approach, processes, cultural orientation, and responsibilities that ensure the effectiveness and efficiencies of the architectures. The following are the benefits derived through effective governance of architectures:

- Interlinking data and IT processes to business goals and strategies
- Establishing industry standards. best practices, and frameworks in the organizations
- Aligning with industry frameworks such as COBIT for planning, implementing, and monitoring IT performance
- Securing the organization's digital assets
- Aligning with legal and regulatory standards such as accountability, security, auditability, and responsibility
- Facilitating risk management and mitigation
- Corporate governance verifies architectural choice and ensures that budgets are directed in an efficient manner
- Minimum level of IT planning maturity is guaranteed

Probability indicator: 👍 👍 👍

What are the architecture governance–critical success factors

To ensure a successful architecture governance it is important to consider the following:

- Establishing best practices for adoption, reuse, and retirement of architecture policies, methodologies, and organizational structures

- Defining organizational roles, responsibilities, and structures to facilitate the governance processes
- Integration of processes and tools to establish the processes, both culturally and procedurally
- Managing the SLA for the control of governance processes, assessments, dispensations, compliance, and OLAs
- Meeting all requirements for integrity, confidentiality, efficiency, effectiveness, reliability and compliance of all governance information, processes, and services

Probability indicator: 👍👍

What do you understand by architecture governance?

Architecture governance is the methodology by which EAs are managed and controlled at an enterprise level. Architecture governance ensures the principles of architecture are well applied to both the system architecture of the underlying IT systems. Governance ensures organizations meet the IT and business and objectives. Architecture governance ensures effective alignment of business and IT, manages risk by reducing the probability of failures in large complex programs, and incorporates cost-efficiencies and business value.

Architecture governance methodology

Architecture governance includes the following:

- **Organization**: Developing a framework that enables accountability to a defined set of stakeholder within the organization.
- **Processes**: Establishing processes for the effective enablement of the governance processes and system of controls to ensure compliance with regulatory and standards bodies.

- **Tools**: Establishing controls over the management of architectural assets, to ensure the efficient evolution of architectures for enterprises.

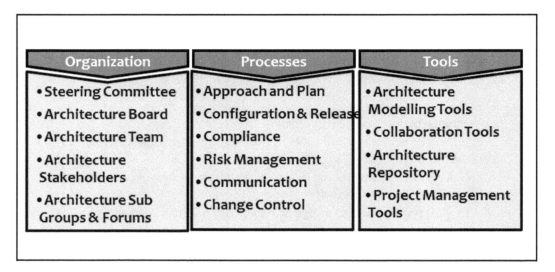

Figure 8: Architectural governance – People, Processes and Tools

Approach

The approach towards achieving architectural governance is as follows:

- Work with enterprise architect teams to establishes the EA ownership and stewardship policies.
- Develop policies and methodologies for EA assets management.
- Plan compliance reviews to ensure compliance with standards, guidelines, and principles.
- Identify potential hotspots where existing policies need change, or new ones have to be introduced.
- Work with the security architect to establish organization security strategies and policies.

Probability indicator: 👍 👍

How can one tell if the enterprise architecture is comprehensive?

There are various approaches to achieving the required comprehensibility for EA. One approach is through periodic reviews of all the architectural deliverables against the business goals, objectives, and requirements. A formal approach to large transformation programs is through architecture governance boards. An architecture governance board ensures the principles of EA are applied to both architecture and design of the underlying IT applications. It also ensures enterprises meet business and IT goals and objectives. Architecture governance ensure effective alignment of IT and business, manages risk by reducing the probability of failures in complex programs, and incorporates cost-efficiencies and business value. There are three important elements of architecture governance strategy that relate to the success of EA within the enterprise:

- Cross-LOB EA board must be established with support from senior management to oversee the governance strategy.
- A comprehensive set of architecture principles should be defined, to guide the method in which an organization is fulfilling its mission.
- An architecture compliance strategy should be enabled to ensure compliance and impact assessments and compliance reviews.

Probability indicator:

What are the objectives for the governance boards architecture compliance reviews ?

Conducting architecture compliance reviews will assist in following:

- Reviews help with architectural alternatives, as the stakeholders from the business guide decisions of what is good for the business, as opposed to the technically best fit option.
- The output from the compliance review is a key asset for the CIO to assist in decision making.
- Architecture reviews make the organization engage with the development teams who might proceed without the involvement of governance.

- Architecture reviews create a swift business outcome for the business community.
- Compliance helps ensure the alignment of IT with business goals and helps identify areas for re-alignment.
- Identifies areas to be considered for integration into the EA as are uncovered by the compliance assessments.

Probability indicator:

How is the architecture compliance review scheduled for the program?

The timing of compliance reviews should be defined with regard to the development of the architectures. Compliance reviews should be held at appropriate checkpoints in the engagement life cycle. Specific checkpoints should be included during the development of the architecture definition itself and implementation of the architecture governance. Architecture scheduling for assessments should be a combination of one of the following:

- Initiation
- Design
- Major design changes
- Ad hoc

The architecture compliance review is targeted at a point in time when requirements and EA are firmed-up, and the architecture is taking shape, but before its completion. The goal is to schedule the review as soon as is practical, at a stage when there is still time to correct any issues. Inputs to the compliance review may come from other parts of the standard process life cycle.

Probability indicator:

Who are the stakeholders for architecture compliance reviews?

A stakeholder is an individual, team, or organization, having an interest in the realization of EA. Many development projects include representatives from different stakeholder groups, although their importance will vary. However, if you do not consider each class, you will have issues in the future. One has to balance and prioritize the needs of various stakeholder groups, so that when conflicts occur, well informed decisions can be made.

The following list as follows:

Stakeholder	Responsibility
Architecture board	Ensures that IT architectures are consistent and support overall business needs.
Project leader (or project board)	Responsible for the entire engagement.
Architecture review co-coordinator	Monitors architecture development and review process and is more business- than technology-oriented.
Lead enterprise architect	An IT architecture SME to ensure that architecture is future-proof and technically coherent.
Architect	Lead enterprise architect's technical assistants.
Customer	Ensures that functional requirements are clearly expressed and articulated. Manages that part of the organization that will depend on the success of the IT described in the architecture.
Business domain expert	To ensure the processes that satisfy the business requirements are justified and understood. Knows how the business domain operates.
Project principals	Ensures that architects have good understanding of the customer business landscape and provide input to business domain experts or architects alike.

Table 1: Architectural governance – Organization

Probability indicator: 👍

What does the architecture compliance review checklists consist of and what metrics are used to validate compliance?

Compliance checklist

The compliance checklists provides a wide range of questions that are leveraged in architecture compliance reviews. The questions include the disciplines of domain architects, methodologies, governance, data management, security, and, monitoring and management. Organizations can leverage the checklists tailored to their needs. The checklists provided have many questions for review and are intended to be tailored to the project.

Checklists consist of architectural principles that provokes a question and a description of what to look for in the response. The extensions to a checklist are intended for smart re-phrasing of the questions and to give the SME a feel for the rationale of the question. They may be expressed orally, as part of interview or working session. The compliance reviews ensure that the architecture domains have sufficient coverage per se the depth and breadth:

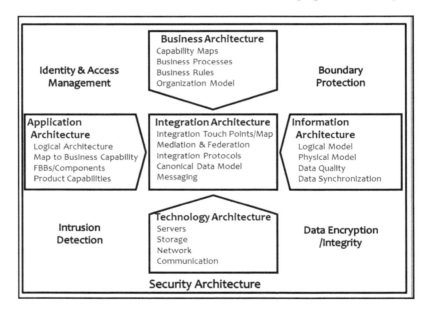

Figure 9: Enterprise architecture domains – EA reference architecture

Approach validating architecture compliance

Metrics should be drawn up with various stakeholders from risk/security, operations, financing/contracts, and business. Metrics will vary for enterprises, but will include conformance with architectural and strategic direction, architecture principles, security requirements, methodologies and processes, domain requirements, and so on. EA is much more than IT solution conformation and requires more than just IT metrics such as performance and reliability to be addressed.

Probability indicator:

How can one evaluate if the solution conforms to enterprise architecture?

Once the EA is defined, a compliance assessment is done. It is critical to engage during the initial phase to ensure architecture compliance processes are leveraged. The compliance assessment ensures architecture conforms to defined requirements. This is also an opportunity to engage project teams and get feedback for EA. The compliance assessment consists of checklists for business, applications, data, infrastructure, security, management, and monitoring domains.

Probability indicator:

Application architecture

In information systems, application architecture is one of several architecture domains that form the pillars of an EA or solution architecture. The term "application architecture" is commonly used for the internal structure of an application, for its software modularization. Application architecture is the methodology for ensuring that the applications suite being leveraged by the enterprise to create the composite architecture is reliable, scalable, and manageable.

What is the methodology for developing application architecture ?

The recommended methodology for developing application architectures is as follows:

- Understand the applications landscape, the basis the application baseline, including business requirements, and it's correlation to business architecture
- Identify logical applications and the best-fit physical components of applications
- Define KPIs for the entire landscape by co-relating applications to services, functions, data, and processes
- Elaborate application architecture by understanding the applications function, and the integration, migration, development, and operational concerns.

What are the typical aspects that you would look for in an application architecture?

Qualities

The following is the comprehensive list for ensuring completeness of an application architecture:

- All modules are well defined, including their functionality and their interfaces to other modules
- The architecture designed can accommodate likely changes and is extensible
- The architecture is independent of the machine and language that will be used to implement it
- The design decision, assumption, risks, and mitigation actions
- The necessary buy versus build decisions are included
- The architecture emphasizes on reusability
- Key aspects of the user interface are defined
- No part is over or under-architected
- Major system goals are clearly stated

- The whole architecture hangs together conceptually
- Motivations for all major decisions are provided
- Diagram depicting application architecture

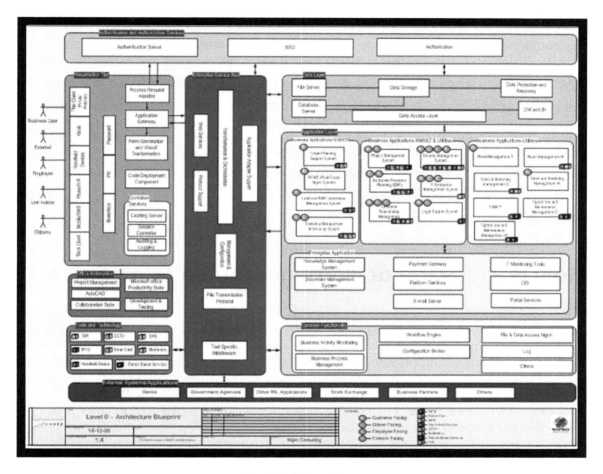

Figure 10: Application architecture

Probability indicator:

How are tiers in an n-tier architecture plumbed together?

This is done through the use of protocols such as SOAP, RMI, and CORBA for building distributed architecture and providing the plumbing mechanism. For example, if the presentation tier and business are designed in .NET, .NET remoting will the right choice. A SOAP web service is the choice if business logic needs to be exposed and accessible outside the domain.

When leveraging a remoting mechanism, such as RMI, the contracts between two tiers is pre-defined. In SOA, the client can dynamically discover the contract. For example, web services expose contracts through the **Web Service Description Language (WSDL)**, which provides decoupling. At times, it is essential to define data contracts or data transfer objects that can be transferred between tiers. Internally, tiers have to convert DTOs to business objects ensuring that the contract doesn't break if the database changes.

Probability indicator:

How is message delivery guarantee to a source system?

One approach to this is through JMS/MQ, which provides queues that store messages if the destination node is not reachable/available. The messages remain in the queue until they are finally consumed by the application end point. JMS is only a specification for messaging services from Oracle and is part of the JEE framework. The corresponding implementation is the MQ series from IBM which provides the API and tools for building JMS compliant applications which are highly reliable. Message queues can be configured to work in a point-to-point model or a publish-subscribe model.

Please refer to the following figure:

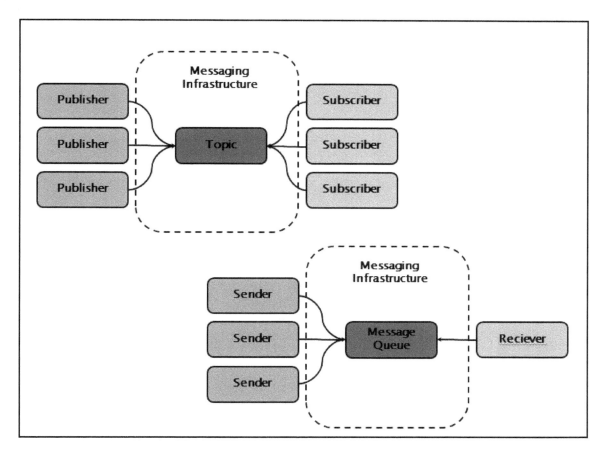

Figure 17: JMS/MQ architecture

Probability indicator: 👍

What is an enterprise resource planning application?

An **Enterprise Resource Planning** (**ERP**) is a business process management product that allows an enterprise to leverage a suite of integrated applications to manage business and automate functions such as customers, administration, logistics, and production. ERP software integrates all facets of operations, including planning, marketing, sales, development, and manufacturing.

ERP is an enterprise software that is targeted to be leveraged by larger enterprises and often requires dedicated SMEs to customize and manage upgrades and deployment. In contrast, small business ERPs are lightweight business management solutions, customized for the specific industry.

Benefits of ERP

The benefits of ERP are as follows:

- Finer controls on financial compliance declarations such as Basel II or Sarbanes-Oxley, as well as other forms of compliance.
- Master data source for products and services, such as data pertaining to customers, vendors, suppliers, products, and orders, drives fast product development and launch cycles which make the company competitive.
- Access to valuable organization data delivers a 360 degree view of the business that drives continuous improvement and establishes performance metrics and measures to gauge business health.
- Facilitates streamlined procurement and sourcing processes and drives alignment to customer demands.
- Facilitates sales and operations planning with access to critical data and fosters **closed loop** processes that ensure the business does not overpromise and/or under deliver to customers.
- Automating business processes such as invoicing and purchase orders within one system improves accuracy and reduces inefficiencies.

- Leveraging a single source of information for billing and customer interactions improves service levels and increases customer satisfaction.

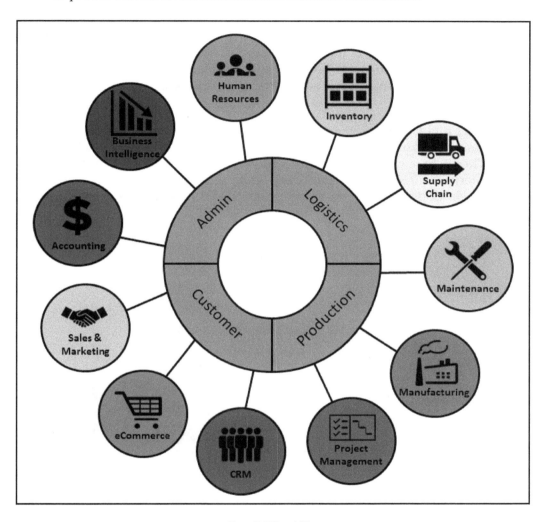

Figure 13: ERP capabilities

Probability indicator: 👍👍

What is customer relationship management? What are the benefits of CRM?

CRM is the acronym for customer relationship management. Customer relationship management entails all aspects of interaction with a customer including sales, services, or marketing domains. While the term "CRM" is leveraged for customer business relationships, CRM also manages business contacts, prospects, clients, contract wins, and sales leads.

CRM solutions provide the customer data to help provide services or products that your customers want, and provide better customer service, cross-selling and up-selling more effectively. They help to close deals, retain current customers, and better understand your customer. Enterprises frequently look for ways to personalize online experiences through tools such as help-desk software, e-mail organizers, and different types of enterprise applications.

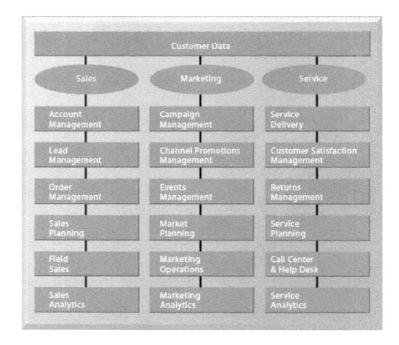

Figure 13: CRM building blocks

Benefits of CRM

Let's take a look at the benefits of CRM:

- Decision making is quick and well supported by real-time reporting across all business teams.
- Marketing capabilities bring quality leads through continually improving, segmentation and campaigns.
- Pipeline reports are trusted and leveraged for reliable sales and production forecasts to increase predictably and efficiency.
- Performance bottlenecks are efficiently identified so timely action can be taken to correct issues.
- Automation removes the inefficient manual processes to cut admin costs and eliminate duplication of efforts so teams can focus on core business activities.
- Customer churn is low as CRM business users have direct access to the relationship details they need to engage clients and provide a good experience.
- CRM integrates with accounting and other back-office solutions to join processes and remove the duplication of tasks.
- Users can quickly check customer order histories to assess buying patterns and identify new sales opportunities.
- Mobile and field teams can work productively with reliable access to customer information they need via their smart devices.
- Sales cycles are shortened and win rates are improved as teams have visibility of which prospects are most likely to close.
- Personalized marketing communications and increased lead generation from customer lists with complete relationship and behavior details are archived in CRM.
- CRM manages customer contacts and customer service calls/tickets

Popular CRM software

The following table illustrates the different types of CRM software:

SAP CRM	Salesforce	Oracle Siebel
OnContact	Sage Act	Prophet
AIM CRM	Relenta	Webasyst
Sugar CRM		

Probability indicator: 👍 👍

Describes the challenges organization faces while incorporating CRM ?

The challenges organizations face while incorporating CRM include:

- Database cleansing ensures client information is in the correct state
- Integrating with other IT applications, whether new or existing
- IT applications are very large and complex, requiring trainers for end users
- Lack of a clear transitional process
- Primary focus on product sales and market segmentation
- Metrics and KPIs are not monitored and tracked
- Weak functional organization of a company
- Lack of responses to customer recommendations and feedback
- Introducing technology solutions without the required frameworks and methodologies

Probability indicator: 👍 👍

Describe the approach leveraged for the product selection phase of the IT architecture

Substantiate a rationale for picking the system over others and the factors that you considered while making the final selection. The following are the key factors for product selection. One can then leverage a decision matrix for the final data consolidation and share it with the customer executives.

The decision matrix is one of the approaches to leverage in this scenario. The decision matrix is one of the approaches to tackling this scenario. This has been explained in *IT strategy and advisory* section.

Cost	Efforts	Timelines
Alignment with overall IT strategy of organization	Existing application's inability to scale or challenges/issues	Existing system not delivering value to the business
Product reached end of life or is built using legacy tools and frameworks		

Probability indicator: 👍👍

Describe what you understand by application performance management (APM)

Application monitoring and performance management helps organizations monitor and optimize infrastructure performance and availability through the use of best practices by identifying and resolving problems in distributed environments. Many organizations begin with no visibility, forcing them into management that is reactive, ad hoc, and slow. The goal is to make sure you have in place the capabilities to assure that you can meet your service level agreements.

Benefits of APM

The benefits are listed as follows:

- Using advanced, robotic monitoring, you can provide an early warning of performance problems, reducing or avoiding the impact of interruptions on users.
- Implementing custom dashboards can enhance your insight into the status of key applications for individual lines of business.
- Deploying agent-based tracking helping you find and remediate difficult-to-isolate, sporadic problems.
- Implementing agentless solutions provides a low-touch approach to discovering and viewing your infrastructure topology and to isolating problems.
- Adding solutions that utilize application agents can improve the accuracy of diagnostics with increased visibility into the key performance indicators of each infrastructure component.

The following diagram depicting APM capabilities:

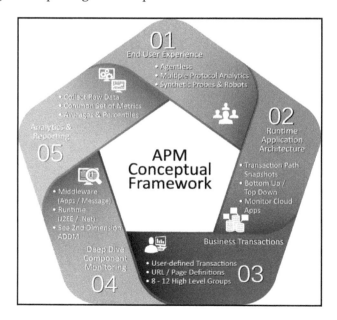

Figure 15: Application performance management capabilities

Probability indicator:

How do you arrive at the costing of a solution while building RFP responses?

There are three major factors to costing a solution. For the first two parts, you will have to engage with the product vendor/ISV to get the information. While there are online tools and data available it's always a good practice to engage the ISV once the solution/building blocks are finalized. The third factor is predominately related to service aspects and will be governed by the billing rates for your organizations. This is calculated through either function points, use case-based, or WBS estimations. This stage will also include finalizing the team organization/structure before working on the effort estimation. This is done with the help from project managers and delivery managers.

This includes:

Component	Description
Part I: Software component	Applications, products, tools, frameworks, monitoring software and antivirus tools.
Part II: Hardware component	Servers, networks, storages, disks.
Part III: Services component	Design, build, and testing phases that will be provided by SI/vendors support and maintained for the next 3-5 years

Table 1: Costing of solution

Probability indicator: 👍👍👍

How to migrate an application from a traditional environment to the public cloud

Approach for cloud migration:

Steps	Description
Cloud assessment	Financial assessment: TCO calculation Compliance and security and technical assessment Identify tools that can be re-used and the ones that need to be procured Create cloud migration plan and measure success through metrics
Proof of concept	Build pilot and validate the technology solution in the cloud
Moving your data	Understand different storage options in the cloud Migrate fileservers, RDBMS, and MySQL
Moving your apps	Forklift and hybrid migration strategy Build cloud-aware layers or tiers Create AMIs for each component
Leveraging the cloud	Automate elasticity and SDLC Harden security Create dashboard to manage resources and leverage multiple availability zones
Optimization	Optimize usage based on demand, improve efficiency, and implement monitoring and telemetry capability Re-engineer applications and decompose relational databases

Table 2: Cloud Migration Approach

Probability indicator:

How can you overcome organizational silo issues?

Challenges

The following are the list of problems with silo organizations:

- Duplication of cost and effort
- Working at cross-purposes
- Lack of synergies
- Little knowledge transfer
- Lack of economies of scale
- The largest problem is a lack of alignment with the overall company strategy

Resolution

In order to correct silo problems, there is no need to re-organize the entire company. Here are the steps that can help break down walls and allow **cross-pollination**:

- Stimulate cross-LOB teams to work on company-wide initiatives. Employees will get to know each other, gain exposure, and even accept assignments in different functional areas.
- Abolish formality in the organizations and the need to go through a chain of commands before involving senior leadership.
- Define standardize systems and platforms across organization and give employees access to the same information. This will discourage information hoarding.
- Plan for comfortable spaces in each facility where cross-LOB teams can come together in a relaxed environment to brainstorm products/services, processes, and create solutions.

Probability indicator:

Business architecture

Business architecture is one domain of EA that describes various architectural aspects of businesses. SMEs that create business architecture are the business architects. Business architecture articulates the functional structure of enterprise including the business process and business capabilities. One of the key outputs of business architecture is business capability models. The business capability is a certain business functionality that delivers business values under specific conditions. The business capabilities are provided via business services and business processes which in turn implement business functionality:

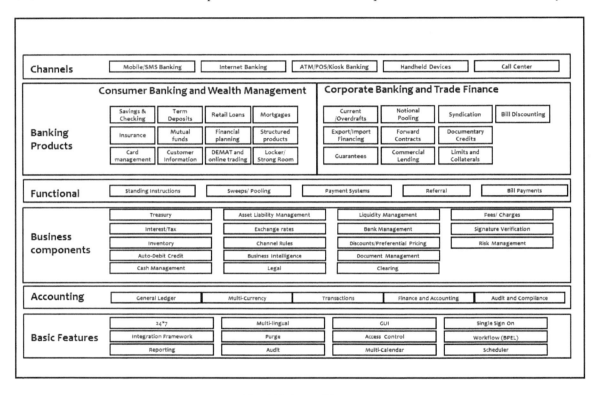

Figure 16: Business capability map

Business architecture is the operating structure and represents the business functions, flows, and information. Business architecture defines key business entities that interact to deliver value to the business stakeholders. Business architecture is a big picture showing all key business functions, operating models, and business flows. Developing BA requires that each function and flow has to be expanded, documented, and road mapped until it properly supports the vision of all stakeholders.

Why do organizations need business architecture ?

Purpose of business architecture

Business architecture enables insight and improvements of operational models. BA shapes people and technology and enables alignment of business and technology to delivery enterprise objectives and goals. Business processes and functions drive the type of technology that implements them. Over time, enterprises transform into technology silos, as a result of take-overs or mergers, or due to lack of processes. The absence of business architects hinders organizations to be able to align to the demands of the future quickly. Non-nimble enterprises in a competitive market fast-past landscape will not last long. The business environment constantly changes requiring enterprises to align with compliance or regulatory measures and frameworks. Business architecture is a vehicle for enterprises to analyze the impact of transformation and respond swiftly to these demands.

By leveraging reusable assets created by business architects, an enterprise can articulate the impact of changes, without expensive investments. Business architects enable appropriate repeatable processes and models to swiftly move from a strategic vision to execution.

Business architecture is a set of strategic tools for aligning capability models and business operations as shown in the following figure:

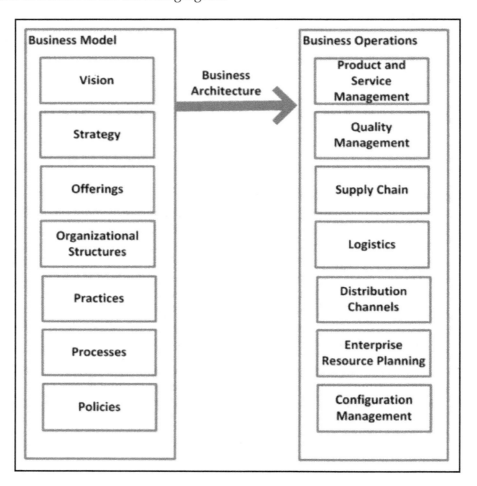

Figure 17: Business architecture

Business reference models examples

The following are examples of business reference models or reference architectures for different industries:

- Federal EA Business Reference Model-US Federal Government DoD Business Reference Model-Defense Open Group Exploration-Mining Business Reference Model
- Frameworx (eTOM) – Telecom **Supply Chain Operations Reference (SCOR)** model -SCM SAP R/3 reference model – ERP
- Oracle Industry Reference Model IRM – Banking Oracle Retail Reference Model-Retail IBM Insurance Framework-Insurance

Probability indicator:

What does Business architecture cover ?

Business architects are the bridge between strategy and execution for enterprises. Business strategy and business requirements drive the business architecture. Business architecture ensures that articulating these objectives into incremental steps can be implemented in a consistent manner across all LOBs to achieve the end results. Business architects drive the definition of business strategy, planning, and organizational processes.

Business architects create the target state business state entities which include process, capability, organization and their interconnections. These entities are the key inputs to the solution design process along with the other EA domains. In all cases, the focus of business architecture is on the following:

- **Organization structure**: The organizational structure, identifying business locations, and relating them to organizational units. The organizational chart can be used to map out this structure.
- **Business goals and objectives**: Business goals and objectives for each organizational unit.
- **Business functions (maps)**: Decomposition of major functional areas into sub-functions/sub-domains.
- **Business services**: This is the services that each of the enterprise units provides to its customers, both internally and externally.
- **Business processes**: The business processes that the organizations supports, including measures and deliverables (KPIs and KRAs).

Relationship to enterprise architecture

Business architecture is one domain of EA and the other domain are application, data, and infrastructure, as illustrated in the following figure will illustrate:

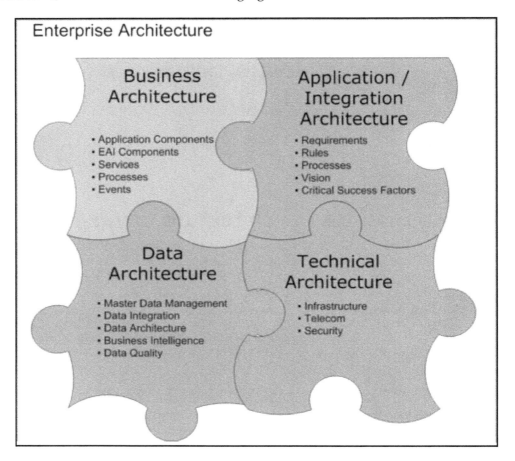

Figure 18: Relationship to enterprise architecture

The five views of business architecture

Business architecture provides a comprehensive asset for organizations or LOBs. Typically, five different views of the enterprise are created:

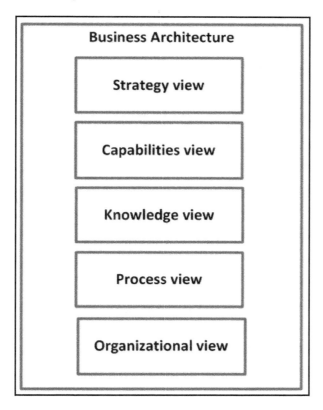

Figure 19: Five views of business architecture

The business architecture is split into:

- **Strategy view**: Strategic roadmap for fulfilling the business goals and KPIs that can be leveraged to track an organization's progress
- **Capabilities view**: Explains business services including core business, business management, customer-facing, and partner relationship capabilities
- **Knowledge view**: Enterprise taxonomy and interconnect between core concepts such as customer, supplier, products, services
- **Process view**: Key business processes and scenarios that cross enterprise boundaries. Describes roles, responsibilities, and resources parts of each process
- **Organizational view**: Mapping of business capabilities to roles, groups, and business units

Current versus target business architecture

Business architecture articulates the current state and the target state basis of the business goals. It is a common mistake to spend too much effort documenting the current state. The current state is required in order to identify and analyze issues and gaps and their impacts. Gaps in capabilities such as people, processes, services, integrations, and technologies are identified and scored.

Value of business architecture

Business architecture is a cornerstone that facilitates accountability and improves decision making .This results in better value in IT investment, improved operations, and legal compliance. This results in benefits such as reduced costs, higher sales, reduced risk, increased customer retention, and better relationships with suppliers and vendors.

Probability indicator: 👍 👍

Describe the Business architecture inputs/outputs ?

These are the typical work products related to the business architecture phase of the TOGAF **Architecture Development Method (ADM)**. The following figure provides a detailed description:

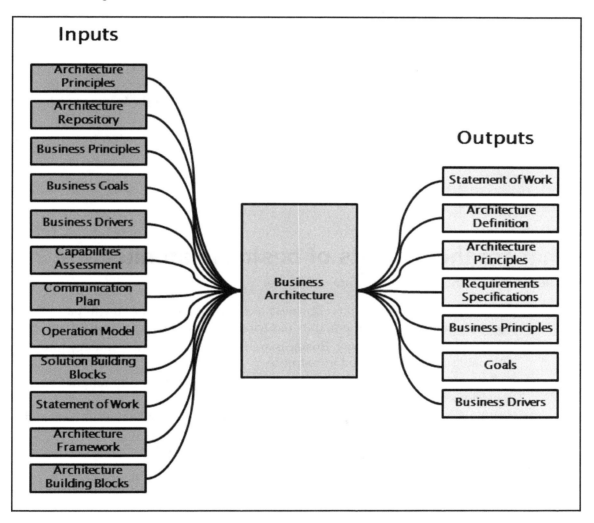

Figure 20: Business architecture inputs and outputs

This list of baseline deliverables serves as a reference. Work products are usually tailored to each organization to meet the organization's needs and conform to other frameworks and standards such as CMMI.

- Business architecture defines current and target business capabilities and processes.
- Business architecture is a library of current business capabilities and strategy for rolling out new capabilities in support of business goals.
- Business architecture models the services, processes, people, and tools the business requires to achieve its strategic goals.
- Business architecture is a current and future view of business capabilities, business knowledge, processes, and organizational structure.
- Business architecture is a disciplined approach to realizing the business vision and goals.
- Business architecture builds a common understanding of the enterprise and is used to align strategic objectives and tactical demands.

Probability indicator:

What are the benefits of business architecture ?

The benefits of business architecture are as follows:

- Better decision-making ability. Business architecture articulates the impact of decisions before making them, thus reducing risk and providing mitigation.
- Driven and cohesive strategy. Business architecture outlines the strategy into actionable steps and aligned investment.
- Higher efficiency and capacity. Business architecture enables and rationalizes operations for efficiency and scale.
- Agility in business and IT execution. An archive of reusable business assets and processes that outlines strategies and expedites the ability to implement changes.
- Business architecture improves organizational competitive advantage by focusing investment on strategic roadmap.
- Business architecture is a foundation to enhance accountability and improve organizational decision-making.

Probability indicator:

How does business architecture increase operational efficient and capacity for growth ?

Methodology

An enterprise can rapidly articulate the impact of changes by leveraging reusable assets produced by business architects, without elaborate investment in current-state analysis. To rapidly move from the strategic vision to execution, business architects put the appropriate repeatable processes in place. The specific organization problems the business architects increase operational effectiveness by assessing the root-causes. The analysis outlays the scope, opportunities, and risks with its resolution.

Leveraging business architecture supports the following:

- Define a new market opportunity
- Enable legacy modernization
- Investment planning and roadmaps
- New product offerings in a marketplace
- Globalization
- IT outsourcing
- Supply chain optimizations
- Regulatory and legal compliance
- LOB restructuring
- During a merger or acquisition integrate capabilities, processes, people, technology and culture
- Transform a large enterprise to a customer-centric model
- Make a decision that significantly guides a government program

Probability indicator:

Explain difference between a business analyst and a business architect?

Let's take a look at the differences:

- **Business architect**: A role within enterprises (business or government) that is focused on collating data on the strategic positioning of a domain including LOB, BU, department, or team and creating a big picture of the capability and its gaps that may impede that area from reaching its full potential.
- **Business analyst**: A role either within an IT department of an enterprise or within a non-IT team but as a key SPOC with an IT department. This role is focused on analyzing the root cause of a business problem and developing the business requirements to address that problem.

Probability indicator:

What are the benefits of business-centric architecture versus technology centric architecture?

Business architecture enables processes supporting corporate goals and establishes the cost of IT. The need for business architecture for growing complexity of organizations is supporting transitioning through activities such as mergers and acquisitions and adherence to regulatory actions. This results in enterprises becoming stronger, efficient, effective and agile. This is the value that business architecture brings to the table.

Business architecture is important to assist in dealing with issues around governance, risk, and compliance. The capability to be able to trace and audit in the organization is crucial. Ultimately, a good business architecture facilitates smart decision making.

It enables your organization to use knowledge effectively in order to react to revenue generation, cost cutting, customer experience, and so on, and will allow you to respond to emerging opportunities.

	Technology Centric Architecture	Business Centric Architecture
Focus	Technology Standards and Portfolios Architecture Patters and Governance Application & Data Architecture	Business Strategies Business Capabilities, Operating Models and Value Chains Business process and Business Services Business Governance
Tools	Technical Maps, Patterns	Value Chains, strategy maps, value streams, business maps
Architects Skills	Technologist SME for application and infrastructure	Business Advisors SMEs for Business Architects

Table 3:Business versus Technology centric architect

Probability indicator:

How are business architecture and BPM-related?

BPM interlinks key activities of business architecture. This establishes a strong connection between business architecture and BPM. BPM is a technique that enables business architecture and provides the mechanism to rationalize IT systems, and optimize processes. BPM implements the well-known principle of *you can't improve what you can't measure*. Documenting the current state processes using BPM allows you to identify:

- Domains where functions are performed efficiently and where processes are unclear
- An existing repeatable process, but is dangling or has no parent
- Gaps in the competency skills which could be solved by staffing or training

The core competency of a business architect is to analyze the business changes to make it operate better; BPM is, therefore, a key competency too. BPM will provide documentation of core processes and will result in pragmatic improvements by the owners of these processes.

Probability indicator:

How to identify business processes organization's value chain?

The Porter's value chain is a good starting point for identifying the key business activities/ processes in an organization. Reference architectures like NGOSS also provide the business architecture components and are a good starting point. Some of the reference architecture/frameworks are, for example, Energetics in oil and gas, DoDAF in defense, BIAN in banking, ACORD in insurance

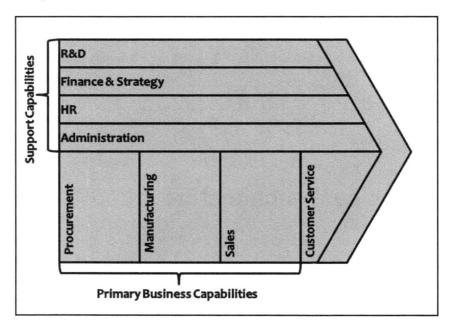

Figure 21: Porter's value chain

Probability indicator: 🔔🔔🔔

What are the core components of an enterprise?

Michael Porter suggested that an enterprise consists of two main categories of activities:

- **Primary activities**: For example, the operational processes delivering the product, services, sales, inbound logistics, outbound logistics and operations

- **Support activities**: For example, HR, finance, administration, and so on

The development activities are a category in itself as a chunk of them, such as business development, strategy, R&D, new products, or capabilities development and they ensure the competitive advantage for organizations. More activities are outsourced and even operations, a core activity once, is outsourced these days. The part that typically remains with the organization is a capability newly added to the operating model, the governance capability, which coordinates all other activities.

Probability indicator: 👍👍👍

Which modeling tools or frameworks have you leveraged and what is the value of these tools to the EA discipline?

Modeling tools:

- **IT disciplines**: **Software Development Life Cycle** (**SDLC**), including an understanding of various SDLC methodologies such as agile, waterfall, scrum, spiral, RUP, and their appropriate benefits.
- **Modeling tools**: **Unified Modeling Language** (**UML**), business process modeling, data modeling

Probability indicator: 👍👍

Data architecture

Data is one of the architecture domains that is the pillar of EA. The other pillars are the application, business, and infrastructure. Data architecture enables the designing and implementations of data resources. Data architecture enables the design, construction, and implementation of business-driven data entities that include real world entities.

The data architecture pillar artifact for the data design is leveraged in the implementation of the organization's physical database. Data architecture can be compared to a house architecture where the descriptions of sizes, materials, roofing, rooms, plumbing layout, and electrical structures are elucidated.

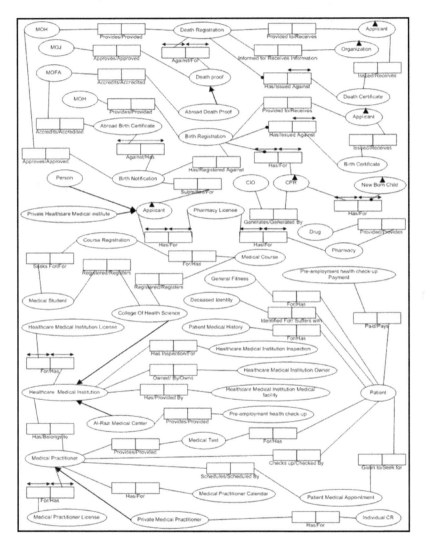

Figure 22: Logical data architecture

Examples for data reference models

The following is a list of various data models for various domains:

TMF SID Telecom	DODAF Logical Data Model	Energetics Epicenter data model
ARTS data model, Pipeline Open Data Standard (PODS) data model	Professional Petroleum Data Management (PPDM) Association data model	

What are the Data principles ?

The following guidelines and rules are envisioned to be enduring and seldom modified, and support the organization in fulfilling its mission.

Principle	Summary
Data is an asset	Data is an asset having value and is managed accordingly within an enterprise.
Data is shared	Business users have access to data to perform their duties; therefore, data is shared across organizational LOBs.
Data is accessible	To perform their duties data is accessible to business users.
Data trustee	Each data element has a trustee accountable for data quality.
Common vocabulary and data definitions	Data is consistently defined across the enterprise, and these definitions are available to all business users.
Data security	Data protection is against unauthorized access and disclosure.

Table 4: Data principles

Probability indicator: 👍 👍

Describe the data modeling process

Beginning with the methodology:

The process starts with a selection of frameworks and models to support the views required, using the selected methodology. Examples of data models include the DODAF logical data model, the ARTS data model, the **Pipeline Open Data Standard** (**PODS**) data model, the **Professional Petroleum Data Management** (**PPDM**) association data model and the Energetics Epicenter data model. Confirm that all stakeholder requirements have been addressed. The recommended process for developing a data architecture is as follows:

- Collate data models from existing business architecture and application architecture assets
- Rationalize data requirements and align with enterprise data catalogs and models. Establish data inventory and ER models
- Develop metrics and KPIs across the architecture by relating data to business services, business functions, processes, and applications
- Elaborate data architecture by examining creation, distribution, migration, security, and archival

Probability indicator: 👍 👍

What are the key capabilities of data architecture?

The key top-level capabilities an organization needs to manage the data and information assets are listed as follows. This is referred to as the reference architecture for the data domain. The high-level capabilities for the data domain are:

- Governance, quality, and life cycle management
- Data security
- BI and DWH
- Data integration and ETL
- MDM
- Enterprise data model
- Content management
- Data infrastructure management

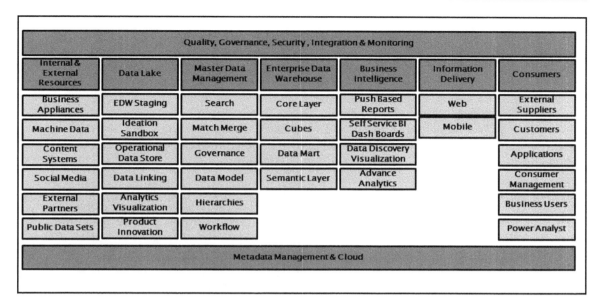

Figure 23: Information capability map

Probability indicator:

What do you understand by data quality? What are the various tools for data quality requirements?

Good quality data means that all data and master data is complete, consistent, accurate, time-stamped and industry standards-based. By improving the quality of data, an organization will be able to reduce costs, improve productivity and accelerate speed to market. A quality organizational data is the foundation to collaboration and synchronization. Data quality improvement involves quality assessment, quality design, quality transformation, and quality monitoring

The tool needed is: Oracle data quality.

Probability indicator:

What are the different backup and recovery strategies?

Strategies

Backup and recovery refer to the mechanisms and methodologies for protecting the organization's database against data loss and re-constructing the data after any such kind of data loss. A backup is a copy of data that can be leveraged to reconstruct that data. Backups are categorized into physical backups and logical backups:

- Physical backups are backups of the physical files used in storing and recovering your databases, such as control files, data files, and redo logs. Every physical backup is a copy of some database information to a different location, either on disk or offline storage such as a tape.
- Logical backups are logical data such as tables or stored procedures that are exported from a database with an export utility and stored in a binary format. This is later imported into a database using the import utility.

Physical backups are the foundation of a sound backup strategy. Logical backups are the useful add-ons to physical backups but are not fool-proof protection against data loss without physical backups.

The tool required is: Oracle data guard

Probability indicator: 👍 👍

What are the KPIs/KRAs data domain ?

The **key performance indicators** (**KPIs**) are like checkpoints for meeting an organization's objectives and goals. Monitoring KPIs will identify progress in terms of customer marketing, sales, and services goals. KPIs are a quantifiable measure leveraged to understand an organizational performance compared to an organizational goal. For a few goals, there could be many KPIs and they are often narrowed down to just two or three key data points known as KPIs. KPIs are those measurements that most accurately show whether a business is progressing toward its target goal/s. Some are listed as follows:

- Transactions per sec (performance, scalability)
- Meantime of a transaction (performance, scalability)
- Mean-latency time for a transaction (performance, scalability)
- Daily mean latency time for a transaction (daily average, scalability)
- Transactions per day (scalability)
- Daily mean latency time for a transaction per transaction (d/e, scalability)
- Total failed logins per day (security) and total failovers per day (availability)
- Daily meantime for failover to a secondary service (availability)

Critical success factors

Critical success factors (CSFs) are the key variables or conditions that depict on how effectively and successfully an organization meets its strategic goals for the program. Businesses have to perform the CSF activities diligently in order to achieve their target objectives and retain a market lead:

- Percentage of entities identified and leveraged for data models
- Percentage of entities identified while delivering logical data models
- Scalability of the data model
- Design for performance
- Data architecture has to be in sync with the business data model
- Is data redundancy minimized to n percentage?

Probability indicator: 👍 👍

What are various data synchronization/integration capabilities? What are the tools that support data integration?

Capabilities

Data synchronization is the mechanism that enables consistency between a source and target storage and harmonizes the data. This is a key to different organizations, including file and mobile synchronizations. There are two different synchronization capabilities:

- **Real time**: Enables real-time data integration and continuous data availability by delivering updates of critical information and providing continuous data synchronization between source and target environments. Companies gain improved intelligence across organizations by leveraging more accurate and timely data and increasing the uptime of the mission-critical applications. For example, Tool Oracle Golden Gate
- **Batch**: Provides high-performance bulk data movement and data transformation capabilities for improved organizational performance and low TCO. Provides a heterogeneous platform support for data integration. Facilitates knowledge management, optimized productivity, extensibility, service-oriented data integration, and management for heterogeneous environments. For example, Tool Oracle Data Integrator

Probability indicator: 👍 👍

What are the different approaches for securing data?

Approaches

The following list describes various approaches to consider for securing stored data:

- Design a tiered data protection mechanism and security model including multiple perimeter rings of defense to counter threats. Multiple layers of defense protect and isolate data in case one of the perimeters is compromised by threats.

- Enable logical (encryption, authorization, and authentication) and physical (locks and restricted access to the server, networking and storage cabinets) security.
- Logical security includes firewalls, DMZs, virus-detection, and antispyware for servers and storage systems. Storage security strategy won't be complete without making sure the applications, databases, filesystems and OS are secure to prevent unauthorized access to critical data.
- Storage and networking tools will facilitate passwords change management at initial installation and on an ongoing basis. Restrict access to tools to those who authorize to leverage them for the organization.
- Techniques to protect data while in-flight include encryption, virtual private networks, and the IPSec protocol.
- Consider different levels of data encryption to counter applicable threats. Enable key management in the environment.

Probability indicator:

What is a data warehouse? What are the benefits of data warehouses?

Data warehouses facilitate reporting on key business processes aka KPIs. Data warehouses help integrate data from various sources and show single-point-of-truth about business metrics. Data warehouses are also leveraged for data mining which helps in pattern recognition, forecasts, trend prediction, and so on. Data warehouses integrate various data sources and archives them to be able to analyze the business, including performance analysis, trends, and predictions, and to leverage results to improve the business efficiencies.

A data warehouse is a data repository, which is leveraged for a management decision system. Data warehouses consist of a wide variety of data that have a high level of business conditions at a single point in time. This is a repository of integrated data available for queries and analysis. The following are the different types of data warehousing:

- Enterprise data warehousing
- Operational data store
- Datamart

A data warehouse stores data for analyzing, where as OLAP is leveraged for analyzing the data, managing aggregations and partitioning. Data marts are designed for one domain. An organization may deploy different data marts pertaining to different departments such as HR finance, R&D, and so on. These data marts are built on top of warehouses. A data mart is a specialized category of data warehousing, and contains a snapshot of operational data, helping business stakeholders to analyze trends.

Probability indicator: 👍 👍

What is the differences between OLTP and OLAP ?

Let's look at the differences:

- **On-line Transaction Processing (OLTP)** is differentiated by a lot of short on-line transactions: UPDATE, INSERT, DELETE. The main emphasis of OLTP is on fast query processing, ensuring data integrity in a multi-access landscape and effectiveness measured in terms of transactions per second. In an OLTP database there is detailed current data and schema leveraged to store transactional databases in the 3NF entity model.
- **On-line Analytical Processing (OLAP)** is differentiated by a relatively less volume of transactions. Queries are often complex and involve aggregations. In OLAP a response time is an effectiveness measure. OLAP applications are leveraged by data mining solutions. In an OLAP database there is aggregated, historical data, stored in multi-dimensional star schemes.

Probability indicator: 👍 👍

What is the differences between big data and BI

Let's take a look at the differences.

Big data is a vast amount of data from various sources generated by various applications, appliances, and systems. One has to perform a lot of cleaning, aggregation, crunching of this data, and also will need to run various algorithms based on the objective of these analysis.

Business Intelligence (BI) is a set of tools and technology that enables you to analyze, report, and visualize data, and provides functions such as deep dive, slice and dice, and other related function. It may or may not use big data as a source of its data for analysis. BI is also known as a **Decision Support System (DSS)** which refers to the technologies and practices for collection, integration, and analysis of the business related data.

Three key points where big data is different from analytics are outlined in the following table:

Data Point	Description
Volume	The global quantity of digital data will grow from 130 Exabytes to 40,000 Exabytes by 2020. A petabyte is one quadrillion byte or equivalent of 20 million cabinets of text.
Velocity	The speed of data is even more critical than the volume. Real-time access to information enables organizations to make quicker decisions and stay ahead of the competition.
Variety	Big data comes in different shapes and forms. It can come in the form of images on Facebook, e-mails, text messages, GPS signals, tweets, and other social media updates. These forms of data are known as unstructured data.

Table 5: Big Data Attributes

Probability indicator: 👍 👍

What are Hadoop and MapReduce ?

Hadoop is not a database, but a software ecosystem that allows massive parallel computing. It is an enabler to types of NoSQL distributed databases, which allows data to be distributed across thousands of nodes with little reduction in performance.

A staple of the Hadoop ecosystem is MapReduce, a computational model that basically takes data intensive processes and distribute the computation across an endless number of nodes referred to as a cluster. It is a game-changer in providing the enormous processing needs of big data; a large data process might take several hours of processing time on a centralized relational database system, but may only take a few minutes across a large Hadoop cluster where all processing is in parallel.

NoSQL

NoSQL represents a different framework of databases that allows high-performance, processing of data on a massive scale. NoSQL is a database infrastructure that has been well-adapted to the demands of big data. NoSQL achieves efficiency because unlike RDMS that is highly structured, NoSQL is unstructured in nature, trading off stringent integrity requirements for agility and speed. NoSQL is based on the concept of distributed databases, where unstructured data may be stored across multiple nodes. This distributed architecture allows NoSQL databases to be horizontally scalable, as data continues to explode, with no reductions in performance. The NoSQL database infrastructure has been the solution to handling some of the biggest data warehouses on the planet, such as the likes of Amazon and Google.

Probability indicator:

What tools and techniques have you used to manage enterprise data and data architecture artifacts?

The below list explains the tools and techniques to manage enterprise data artifacts:

- The ability to create data usability proposals such as data integration data cleansing tools, data dictionaries, master data management, and data warehouses
- Sound knowledge of data architecture approaches, standards and best practices
- Strong technical competencies with data technologies (for example, MDM, data warehouses, data marts, DBMS, and BI)
- Practical expertise in design approaches for data warehouses
- Expert data modeling skills such as conceptual, logical, and physical modeling
- Expertise in ETL concepts, Cognos, and OBIEE tools
- Expertise in MDM

Probability indicator:

What is ETL?

ETL stands for Extract, Transform, and Load. ETL is leveraged to read data from a specified source and extract a desired subset of data. Next, it transforms the data using rules and tables and converts it to the target state and resulting data is loaded into the target database.

Probability indicator:

Infrastructure and security architecture

Infrastructure architecture is one architecture domain that form the pillars of EA. It describes the structure of the technology infrastructure of the enterprise. It includes the nodes of hardware, the infrastructure applications that run on them, the infrastructure services they offer, the protocols, and the networks connecting applications. Infrastructure architecture also addresses issues pertaining to performance, resilience, storage and backup.

What are the principles of infrastructure domain?

Principle	Summary
Requirements-based change	Changes to IT applications are made in response to business needs only
Responsive change management	Changes to enterprise landscape are implemented in a timely fashion.
Control technical diversity	Technological diversity is controlled to minimize the non-trivial cost of maintaining expertise in and connectivity between multiple processing environments.
Interoperability	IT infrastructure should conform to organizational standards and frameworks that enable interoperability for applications and data.

Table 6: Infrastructure Domain Principles

Probability indicator:

What does the infrastructure architecture cover?

The infrastructure architecture typically covers the following aspects:

- Servers, databases, backups, storage, and hardware
- Networks, switches, and routers
- SDLC environment, for example, Dev, staging, pre-prod, and production
- Identification and authorization, SSO, audit trail, and logging

The characteristics to look for when evaluating and selecting architectural building blocks are:

Scalable vertically and horizontally. It is possible to repeat the solution blocks many times to scale for the required level of services.

- Solution blocks support different kinds of applications standards.
- The solution block can be leveraged for different applications with minimum customization.
- Solution blocks can be reused to build other solutions. For example, Enterprise Java Beans (EJBs) can be reused to enable different capabilities.
- The solution blocks are portable across platforms.
- Solution blocks have standardized interfaces that make them easy to integrate across landscape components.
- Leveraging building blocks facilitates asynchronous communication. Building blocks facilitate standards for interfaces and communications flows.

Systemic Components	Application Tiers				
	Resource	Integration	Business	Presentation	Client
Security servers	Database servers	EAI servers	Application servers	Portal servers	Cell Phones
Load balancing servers	Legacy systems	Directory servers	Calendar servers	Web servers	Pagers
Certificate servers	Directory servers	Wireless servers	Mail servers	Caching servers	PDAs
Monitoring servers	FTP servers	EII severs	Vending machines	WAP servers	Web browsers

Figure 30: Infrastructure Building Blocks

Probability indicator: 👍 👍

What is SSO?

Single Sign On (SSO) is a user session authentication mechanism that permits a user to enter one set of credentials to access multiple landscape applications. SSO authenticates the end-user for all the applications at once and are given rights to and eliminates further prompts when switching between applications during session. You can check the following figure for a better understanding:

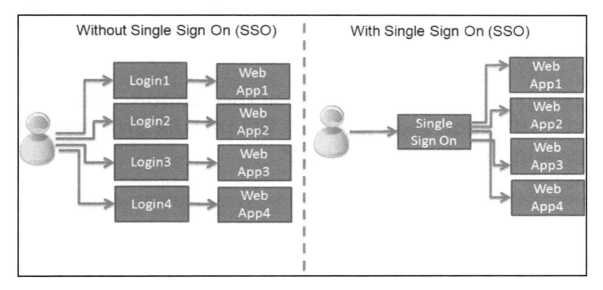

Figure 31: SSO architecture

Benefits of SSO

The benefits of SSO are as follows:

- Lowers the cost of administration if the end user loses their credentials and can reset them using a simple Q&A mechanism.
- Increases productivity by reducing the password related call center processes. Customers can retrieve the forgotten credentials, without interventions of the helpdesk.
- Simplifies the customer journey as SSO allows just one time login and enables a seamless experience across IT platforms.

- Instead of registering via traditional time-consuming process, SSO accelerates user access using social network data, for example, signing in via Facebook
- SSO enables automatic logging policies to prevent unauthorized access, increasing security posture. For example, if the user is inactive for some time period they are automatically logged out.
- With a fraudulent technique where victims are tricked into giving sensitive information, SSO increasing security for users.

Probability indicator:

What is an authentication, authorization, and identification mechanism? What tools are used to provide such a capability?

Authorization authentication, and accounting is a mechanism for a framework for access control to IT resources, enabling policies, auditing, and providing billing capabilities. These processes are key for effective network security and management.

Authentication provides a capability of identifying a user, by having them enter a user name and password before granting access. The process of authentication is based on each user having unique credentials for gaining access. The server compares stored credentials with the user's entered credentials and if these match, the user is granted access. If the credentials differ, authentication fails, and access is denied.

The user has to gain authorization for performing various tasks. After logging into a system, the user may try to execute commands. The authorization process determines whether the user has the authority to execute commands. Authorization is the mechanism of enforcing policies: determining the types of activities or resources a user is allowed. Authorization occurs within the context of authentication. Once a user is authenticated, they are authorized for different types of activity.

The final cog in the AAA framework is the accounting mechanism that measures resource consumption. This includes the amount of time or amount of data a user has sent and/or received during a session. Accounting is carried out by logging session statistics and usage data and is leveraged in billing, trend analysis, resource utilization, and capacity planning. Authentication, authorization, and accounting are often enabled by a dedicated AAA infrastructure. The AAA framework leverages leverages a radius mechanism for the entire mechanism.

Important considerations for authentication and authorization

The key points are as follows:

- Divide unauthenticated and authenticated resources that can be split into separate deployable units
- Ensure centralized configuration for authenticated resources' proper use of filters
- Leverage a standards framework such as Spring security to build authorization

The tools used are as follows:

- Identity
- Access manager

Probability indicator:

What is federated identity management?

Federated identity is a mechanism that lets subscribers leverage the same credentials to gain access to the all enterprise networks within the group. The use of such a mechanism is also called identity federation. Identity federation offers cost advantages and convenience to enterprises and their subscribers. For example, multiple enterprises can share a single application, with resultant cost savings and resources consolidation.

In order for FIM to be effective, the partners must have mutual trust. Authorization messages among partners are transmitted using **Security Assertion Markup Language** (**SAML**) or similar XML standards.

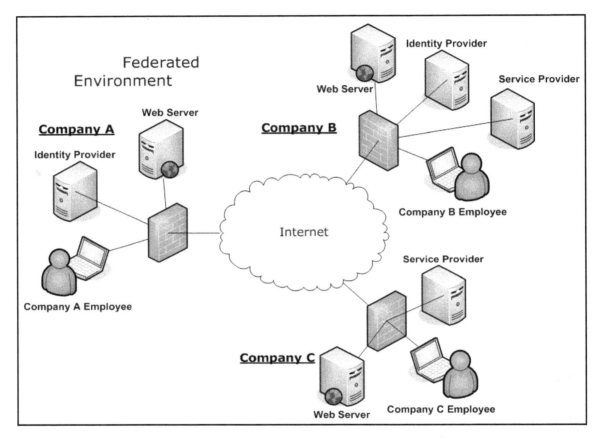

Figure 32: Federated Identity

Probability indicator:

What are the various options for implementing security?

The approach consists of planning and assessment to identify risks across key business areas, including people, processes, data, and technology throughout the entire organization. It is important to take a holistic approach to facilitate business driven security assets and that can act as an effective defense for the entire enterprise IT. An IT organization can implement a security program in four steps:

1. Identify a security framework/standard that will be the basis of the security program.
2. Perform a security audit.
3. Review the audit findings in the context of the selected framework/standard.
4. Identify risk levels and establish a priority for developing policies, procedures, and controls.

Security related consideration for an enterprise application can be split into these parts:

- User authentication and authorization
- Web domain issues
- External IT interfaces
- Infrastructure security

Probability indicator: 👍👍

Explain the public-key cryptography ?

Asymmetric cryptography is a mechanism in which a pair of keys are leveraged to encrypt and decrypt a message so that the message is transmitted securely. Initially, the user requests a public and private key pair. A user willing to send an encrypted message can get the recipient's public key from admin. Initially, the user receives a public and private key pair from a certificate authority.

The user willing to send an encrypted message gets the recipient's public key from a directory. They leverage this key to encrypt the message, and they send it to the recipient. When the recipient gets the message, they decrypt it with the private key, which no one else has access to:

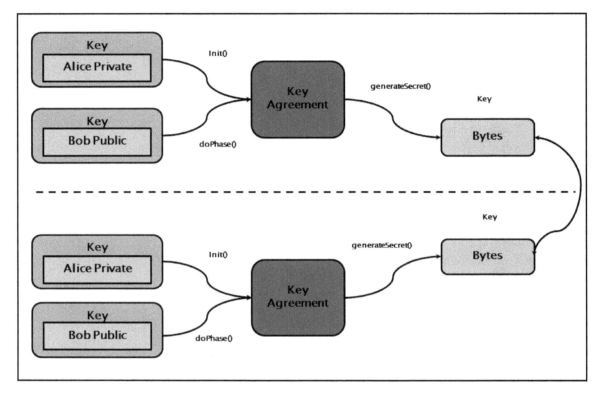

Figure 33: Cryptography

Probability indicator: 👍👍👍

What is more important to focus on, threats or vulnerabilities?

Threats versus vulnerability

A threat is a possible action against you. A vulnerability is a specific window by which the threat can be realized. Threats and vulnerabilities exist in different forms. The threats represent aspects that could happen in the future while vulnerabilities are in the system all along.

The response to a vulnerability is to eradicate it. Eliminating a vulnerability does not eliminate concerns and in fact it may introduce a new vulnerability. The response to threat is to reduce the exposure. One can reduce the exposure by eliminating vulnerabilities and take steps to reduce the damage, but eliminating is not a feasible goal.

Probability indicator: 👍 👍

What do you understand by phishing, SQL Injection, Man-in-the-Middle, and cross-site scripting?

Principle	Summary
Phishing	This is an attempt to gain sensitive data such as usernames, passwords, and credit card information by masquerading as a trustworthy entity. Communications purporting to be from popular social web sites, auction sites, online payment processors, or administrators are commonly used to lure unsuspecting individuals. Typically carried out by e-mail spoofing or instant messaging, and it often prompts users to enter details at a fake website whose look and feel are identical to the legitimate one.
Denial-of-Service	A DoS attack is an attempt to make an IT resource unavailable to its intended end users. Consists of efforts to temporarily or indefinitely suspend services of a host connected to the Internet.

Cross-Site Scripting (XSS)	This occurs when the attacker uses a web application to send malicious code, in the form of a script, to a different end user. **Cross-site scripting (XSS)** is a type of security vulnerability found in web applications. XSS enables attackers to inject client-side script into web pages viewed by other users. XXS vulnerability may be used by attackers to bypass access controls.
SQL Injection	This is a mechanism that enables an attacker to perform unauthorized SQL queries in web applications using dynamic SQL statements. Using SQL Injection, attackers might be able to retrieve data you didn't intend for the user to see. Measures to prevent it are: escape user input, validate user input, and use Java Prepared Statements rather than Statements.
Man-in-the-Middle (MitM)	This is a mechanism where an attacker intercepts a user's session, inspects its contents, and modifies its data, or otherwise uses it for malicious purposes. A measures to prevent this is to use encryption of sensitive data and prevent the data being read.

Probability indicator: 👍 👍

What are the important security factors to consider for web applications?

Security for web services is handled at two levels:

- **Transport level**: SSL is leveraged to exchange certificates to ensure transport level security. This ensures that the server and client are mutually authenticated. It is possible to use one-way SSL authentication as well.

- **Application level security**: This is implemented by transferring encrypted information in the message header or SOAP header. This helps the server to authenticate the client and be confident that the message has not been tampered with.

Important factors to consider are as follows:

- **Data validation**: Ensure they have also validated in business layer.
- **SQL injection**: Never build SQL queries using string concatenation. Use a Prepared Statement. Even better, use the Spring JDBC Template or frameworks such as Hibernate and iBatis to handle communication with the database.
- **Cross site scripting**: This ensures one checks against a whitelist of input characters.
- Avoid using old versions of software.

Best practices

- Threat modeling: Define threat modeling and understand the various security threats posed by the application.
- Leverage a static security analysis tool such as Fortify.
- Most importantly, developers and testers should be aware of the latest security threats.
- A key aspect of the release cycle (preferably as early as possible) is the dynamic security tests performed by a security testing team.

Probability indicator: 👍 👍

Summary

This chapter covered the Q&A for enterprise architecture and modernization domain. Enterprise Architecture is a collection of strategic information that describes business, application, data and infrastructure to operate the business. This also includes mission & goals, business processes, roles, organizational structures, information, applications and systems. The section also covered the Q&A for the enterprise architecture, application architecture, business architecture, and data architecture, infrastructure and security and architecture governance. The key skills SMEs will learn will be methodologies, best practices and frameworks, common pitfalls to be avoided and patterns to leverage, architecture governance concepts, principles and guidelines for various domains, best practices architecting, KPI and success factors.

4
SOA and Integration

This section covers the Q&A for SOA and the integration domain. SOA is a set of design principles for building a suite of interoperable, flexible and reusable services based architecture. This section include Q&A for SOA key capabilities, SOA ROI, SOA modernization approaches, SOA entry points, ESB, BPEL, BPM, SOA and security, SOA KPIs, OSIMM, top-down and bottom-up approaches, and SOA patterns.

Service-oriented architecture and Integration

Service-oriented architecture (**SOA**) is an architecture principle for creating flexible and interoperable service-based solutions. The key principle consists of discoverable contracts, service abstraction, loose coupling, service autonomy, service reusability, statelessness, and composability.

Rolling out successful SOA capabilities reduces IT costs by facilitating reusability in the IT landscape. SOA's ability to provide flexibility and agility to service applications reduces the time to market. SOA enables leveraging of existing IT investments by wrapping legacy solutions in reusable services.

What are the key capabilities of SOA and the benefits of SOA?

SOA is an architectural style that enables service orientation. Service orientation is a way of thinking in terms of services and service-based outcomes.

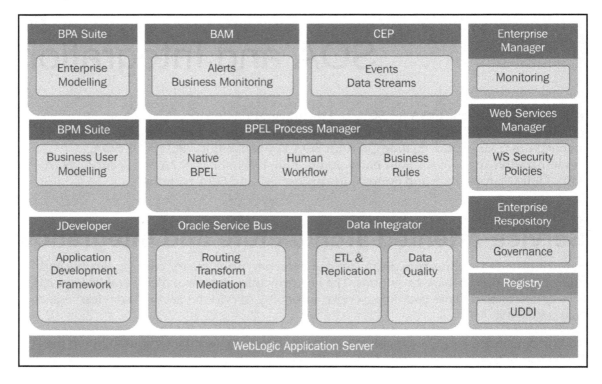

Figure 1: SOA capabilities

The following are the benefits:

- SOA creates business and IT alignment, while lending flexibility to the IT landscape
- Market competition requires the flexibility that SOA provides as business trends change fast

- SOA facilitates the reuse of existing IT assets and new services in the IT landscape
- SOA ensures efficient integration by leveraging standardized interfaces between various services
- It defines a model for integrating business partners, vendors and suppliers into the ecosystem, thus reducing IT costs and improving the customer's journey

Probability indicator: 👍👍👍

What are the key components of the SOA tiers?

SOA covers IT infrastructure, tools, and processes that enable creation of interoperable services that can be combined into meaningful processes, enabling various business scenarios. SOA provides a comprehensive suite of components for developing, securing, and monitoring applications. The following list gives the key components of the SOA stack:

Components	Description
Function	A function is a business capability. Services are functions and have functions, but functions may not necessarily be services.
Business service	A business service is what a business does that has an interface and contract with consumers. A business service is supported by process, technology, and people.
Information system service	IT systems are supported by applications and are interlinked with SOA interfaces.
Application component	An application component is an independently governed entity providing IT services. They can be physical applications or logical applications grouping applications of a similar type.
Technology component	A technology component is a software or hardware entity that can be purchased, configured, combined, and deployed to produce larger solution components.

Table 1: SOA key components

You can get more insights by looking into the diagram:

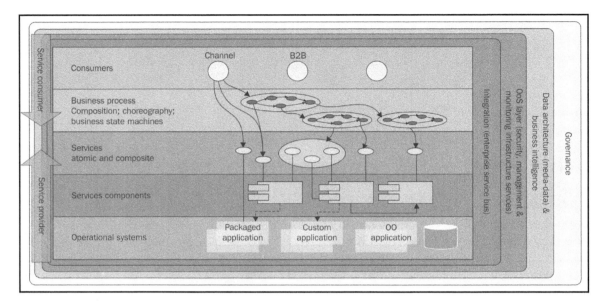

Figure 2: SOA components

Probability indicator:

How do you calculate the ROI for SOA?

There are Excel tools for calculating ROI and these come in handy. The most common approach is to roll up your sleeves, open a spreadsheet template, and create the cost/benefit justification. Despite the extensive amount of time it will take, this may very well be the ideal approach.

The following steps describes calculating ROI for a SOA initiative:

1. The process of ROI calculation for an initiative starts with defining the objectives for the SOA initiatives. These objectives are mapped to the overall SOA roadmap.
2. The next step is to identify the challenges and issues in the existing IT landscape.

 Since ROI has to be a dollar term, the preceding attributes need to be calculated in terms of dollars.

3. Add the costs of all the initiatives in the existing IT environment, and this would be the cost that an organization is bearing without going to the SOA route. This cost also reveals returns in the future, as in our example-consolidated cost of building address update function (assume the SOA route). Or, in other words, having the same address update functionality is each application in future (assume a non-SOA route).

4. Add all the costs for future initiatives. This would give a consolidated number of dollars saved because of the current initiative.

5. Add these costs in a worksheet format and categorize them.

6. Finally, add up the cost involved in building the initiative/project:
    *   *ROI = Cost saving in the current systems + Cost saving in the future endeavors*
    *   *Profitability index = Return On Investment – ROI / (Total Cost of the SOA Initiatives)*

Probability indicator: 👍👍👍

What are the different SOA modernization strategies?

There are different strategies to enable the modernization of legacy applications using SOA. Enterprises need to select one strategy and evaluate it against these strategies. The key strategies include service enablement, language conversion, re-architecting and re-hosting. The following table provides further details:

Strategy	Description
Service enablement	Through services hosted by integration platforms or containers, this strategy enables access to legacy applications.
Language conversion	This approach converts applications written in legacy languages into a new language that facilitates service orientation. This works if the conversion is successful, but re-architecting may be necessary if the software is complex and interlinked.
Re-architect	This approach involves re-architecting and restructuring the business logic of legacy applications.
Re-hosting of applications	To reduce the cost of the mainframe and legacy, the majority of business-critical parts are distributed on a cloud model.

Wrappers	Legacy applications are key to any IT landscape. We need to identify discrete entities and wrap them in service interfaces to leverage in a SOA environment.

Table 2: SOA Modernization Strategies

Probability indicator:

What are SOA entry points? How do you start an SOA initiative? What are the SOA design principles?

SOA entry points mean the five entry points into SOA, and any of these five entry points provides an effective starting point for SOA initiatives. SOA entry points enable organizations to pursue SOA by leveraging a project-based methodology and demanding that each project must deliver business value. Each entry point provides a key SOA-related solution:

Entry point	Description
People	Collaboration is improving productivity by giving employees and partners the ability to create a personalized, consolidated way to interact with others
Process	Optimizing processes and monitoring the efficiency and effectiveness of the amended processes
Information	Enhancing business insights and reducing risk by leveraging trusted information services
Reuse	Reusable services are the building blocks of SOA, which give flexibility and reduce time to market to eliminate duplicates
Connectivity	SOA connectivity has value and provides flexibility to the landscape and future SOA initiatives

Table 3: SOA Entry Points

SOA design principles

The success of software engagements on any paradigm is not typically assured. Software developed leveraging SOA paradigm carries higher risks. This is because a service-oriented architecture usually spans multiple Business Units (BUs) and Lines of Business (LOBs) and requires elaborate and substantial groundwork initially. Hence, SOA without concrete guidelines and principles is likely to fail. To ensure that the SOA initiative delivers as per the promise, it is critical to adopt a set of principles and guidelines. Please find the list of SOA principles for designing SOA applications:

- Standardized service contract: services adhere to a service description
- Services minimize dependencies due to loose coupling
- Service abstraction hides the logic from the outside world
- Service logic is designed with the intent of maximizing reuse
- Service autonomy, that is, services control the logic they encapsulate
- Service statelessness, that is, ideally, services should be stateless
- Service discoverability, that is, services that can be discovered via a service register
- Service composability is breaking large problems into smaller problems
- Service interoperability is leveraging standards that facilitates various subscribers to use services

Probability indicator:

How does ESB enterprise service bus relate to SOA? What are the advantages and disadvantages of SOA?

Enterprise Service Bus (**ESB**) is a critical and core component of the SOA landscape. ESB facilitates end-to-end connectivity between services and with partners, vendors, and suppliers. This component provides routing, mediation, and transformation in the SOA environment. Depending on the goals, ESB facilitates integrating services within the SOA landscape such as business process management services or information services. ESB is leveraged to integrate different applications and IT systems in the landscape. ESB provides business connectors that facilitate different applications to interact using different technologies and protocols. The SOA reference architecture is a reusable asset that helps building SOA capabilities that meets organization's needs. ESB is a core component of this reference architecture and provides one of the key capabilities in the SOA landscape.

The following are the advantages of SOA:

- Faster and cheaper integration of landscape applications and systems
- Increased flexibility in the landscape as it is easier to modify as business requirements change
- ESB is based on industry standards and best practices
- Scalable and can be deployed as a point solutions or distributed bus enterprise-wide deployment
- Out-of-the-box components and rules that are ready for use, hence more configurable than coding
- No central broker and no central rules-engine model
- Enterprise becomes refactorable with incremental patching and zero downtime

The following are the disavantages of SOA:

- Requires a message model, resulting in additional overhead. Potential difficulties are in integrating disparate applications to collaborate through message models and standards.
- Requires continuous management of message standards' versions to ensure the benefits of loose coupling. Incorrect or incomplete management may result in tight coupling.
- An ESB requires more hardware than simple point-to-point messaging.
- Middleware competency skills are needed to manage and configure an ESB.

- Extra overhead and latency are caused due the additional ESB layer, compared to a point-to-point mechanism, and increased latency is a result of additional XML transformations.
- ESB may become a single point of failure.
- While ESB requires significant time and effort, it won't produce value without subsequent development of SOA capabilities in the landscape.

Probability indicator:

How do ESB fit in this landscape? What are the alternatives to ESB?

ESB is a critical and core component of any SOA. ESB provides many-to-many connectivity between applications and systems within the landscape, and also with suppliers, partners and vendors. But SOA is not just creating and managing an ESB. Depending on the business objective and goals, ESB can be leveraged to integrate systems such as BPM services, information services, interaction services, **Information Technology Infrastructure Library** (**ITIL**) services, or development services. SOA reference architecture is a key asset that will help outline an SOA capability that meets the priorities and needs of the businesses. ESB capabilities is a key component of this reference architecture and provides the backbone for SOA.

Alternatives to an ESB

- Distributed services can often be provided by application servers exposing services via point-to-point protocol web services over HTTP.
- To leverage a specific protocols, one can build a client that responds to those protocols. If the requirement is constrained to one or two protocols, it may not be worth investing in an ESB.

Probability indicator:

What are BPM and BPEL?

Business Process Management (**BPM**) is management of the business processes. BPM is a simple yet powerful capability that increases the effectiveness and efficiency of business processes. BPM is a combination of technology and processes that facilitates the execution and monitoring of business processes. The term *workflow* is synonymous with BPM but is intended for human-to-human interaction scenarios. The term "business process" represents more scenarios where IT applications and human entities inter-connect to achieve business objectives and goals.

Business Process Execution Language (**BPEL**) is a standard and defines interactions between applications in the landscape using XML standards. This standard is adopted by many organizations to enable application interaction but lacks human interaction. This is related to integrating applications that are exposed via web services.

Probability indicator:

How do you handle security in an SOA project?

Enterprises need to build business services that are inherently secure, meaning that security is intrinsic to their business processes, development, and day-to-day operations. Security has to be factored into the initial design, not bolted on later. This enables enterprises to securely adopt new forms of technology, such as cloud computing and mobile device management; and business models and IT outsourcing can be safely leveraged for cost benefit, innovation, and shortening time to market. An SOA environment needs to emphasize the following key security areas:

- Users and services identities and propagation of these across LOBs
- Seamless connectivity to enterprises on a real-time, transactional basis
- Ensuring that proper security controls are enabled for services and applications
- Managing identity and security across the IT landscape, implemented in a heterogeneous mix of technologies
- Protection of data at rest and in transit
- Compliance with a growing set of regulatory and legal frameworks.

Probability indicator:

What are the KPIs for SOA?

Metrics are the key to continuous improvement and justification of any SOA initiatives. Initially, it starts with a baseline measurement and then it is measured at appropriate intervals.

KPIs provide a yardstick for measuring the business value of SOA initiatives. KPIs are leveraged to know the critical area in the landscape and on delivering business value so as to align IT investments with business goals and priorities. KPIs target the critical areas to help focus activities; fine-tune performance; and model processes up, down, and across to achieve the goals.

KPIs help transform an IT role into a proactive business advocate as one can work consultatively with colleagues to analyze IT spending to improve the organization's performance. Here are the metrics for SOA:

SOA KPIs	Description
Application usage	SOA provides services that are leveraged by many consumers. The usage of the application before and after SOA.
Cost reduction	The IT budget ratio between the projects driving business growth initiatives and the projects for legacy maintenance. Define different cost heads, for example, operations, development, license, and facility.
Functional reuse	Define and measure functional reuse before and after SOA enablement. The metrics are measured and reported across LOBs.
Quality of service (QoS)	QoS include availability, performance, scalability,capacity
Revenue	SOA will lead to added revenue by exposing processes/functionality to the outside world.
Time to market	Leveraging SOA enables reusable and standardized services deployed to access legacy systems, this reduces the time to market of these capabilities in the landscape.
Security KPIs	Ensure that services have security controls enabled, which helps monitor frequency and severity of security incidents after SOA-fictions.

Table 4: SOA key components

Probability indicator: 👍 👍

Which approach works better for service identification? Top-down or bottom-up?

A key technique of the SOA identification journey is to employ a meet-in-the-middle approach and is a combination of bottom-up, top-down, and middle-out techniques. In many scenarios, only the bottom-up approach is leveraged. However, this approach typically leads to poor service identifications driven by the architecture of legacy applications and does not consider the business perspective. The following list explains various approaches:

- Domain decomposition is a top-down approach where business domains are decomposed into functional areas across the value chain. After the initial decomposition, each area can be further decomposed into processes and sub-processes. As best practices, the use cases are good candidates for service exposures.
- Existing asset analysis represents a bottom-up approach where we analyze models, transactions, and APIs from legacy applications as potential candidate services.
- Goal service modeling facilitates a middle-out methodology that relates services to metrics, goals, sub-goals, and KPIs of the organization. This mechanism provides validation and may reveal candidate services that were not identified through the earlier approaches.

Probability indicator:

What is service-oriented modeling and architecture methodology (SOMA)?

A key approach in SOA development is to leverage a development methodology or framework to identify, design, and build SOA entities. The **service-oriented modeling and architecture** (**SOMA**) defines a set of product- and technology-agnostic modeling frameworks for analysis and design activities for defining SOA. The SOMA process consists of three major steps: identification, specification, and realization.

The SOMA service identification approach leverages the approach combining top-down, bottom-up, and middle-out techniques. In a few occasions, a bottom-up approach is taken, but this approach typically leads to poor service definitions that are mainly driven by legacy architecture and not the business perspective.

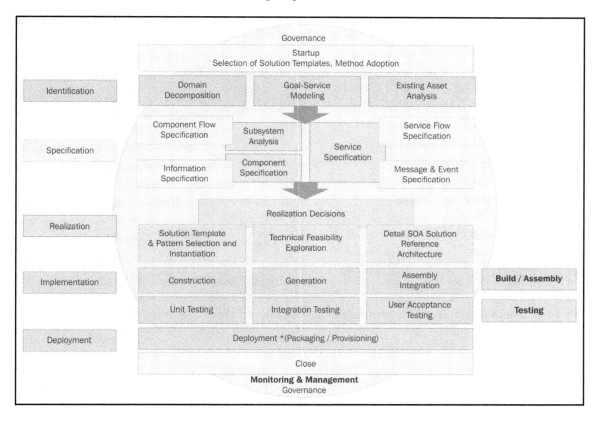

Figure 3: SOMA

Probability indicator:

How can services supporting long-running processes be scaled effectively?

There are two main approaches to scaling:

- Scaling up involves upgrading the existing hardware, replacing existing components, such as CPU or memory, or adding new hardware components. The critical components that affect performance and scalability are CPU, memory, disk, and network cards.
- Scaling out involves adding more servers to the landscape to increase application load processing. This increases the overall processing capacity of the solution.

Probability indicator:

What is OSIMM?

The **Open Group Service Integration Maturity Model** (**OSIMM**) framework guides enterprises in their SOA transformation journey. OSIMM model enables enterprises to benchmark their current SOA deployment and develop roadmaps for transformation to the target state. This is also leveraged by **Independent Software Vendor** (**ISVs**) to position their products and software against such benchmarks. OSIMM serves as a framework for the SOA transformation process that can be customized to suit the needs of different enterprises.

OSIMM helps create an incremental transformation IT roadmap for more mature target levels in order to achieve benefits for the higher maturity levels. OSIMM establishes SOA characteristics desirable to achieve a new maturity level. This enables determining whether issues at the current level of integration maturity can be solved by next levels.

This process consists of the following steps:

- Prepare OSIMM assessment assets, frameworks, and models
- Define the current level of services integration maturity
- Define the target level of services integration maturity
- Identify the transformation path to achieve the target level of maturity

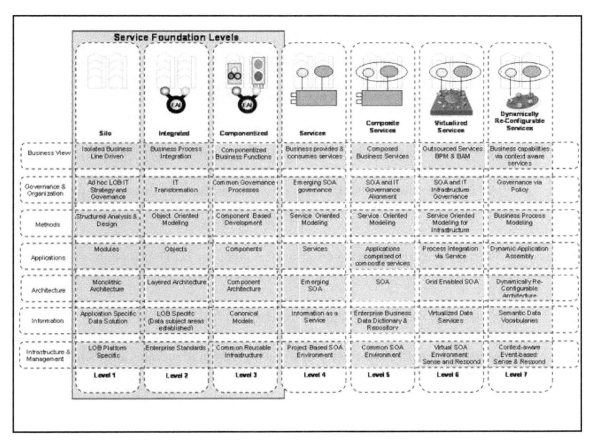

Figure 4: OSIMM

Probability indicator:

What is the difference between SOAP and REST?

Simple Object Access Protocol (**SOAP**) is a communication protocol. This protocol establishes a set of rules for communication, leveraging XML standards. Microsoft developed SOAP as a mechanism for interaction on the Internet, succeeding its predecessors **Common Object Request Broker Architecture** (**CORBA**) and **Distributed Component Object Model** (**DCOM**). The reason for SOAP's success was that it leveraged XML communication, unlike binary systems such as DCOM and CORBA. The following lists the capabilities of SOAP

- SOAP is a heavyweight protocol but a distinct advantage is its language and platform
- Importantly, it is independent of transport protocols
- It is extremely extendable and supports a set of web services extensions
- SOAP is reliable and standardized
- Another benefit is that it is designed for distributed models
- SOAP is widely used for asynchronous processing of data for web applications
- SOAP is secure and compatible, and this ensures that services are not firewalled
- Different languages enable automation of SOAP services

Representational State Transfer (**REST**) is not based on communication protocols but has a standard architecture principle leveraged to transfer data over HTTP protocols. REST is a web service that is the result of an alternative to distributed SOAP services. The following is a list of the capabilities of REST

- REST is based on a light-weight architecture
- It needs no tools for creation and is very easy to implement
- It is leveraged in the device service implementation in mobiles and PDAs, where they need less overheads
- REST supports only standard methods (GET, PUT, POST, or DELETE)
- It is a stateless communication protocol
- REST is quick and efficient but with a disadvantage in web caching

Advantages of RESTful web services over SOAP Web Services:

- Lightweight and easy to consume from smart devices.
- Easy to expose with no restrictions on communication protocol and output format.
- RESTful services leverage HTTP. The entire Web is based on HTTP and is built for efficiency. HTTP caching capabilities enable REST to be efficient and effective.
- High performance, as low XML and SOAP overhead and caching enable REST to be highly performant.

Probability indicator:

What are important constraints for a RESTful web service?

The five key constraints while creating RESTful services are:

- The client-server model; there has to be a service producer and a service consumer.
- The interface URL is uniform and exposes resources.
- The service is stateless. If the service is called many times, the result will be the same.
- The service result should be HTTP cacheable.
- Layered architecture. The client does not have a direct connection to the server-it will be getting info from a middle layer cache.

Probability indicator:

How do you transform a business by leveraging SOA?

Transforming a business to SOA includes standardized contract, reusability, abstraction, loose coupling, composability, and so on. SOA is a technology-agnostic architectural paradigm, and enterprises can pursue service-oriented strategic goals by leveraging different technologies. The current trend is that web services are technology platforms that enable SOA principles and are mostly leveraged to build this architecture. A strategy for achieving loose coupling is the WSDL service interface, hiding the implementation from stakeholders. Loose coupling is addressed by encapsulating the implementation that limits the impact of changes to the implementation on the service interface.

Best practices is that SOA services are stateless. The state data must be retained only during the request/response mechanism. This is because the state management consumes a lot of resources, affecting scalability and availability of the service.

Probability indicator:

What is the composition of a service?

Composition is a technique of combining different services to create a composite application. A composite application is an aggregation of various services for producing an enterprise process. A composite service consists of aggregation of different services to produce another reusable service.

Probability indicator:

What are common pitfalls of SOA?

A common pitfall is to consider SOA as a target state rather than a **journey**. Architects, rather than solving business problems via SOA, are likely to create large and complex interconnections between IT assets. Another pitfall is trying to solve multiple issues at one go rather than solving smaller problems. A top-down approach starting with enterprise-wide infrastructure investments often fails to highlight results in a given timeframe or compelling ROIs. SOA needs a different thought process for building SOA solutions. Instead of thinking of technology first, SMEs must think in terms of business solutions. The adoption of SOA will result in business departments, creating service-oriented IT organizations instead of technology-oriented IT organizations.

Probability indicator:

Do we really need SOA?

SOA delivers business benefits and IT cost efficiencies, but needs a disciplined approach to governance to be effective and successful. In a few cases, the cost of enforcing principles may be higher than the benefits, and therefore may not be a sound initiative. The SOA model is leveraged for building business applications using loosely coupled services that are orchestrated to specific business goals by inter-linking.

Probability indicator:

Explain the different levels of enterprise integration

Enterprise integration is focused on transferring data from one database to another database, but the current trends have challenged this methodology. There are five levels of enterprise integration, and each level represents efficiency improvement:

Level	Description
Business process integration	This is integration at the process level and is typically accomplished with ERP API or workflow tools.
Web content integration	This is enabled through mashups or portals and facilitates process across multiple information areas leveraging web frameworks and tools.

Automation integration	Integration at a sub-process level.
Service integration	Services that provide CRUD data and provide process automation, and this is accomplished through SOA principles.
Database integration	This consists of transferring data from one database to another. This approach is overused and is more efficient to integrate at a higher level.

Table 5: Integration Levels

Probability indicator:

What is a web service? Are web services SOA?

A web service is a service offered over the web through the HTTP protocol. When browsing the Internet, we leverage different web services. Even loading google.com involves web services. When we type in google.com in the browser, the following steps happen in the background:

1. The browser invokes the get request on google.com.
2. google.com returns an HTTP response with HTML contents.
3. The browser renders the HTML contents for the end user.

Web services are classified based on data exchange protocol. There are two popular web services:

- **SOAP:** All web services using SOAP protocol are called SOAP web services
- **RESTful:** All web services satisfying the REST architectural constraints are called RESTful web services

Probability indicator:

Web Services and SOA

SOA is an architectural paradigm, and a web service is the technical approach to implementing it. Web services are preferred standards of achieving SOA. Web services communicate using loosely coupled SOAP. SOA services are catalogued in a directory. UDDI is a SOA registry and describes the mechanism to get to these web services.

Probability indicator:

What are SOA patterns?

SOA patterns are reusable components which can be applied to commonly occurring design problems. Key SOA patterns include:

- ESB facilitates data transformations, message queuing, message transformation, service brokers, and reliable messaging.
- A File gateway is introduced between a service and legacy file, and acts as a mediator for data transformations.
- Event-driven messaging notifies its consumers of events through messages.
- Service callback provides a callback, mechanism for the service to respond and is an asynchronous communication model.
- Service grid stores the service state which facilitates redundancy and replication.

Probability indicator:

Summary

This chapter covered the Q&A for SOA and integration domain. This section had Q&A for SOA capabilities, SOA ROI, SOA modernization approaches, SOA entry points, ESB, BPEL, BPM, SOA and Security, SOA KPIs, OSIMM framework, top-down and bottom-up approaches and SOA patterns.

The next chapter will covers the Q&A for the solution architecture and design domain. The Q&A will include the **Java Enterprise Edition (JEE)** framework, **Object Oriented Analysis and Design and Unified Modelling Language (OOAD – UML)**, session management, distributed DB, replication, performance issues, spring framework, Hibernate, agile model, MVC, and design patterns

5
Solution Architecture and Design

Solution architecture is a practice of defining and describing an architecture of a system defined in the context of a specific business domain solution and it may encompass the description of an entire system or only its sub-parts. The creation and definition of a solution architecture is led by solutions architects.

A solution architect is a practitioner of solution architecture. Typically part of the solution development team, the solution architect translates business requirements defined by business analysts into solution architecture describing it through architecture and design assets. The development team leverages these assets to implement and deploy the solution. The solution architect's process typically involves selecting the most appropriate technology framework for the problem.

Solution architecture

This chapter covers the Q&As for solution architecture and the design domain. The Q&As cover the following areas: the JEE framework, OOAD – UML, session management, distributed DB, replication, performance issues, the Spring framework, Hibernate, the agile model, MVC, and design patterns.

What are the most important technologies/specifications in Java EE?

The capabilities of Java EE 7.0 are as follows:

- Components are logically divided into three tiers: the business, middle, and web tier. This is the logical grouping, and components can be mapped to different tiers based upon business requirements.
- JPA and JMS provide services for messaging and databases. JCA facilitates integration with legacy applications.
- Enterprise Beans provide a simplified model leveraging POJOs to use basic services.
- CDI, interceptors, and common annotations provide type-safe dependency injection, addressing cross-cutting concerns and a set of annotations.
- CDI extensions facilitate extending the framework beyond its existing capabilities.
- Web services such as JAX-RS and JAX-WS, JSP, JSF, and EL enable models for web applications. Web fragments facilitate the registration of third-party frameworks in a natural manner.
- JSON provides parsing and generation of JSON structures in the web layer.
- Web sockets facilitate bi-directional, full-duplex communication over a TCP connection.
- Bean validation provides a means to declare constraints and validates them across different technologies.

This following diagram depicts the JEE framework 7.0 capabilities:

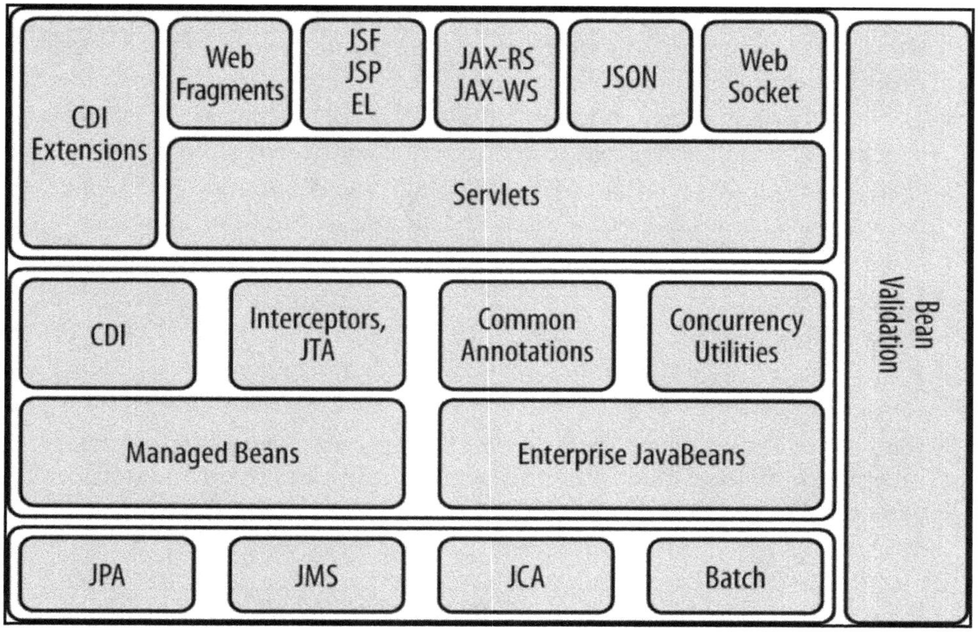

Figure 1: Capabilities of Java EE 7.0

Probability indicator: 👍 👍

What are the improvements in EJB 3 and later versions of EJB?

SMEs have observed that EJB 3 is an entirely different ball game. It includes configuration, annotations, dependency injection, and aspect orientation making EJBs a lean alternative to JAR-heavy frameworks. EJB technology is lean and weightless. There is no longer a need for JARs, XML configuration, or added frameworks. They integrate Java persistence API, are scalable on multicore machines; and are only vendor-neutral solution for enterprise applications. EJB 2.1 specification was not concise and violated the **Don't Repeat Yourself** (**DRY**) principle. The EJB component was spread across remote, home interfaces, bean classes, and the deployment descriptor. Without tools, refactoring was tedious and IDEs weren't good at refactoring.

The following are the list of improvements in EJB 3 over the previous implementations:

- It simplifies the process of developing EJB. It reduce significantly the overhead of using Java language annotations as configuration, improving developers' productivity.
- The specification of programmatic defaults and metadata reduces the need to specify expected behaviors and requirements of the container.
- Encapsulation of dependencies and JNDI access through the use of annotations, dependency injection mechanisms, and simple lookup mechanisms.
- EJB support inheritance and polymorphism.
- Lightweight CRUD operations with the JPA entity manager API.
- Enhanced query JPA capabilities.
- A life cycle's callback methods can be defined in EJB itself or in a bean listener class.
- Interceptor facility listeners for session beans and message-driven beans. An interceptor method may be defined on the bean class or on an interceptor class associated with the bean.

Probability indicator:

What do you understand by separation of concerns?

Separation of Concerns (**SoC**) is a design principle for separating a program into different sections, so that each section addresses a different concern. A concern is a set of information that affects the code of a program. A concern can be as general as the details of the hardware the code is optimized for, or as specific as the name of the class to instantiate.

A program that embodies SoC is called a modular program. Modularity, and hence separation of concerns, is achieved by encapsulating information inside a section of the program having well-defined interfaces. Encapsulation facilitates information hiding. Layered designs are another embodiment of separation of concerns (for example, presentation, business, data access, and persistence).

Benefits of SoC

The value of separation of concerns is in simplifying the development and maintenance of implementations. Well-separated, concerned facilitates the reuse of individual sections, as well as independent development, with the ability to modify one section of a program without having to know the details of other sections.

Probability indicator:

What is session management?

HTTP is a stateless protocol, and a web server in a cluster can potentially process an application client request. Session management allows a user's session state to be persisted.

For example, after a user has been authenticated by the web server, there is no need to re-authenticate at the next HTTP request if the user's authentication persists in the user's session state. The convenience of session management, however, comes with a price. Applications that use session management must maintain each user's session state, which is usually stored in memory. This can greatly increase an application's run-time memory footprint and tends to link user sessions to specific servers, requiring those sessions to be migrated to another node if the server is taken offline or fails. If session management is not implemented, applications can have a smaller footprint, and any cluster node can service requests from any user.

Approach

The user sessions are stored in cookies or in a hidden entries on a HTML page. An application can allocate a unique identifier to a user and then track the user's progress on the site. A user's interaction spans across multiple web pages by archiving the user's session state, and the application can capture the user's recent interaction with the website. In some instances, the user's session state is persisted to moderate subsequent visits. Some applications apply the user's session state to dynamically pages based on a user's preferences and patterns. Session cookies are stored often in a cryptographically signed format, but the data is usually unencrypted. Session data stored in cookies should not contain any sensitive information such as credit card data or other personal data. User sessions are also stored in a database or via Memcached. There are scripting frameworks such as PHP WASP and Zend that offer session management features.

Probability indicator:

What is session tracking and how is tracking done in servlets for user sessions?

Session tracking is a technique leveraged by application servlets to maintain the state of user requests across a time span. The different techniques for session tracking are:

- User authentication is enabled through a web server to the resources to those clients logging using authorized credentials.
- Hidden fields are added to HTML and are not displayed in the browser. When the HTML with the fields is submitted, these fields are sent to the server.
- All the URLs the user clicks is dynamically re-written to include extra session data. The extra data is in the form of path information, parameters, or some URL updates.
- Cookies are the data that is sent from the web server to the browser and can later be read from the browser.
- HTTP session objects are also leveraged for session data but they put a maximum cap on the number of sessions that can co-exist in the memory.

Probability indicator:

What is the purpose of sessions and cookies, and what are the difference between them?

Sessions and cookies are leveraged to store the user data. A cookies stores user information on the client side and a session does it on the server side and this is the key difference between cookies and sessions. Sessions and cookies are leveraged in the application for preferences, authentication, and application parameters across multiple user requests. Both sessions and cookies are meant for the same purpose. A cookie is leveraged for storing only textual information. The session can be used to store both textual information and objects.

Probability indicator:

How is the Java EE application session replication enabled?

Configuring the distributable tag in web XML enables an application to support session replication but it may not guarantee it will work fine in a session replicated environment.

A JEE application needs to enable the following during application development:

- All the attributes saved in HTTP session including all custom objects should be made serializable.
- Session APIs must be leveraged for making changes to session attributes. A reference to Java objects set in a session previously must call session APIs every time you make any amendments.

Options for enabling session replication

Session replication between clusters can be done in a variety of ways but the efficient approach depends on the type of application. The following are a few common techniques that are leveraged:

- Leveraging session persistence and saving sessions to a shared filesystem allows all nodes in a cluster to access the persisted session
- Leveraging in-memory-replication will create an in-memory copy of a session in all the cluster nodes

Probability indicator: 👍 👍

How do you version a service inventory?

There may be a requirement to modify service logic or to add a functional scope of the services. In these cases, a new version of the service logic or service contract will need to be introduced. To ensure that the versioning of a service can be carried out with minimal impact and disruption to consumers that are dependent on the service, a formal service versioning technique needs to be in place which is the service inventory.

Approach

There are different versioning strategies, each of which introduces its own set of rules and priorities when it comes to managing the services compatibilities including the contracts. The service versioning phase is associated with SOA governance because it is a recurring part of the overall service life-cycle processes. Governance processes guide the service versioning and will have a significant influence on a service which will evolve over time. Because this stage also encompasses the retirement of a service, these influences are further factored into the service's overall life-span.

Probability indicator:

What is the key reason behind leveraging frameworks and libraries in application development?

The explanation is as follows:

A library is a collection of routines or class and facilitates simple code reuse. The routines or classes define specific operations in a specific domain area. For example, there are libraries of mathematics call the function without redo the implementation algorithm.

In the framework, all the control flow is already there, and there's are pre-defined white spots that one should fill out with custom implementation. A framework is more complex than a library and defines a skeleton where the application needs to fill out this skeleton. The benefit is that we do not worry about whether a design is good or not, but just about implementing domain-specific features.

The key difference between a framework and a library is inversion of control. When one calls a method from a library, one is in control but with a framework, the control is inverted, that is, the framework calls you.

Probability indicator:

What is code refactoring?

Applications have a tendency to increase in complexity over a period of time and thus become difficult to maintain and modify. They also become difficult to articulate. Refactoring is a modularization technique that deals with the separation of responsibilities. Refactored implementation makes code more reusable by virtue of loose coupling and minimum dependencies.

Refactoring has merits in terms of correctness and quality, but refactoring pays off the most with software maintenance and upgrades. Often a mechanism to add new requirements to a poorly factored implementation is to refactor the code and then add these features. This takes less effort than trying to add the new feature without refactoring, and it's an excellent way to enhance code quality.

Benefits

Refactoring can have multiples incentives:

- Improved code readability
- Simplified code structure
- Improved maintainability
- Improved extensibility

Probability indicator:

What is the difference between Object Oriented and Aspect Oriented programming?

Object Oriented Programming (OOP):

- OOP enables applications as a set of collaborating objects. OOP code scatters system code such as logging and security with business logic code.
- OOP works on entities such as classes, objects, interfaces, and so on.
- OOP provides benefits such as reuse, flexibility, maintainability, modularity, time, and effort, with the help of OO principles.

Aspect Oriented Programming (AOP):

- AOP works in complex software as a combined implementation of multiple concerns such as business logic, persistence, logging, security, thread safety, errors, and exception handling. It bifurcates business logic from the system code and one concern remains unaware of the other.
- AOP has join points, point cuts, advice, and aspects.
- AOP implementation coexists with OOP by leveraging OOP as the foundation

Probability indicator:

What do you understand by entity model/domain model?

The domain model is a conceptual or logical model of the specific domain related to a specific business domain. It explains entities, attributes, roles, relationships, and constraints that govern the problem domain but not the solutions to the problem. The domain model is defined as the vocabulary and concepts of the problem domain or the business domain. The domain model establishes the relationships between the entities in the scope of the problem domain and identifies their properties. The domain model encapsulates methods within entities and is properly associated with object oriented models. The domain model enables a structural view of the domain complemented with other dynamic views, such as use cases.

Probability indicator:

Describe the architecture of a medium-to-large scale system

This will be based on your past expertise and be prepared with a key engagement as a case study and to answer details pertaining to the following:

- Design decision made or options considered or rejected
- Frameworks leveraged and why
- Methodology or process that was leveraged to arrive at the target architecture or solution

- Security considerations/mechanism recommended
- Addressing non-functional requirements pertaining to availability, scalability, performance and reliability, and so on

Probability indicator:

What are distributed databases?

A distributed database is an architecture in which parts of the database are stored on a different server in a network. Users have access to part of the database at their location to access data relevant to their processes. A centralized distributed database management system (DBMS) manages the database as a single entity. DBMS syncs all data at regular time intervals. In cases where multiple users access the same data, DBMS ensures that updates that are performed on the data at one location are reflected in the data stored in others.

The following are the benefits of distributed databases:

- Efficient handling of distributed data with varied levels of transparency such as networks, fragmentation, replication, and so on
- Increased availability, reliability, and flexibility
- Database fragments relating to organizational structure are stored within the departments
- Autonomy is enabled as departments can control the data they work with and they own data
- During a catastrophe such as an earthquake, the data will not be in one place, but will be distributed in multiple locations, thus providing protection
- Data is located near the site of demand, and databases are parallelized, enabling load balancing and providing excellent performance
- Due to architecture modularity, the components can be modified without affecting other modules in the DBMS
- Reliable transactions are enabled due to database replication and location independence
- As the model is distributed, a single-site failure does not affect the performance of the overall system, thus facilitating continuous operation, even if nodes go offline

Probability indicator:

What is database sharding? Is database sharding the same as master-slave configuration?

Database sharding means horizontal partitioning in a database. The purpose is to split data between multiple nodes while ensuring that the data is accessed from the correct location. Sharding is sometimes referred to as horizontal scaling or horizontal partitioning. Sharding is a proven database scalability technique and is leveraged in some of the world's most popular web applications. With sharding, instead of storing data in just one database instance, it's distributed across multiple instances.

Sharding is an architectural technique that distributes one logical database system into a cluster of machines. In sharded database systems, the database rows of a table are stored separately, instead of being split into columns like normalization or vertical partitioning. Each partition is then a shard, and is independently locatable on a separate database node.

The total number of rows in a database table is reduced since the tables are distributed across multiple nodes. This also reduces the index size, providing excellent performance. Hashing of a unique ID in the application is the most common approach for defining shards.

The downsides of sharding include:

- The application has to be aware of the multiple data locations
- Any addition or deletion of nodes from the system will require re-balancing in the architecture
- Where there are a lot of cross-node join queries, performance will be poor and thus a knowledge of the data purpose and the way it will be leveraged for querying will be the key
- An incorrect sharding technique will result in poor performance

The difference is as follows:

A master/slave approach is only for replication. This method only improves performance for applications dealing with static data since only the master can receive and update information. Sharding does not replicate anything. It simply partitions the data in different files, which may be located in different folders, filesystems, or even machines.

Probability indicator: 👍 👍

What is active and passive and active/active load balancing?

The two popular techniques to achieve this are to use clustering to deal with failover and load balancing. The Active/Active mode is enabled to provide for database or session replication and redundancy. Load balancers can be deployed to route requests according to server performance and on the basis of the algorithm.

Active/Passive mode

Active/Passive configuration offers advantages in that the primary load balancer distributes the network traffic to a suitable server while the second load balancer operates in listening mode to monitor the performance of the primary load balancer, ready to take over the load balancing duties should the primary load balancer fail.

Load balancers, when configured in Active/Passive mode, provide the ability to sustain uninterrupted customer services. One more advantage is the ability to deal with either planned or unplanned outages. Business today requires a 24/7 service for customers and any outage is costly in terms of lost as well as damage to the reputation.

Active/Active mode

In the Active/Active mode, two or more servers aggregate the network traffic and, working as a team, distributes it to the server clusters. The load balancers remember information requests from users and keep this information in the cache. Should the user return, the user will be locked onto the load balancer that previously served them and the information provided again from the cache, therefore reducing network traffic load. One potential disadvantage is that you run them near full capacity.

Probability indicator:

What are the most important performance issues in Java applications?

The following are the performance issues:

- Too many database calls due to many database queries triggered by request response transactions
- In a high work-load environment, over-synchronization will lead to poor performance and scalability issues

- Multiple calls across these remote boundaries and too chatty applications will result in poor performance and scalability issues
- Unexpected performance and scalability issues will result from the wrong usage of O/R-Mappers or frameworks
- As a best practice implementation, it is key to release object references as soon as they are no longer needed, as GC does not prevent such memory leaks
- At times, there are issues with third-party frameworks and components and therefore validation of frameworks is mandatory.
- Wasteful handling of scarce resources such as memory, CPU, and I/O databases is costly and thus the lack of resource access by others will ultimately leads to performance and scalability
- There may be bloated web tiers as many pack unwanted stuff
- It is necessary to verify which objects to cache and which not to cache as incorrect cache strategy leads to excessive garbage collection
- Intermittent problems are the hardest to locate as they occur with specific parameters or are sporadic
- Different serialization types will have different impact on performance, scalability, memory usage, and network traffic.

Probability indicator: 👍👍

What are the tools for performance tuning and analysis of bottlenecks?

The descriptions are explained in the following table:

Tools	Description
Thread and dump analyzer	Analyzes Java core dump files. Locates bottlenecks, deadlocks, and resource contention
Garbage collection and memory visualizer	Analyzes and visualizes verbose GC logs. Identifies memory leaks, the size of Java heaps, and selects GC policy.
Heap-analyzer	Analyzes dumps to find memory leaks.

| Performance monitoring infrastructure PMI | Dashboards can be viewed in the performance viewer Monitors JDBC pools, JVM runtime, heap size, request counts, and average time by servlet |

Table 1: Performance Tools

Probability indicator: 👍 👍

How do you reduce DB communication and application bottlenecks?

DB resolution: Query optimization, restructuring indexes, DB caching tuning leveraging ORM frameworks

- Tacking bottlenecks:
    - **Reduce demand**: Caching, tuning code, tuning database, and tuning application server
    - **Increase available resources**: Horizontal or vertical scaling, memory, CPU
    - **Reduce slowdown due to synchronization**: Effective collections and effective locking

Probability indicator: 👍 👍

What are the options for making asynchronous calls within a Java EE 6?

Java EE provides various ways and APIs to facilitate async capabilities. The following table illustrates the Java EE spec capabilities that provide the async feature:

Async Capabilities	Description
JAX-RS 2.0	Async processing of requests is a new feature in edition 2.0 of JAX-RS in Java EE 7. To execute an aysnc request using JAX-RS APIs, one needs to inject a reference to an AsyncResponse interface in the JAX-RS resource method. The parameter puts the request execution in async mode and the method proceeds with its execution.
Websocket 1.0	Websocket API is a new addition to Java EE 7. It facilitates bi-directional full duplex communication
Concurrency utilities 1.0	Java concurrency utilities is a great addition to Java EE 7. It provides a standard way of spawning threads that are managed by containers and not just isolated/orphan threads
Servlet 3.0	Asynchronous HTTP was introduced in Servlet 3.0, basically providing the capability to execute the request in a separate thread and suspend the original thread to handle client invocation.
EJB 3.1	EJB message driven beans were leveraged to fulfill async related requirements. MDB listens to messages sent to a queue/topic and executes business logic. The important thing to understand is that the client which sends the message to the queue/topic is unaware of the decoupled MDB and does not wait/remain blocked until the end of the execution

Table 2: Asynchronous Options JEE

Probability indicator: 👍👍

What are the various persistence mechanisms in JEE applications?

Persisting data and querying it back is a major consideration. Here are a few ways of designing your persistence tier:

- Using JEE JPA and **Object Relational Mapping (ORM)** frameworks such as Hibernate
- Creating DB stored procedures and then leveraging a data tier to consume them in the EIS layer
- Generating strongly typed classes, basic database tables, leveraging code generation techniques, and JDBC

Probability indicator:

What is the difference between performance, load, and stress testing?

Performance testing: Performance testing is done to establish how the application components are performing, under a simulated situation. Resource usage, scalability, and reliability are validated under this testing. This testing may be a spin-off of performance engineering, which is focused on tackling the performance issues architecture of software applications.

The primary goal of performance testing is establishing the benchmark behavior of the application.

Load testing: Load testing tests the application by constantly and incrementally increasing the work load on the application until it reaches the threshold limit. It is the easiest form of testing and leverages automation tools such as Load Runner. Load testing is also known as volume or endurance testing. The purpose of load testing is to assign the largest job to the application so that it can test the endurance results.

The target of load testing is to determine the upper limit of all the components of the applications such as databases, hardware, networks, and so on, so that it can manage the anticipated load in future.

Stress testing: In stress testing, various tasks to overload the applications are executed in an attempt to break the application. Negative testing, including the removal of components from the application is also done as a part of stress testing. This is also known as fatigue testing. This testing establishes the stability of the application by testing it beyond its bandwidth capacity. The objective of stress testing is to ascertain the failure and to monitor the recovery gracefully.

The goal is to analyze crash reports to define the behavior of the application post-failure. The challenge is to ensure that the application does not compromise the security of sensitive data after the failure.

Best practices for load and performance testing include:

- Set precise performance objectives or parameters and define peak load, expected response time, and availability
- An application does not work on its own as it needs to interconnect with external interfaces and hence establish performance goals with external interfaces
- Validate early and ensure performance testing early in the life cycle
- A testing environment and the production environment should be identical
- Make it a practice to leverage application profilers in the IDE (for example, JProfiler)
- Optimization decisions should be based on past experience and should not be premature optimizations
- Set a strategy for expected and peak load, server configuration, clustered environments, and load balancers

Probability indicator:

Explain use case diagrams

Use case diagram explains IT application objectives from the user perspective. Use cases are added in requirement specifications to depict clarity regarding an application. There are three key parts to use cases: scenario, actor, and use case:

- **Scenario**: This is a sequence of events than are triggered when a user interacts with the IT application.
- **Actor**: The actor is the end user of the IT system.
- **Use case**: The use case is a goal performed by the end user. As use cases represent action, they are normally defined by strong verbs.

Primary and secondary actors

Actors are represented by a stick man symbol and use cases by an oval shape. Actors are further classified into two categories: primary and secondary. Primary actors are the users that are active participants, and they trigger the use case, while secondary actors passively participate in the use case.

Probability indicator:

Explain the difference between abstraction and encapsulation?

The explanation is as stated as follows:

- An abstraction resolves the design level problems while encapsulation solves problems at implementation levels
- An abstraction is leveraged for hiding unsolicited data and providing relevant data while, to protect from external entities, encapsulation is about hiding the code and data in a single unit
- Encapsulation means hiding the internal mechanics of an object while abstraction puts emphasis on the object interface

Probability indicator:

Explain composition and aggregation and in class diagrams?

There are two types of association: aggregation and composition:

- **Aggregation**: An association establishes that the entire object exists without the aggregated object. For example, in the diagram there are three classes: university, department, and professor. The university cannot exist without the department; the university will be shut as the department is shut. This means that the lifespan of the university depends on the lifespan of the department. The filled diamond represents the aggregation.

- **Composition**: The diagram also defines the second association between the department and the professor. In this case, if the professor leaves the department the department still continues to exist, meaning the department is not dependent on the professor. The empty diamond represents the composition.

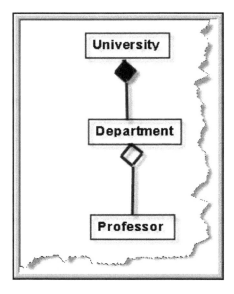

Figure 2: Aggregation and composition in action

Probability indicator:

Explain specialization and generalization?

Specialization and generalizations define parent-child relationships between the classes. In many instances, classes may have the same operation and properties and these classes are called **super classes** and later one inherits from the super class to create sub-classes with their own custom properties. In the diagram, there are three classes for showing generalization and specialization relationships. All the phone types have a phone number as a generalized property, but depending upon landline or mobile you can have wired or sim card connectivity as a specialized property. In this diagram, the cell-phone represents generalization whereas **clslandline** and **clsmobile** represent specialization.

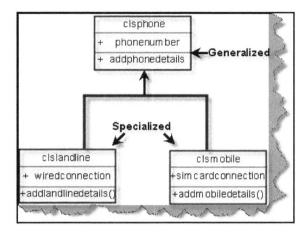

Figure 3: Generalization and specialization

Probability indicator: 👍

Explain the difference between compositions and inheritance?

- Inheritance **is a** relationship whereas composition **has a** relationship
- In inheritance there is only one object in the memory, the derived object, whereas in composition , the parent object holds references to many other objects
- Inheritance is an object inheriting reusable properties of the super class and composition is an object that holds another object.

Probability indicator: 👍👍

What are the benefits of the Spring framework?

The Spring framework helps build simple, portable, fast, and flexible JVM-based applications. Spring is a lightweight open source framework for developing enterprise applications. The Spring framework resolves the complexity of enterprise application development and provides a cohesive framework for application development based on dependency injection and inversion of control and design patterns.

The benefits of the Spring framework include:

- The Spring framework enables building enterprise-class applications using POJOs. The benefit of using only POJOs is that one does not need an EJB container and it is not complex.
- The Spring framework is structured in a modular manner. In Spring, even though the number of packages is substantial, one is to understand one the few they need while ignoring the rest.
- The Spring framework doesn't reinvent the wheel as it makes use of the existing technologies such as ORM frameworks, logging frameworks, and timers.
- Spring's framework also has a well architected MVC framework, providing an alternative to web frameworks such as Struts or other less popular web frameworks.
- Spring provides a simple API for translating technology-specific exceptions into consistent, unchecked exceptions.
- The Spring framework provides a consistent transaction API that can scale down to a local transaction.
- Testing an application written with the Spring framework is easy because the environment-dependent code is moved into this framework.

Probability indicator: 👍 👍

What is database deadlock and how can it be avoided?

When multiple entities are trying to access the DB locks they go into the cyclic wait state, making it unresponsive. Deadlock is a condition that occurs with multiple threads for any applications, not just on a RDBMS.

For example, a thread in multithreaded an OS might acquire one or more resources, such as blocks of memory. If the resource being acquired is currently owned by another thread, the first thread will have to wait for the owning thread to release the resources. The waiting thread is said to have a dependency on the owning thread. In the instance of the database engine, sessions can deadlock when acquiring non-database resources, such as memory or threads.

Few listed as follows:

- Creating a queue can verify and order the requests to the DB.
- Ensure that the transactionsh are small
- Keep transactions short and in one batch.
- Avoid user interaction in transactions.
- Efficiently leverage DB cursors as they lock the tables for a long time.

Probability indicator:

Explain the difference between the DOM and SAX parsers?

The **Document Object Model (DOM)** parser creates a tree structure in memory from a document. In a DOM, the parser serves the application with the entire document. In contrast, the Simple API for XML SAX parser does not create any internal structure. A SAX parser always serves the client application only with part of the document at any given time.

The SAX parser, however, is much more space efficient if dealing with a big document whereas the DOM parser is rich in functionality. Leverage the DOM parser if you need to refer to different document areas before giving back the information. Leverage a SAX parser if you just need unrelated nuclear information from different areas.

Examples: Crimson are SAX Parsers whereas XercesDOM, SunDOM, and OracleDOM are DOM parsers.

Probability indicator:

What is connection pooling?

The connection pooling technique allows multiple clients to make use of cached shared and reusable connection objects, providing access to a database. Connecting to a database consists of several time-consuming steps. A physical channel such as a socket or a named pipe must be established, the handshake must occur, the connection string information needs to be parsed, and the connection must be authenticated by the server.

In practice, applications leverage only a few configurations for connections. This means that during the application execution, many similar connections will be repeatedly created and closed. To minimize the cost of connections management, an optimization technique called connection pooling is leveraged. Connection pooling reduces the times that new connections need to be opened. The pool maintains ownership of these physical connection. It manages connections by ensuring a set of active connections for different connection configurations.

Connection pooling provides the following benefits:

- Reduces the number of times new connection entities are created
- Promotes connection object reuse
- Fastens the process of getting a connection
- Reduces the effort to manually manage connection objects
- Minimizes the number of stale connections
- Reduces the amount of resources spent on maintaining connections

Probability indicator:

What are the advantages of Hibernate?

Hibernate is an ORM framework and has numerous pros and cons. This section mainly lists the advantages of using Hibernate.

The advantages are as follows:

- Hibernate is independent of the database engine. A list of Hibernate dialect is leveraged for connecting to different databases.
- Java Persistence API – JPA is a specification. Hibernate is a standard ORM solution, and has a JPA capability. Hence, leveraging Hibernate will help you leverage all capabilities of ORM and JPA.
- Hibernate has integrated automatically with most reliable connection pool mechanisms.
- Hibernate is a layered architecture so that we are not bound to leverage everything provided by Hibernate. We just leverage those features that are needed for the project.
- Hibernate supports inheritance, associations, and collections.

- Hibernate supports relationships such as Many-to-One, One-to-Many, Many-to-Many-to-Many, and One-to-One.
- Hibernate also supports collections such as lists, sets, and maps.

The following are differences between Hibernate and JPA.

Java Persistence API is a specification for ORM implementations whereas Hibernate is the actual ORM framework implementation. JPA is a specification that guides the implementation of ORM frameworks. Implementations abiding by the specification would mean that one can be replaced with others in an application without much hassle. Only the features that are added to the specification need to be taken care of if any such change is made.

Probability indicator: 👍 👍

Why is String immutable in Java?

String is immutable for several reasons; here is a summary:

- Security: Parameters are leveraged as String in network connections, database connection usernames/passwords, and so on. As they are immutable, they cannot be changed easily.
- Synchronization and concurrency, by making String objects immutable, automatically make them thread safe, thus solving the synchronization issues.
- When a compiler optimizes the String objects, if two objects have the same value, you need only one string object.
- String is leveraged as arguments for class loading but if it is mutable, it could result in the wrong class being loaded.

Probability indicator: 👍 👍

Does garbage collection guarantee that the application will not run out of memory?

Garbage collection does not guarantee that a program will not run out of memory. It is possible for programs to use up memory resources faster than they are garbage collected and it is possible for programs to create objects that are not garbage collected.

The methodology used is as follows.

The Java runtime environment deletes objects when it determines that they are no longer leveraged and this is known as garbage collection. The Java runtime environment provides a garbage collector that periodically frees the memory used by objects that are no longer needed. The Java garbage collector scans Java's dynamic memory areas for objects, marking those that are referenced. After all possible paths to objects are investigated, those objects that are not referenced are garbage collected.

Probability indicator: 👍 👍

Does Java support multiple inheritance and what is the difference between checked and unchecked exceptions?

Java doesn't support multiple inheritances. Interfaces don't facilitate inheritance and hence the implementation of multiple interfaces doesn't make multiple inheritances.

Checked exceptions are checked at compile time. If some code within a function throws a checked exception, then the function must either handle the exception or it must specify the exception using the throws keyword.

Unchecked exceptions are not checked at compile time. In C++, all exceptions are unchecked, so it is not forced by the compiler to either handle or specify the exception. It is up to the programmers to decide and catch these exceptions.

Probability indicator: 👍 👍

What is casting?

Casting means taking an object of one type and turning it into another type. There are two types of casting, casting between object references and casting between primitive numeric types. Casting between numeric types is leveraged to convert larger values, such as double values, to smaller values, such as byte values. Casting between object references is leveraged to refer to an object by a compatible class, interface, or array type reference.

Probability indicator: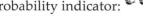

What is a final variable? What is a final method? What is a final class? What is an immutable class?

The final variable is a constant variable. The variable value can't be changed after instantiation. A method that cannot be overridden in the subclass. A class that cannot be sub-classed. A class using only immutable; objects cannot be changed after initialization can be created.

Probability indicator:

Explain thread states?

The thread is a lightweight process, the smallest unit of a scheduled execution. An instance of the `Thread` class in Java could be in one of the following states. A thread can only be in one state at a given time. These states are virtual machine states which do not reflect any operating system thread states.

The following diagram depicts different thread states:

- **Runnable**: The thread is waiting for its turn to be picked for execution by the thread scheduler based on priority
- **Running**: The CPU is actively executing the thread and will run until it becomes blocked, or voluntarily gives up
- **Waiting**: The thread is in a blocked state while it waits for external processing, such as a file I/O, to complete
- **Sleeping**: Threads are forcibly put to sleep or suspended and resume using Thread API
- **Blocked on I/O**: The thread will become runnable after an I/O condition is complete
- **Blocked on synchronization**: The thread will move to Runnable when a lock is acquired
- **Dead**: The thread is finished working

Probability indicator:

Explain the advantage of collection classes over arrays?

The advantages are as follows:

Arrays: An array is a collection of objects of similar type. Because arrays can be any length, they are leveraged to store thousands of objects, but the size is fixed when the array is created. Each item in the array is accessed by an index, which is a number that indicates the position where the object is stored. Arrays can be leveraged to store both value or reference types.

Collections: An array is just one of the different options for storing data. The option selected depends on various factors, such as how you manipulate or access the data. For example, a list is generally faster than an array if you must insert items at the beginning or in the middle of the collection. Other types of collections include maps, trees, and stacks; each one has its own advantages:

- Collections are re-sizable and can increase or decrease the size as per requirements
- Collections can hold both homogeneous and heterogeneous data
- Every collection follows standard data structures
- The collection provides built-in methods for traversing, sorting and, search

Probability indicator: 👍 👍

Why is Java considered a portable language?

Java is a portable language because without any modification we can use Java byte code in any platform (which supports Java). So this byte code is portable, and we can use it in any other major platform.

Probability indicator: 👍 👍

What is the difference between threads and processes?

The differences are as follows:

Processes: Processes are often synonymous with applications, but what the user sees as a single application is, in fact, a set of cooperating processes. A process has a self-contained execution environment which includes a private set of basic runtime resources and its own memory space.

Threads: Threads are lightweight processes and both processes and threads provide an execution environment, but creating a new thread requires fewer resources than processes. Threads exist within a process; every process has at least one thread. Threads share the process's resources, including memory and files.

Comparison:

- When an OS wants to start running the program, it creates a new process and every process has at least one thread running.
- A thread is a path of execution in a program, which has its own local variables, a program counter (a pointer to the current execution being executed), and lifetime.
- When the Java VM is started by the OS, a new process is created. Within that process, many threads can be created.
- Within a process, every thread has an independent path of execution, but there may be a situation where two threads can interfere causing concurrency and deadlock.
- As two process can communicate, in the same way two threads can also communicate with each other.
- Every thread in Java is created and controlled by a unique object of the Thread class.

Probability indicator:👍 👍

What is the difference between String buffers and String classes?

A string buffer creates a mutable sequence of characters. A string buffer is a string but can be modified. It contains some sequence of characters, but the length and content of the sequence can be changed through method calls. The String class represents character strings. All string literals in Java, such as "xyz", are constants and implemented as instances of the string class; their values cannot be changed after the initial creation.

Probability indicator:👍 👍

What is ORM?

Object Relational Mapping (**ORM**) and O/R mapping is a technique for converting data between incompatible types in OO languages. This creates, in effect, a "virtual database" that can be leveraged from the programming language.

The benefits of ORM include:

- Productivity
- Application design
- Code reuse
- Application maintainability

Probability indicator:👍 👍

What is the difference between a .jar, .war and .ear file?

In JEE applications, the modules are packaged as WAR, JAR and EAR based on functionality:

- **JAR**: EJB modules containing enterprise Java beans, class files, and EJB deployment descriptors are packed as JAR files with the `.jar` extension
- **WAR**: Web modules containing Servlet class files, JSPs, GIF, and HTML are packaged as JAR `file.war` extensions
- **EAR**: All the `.jar` and `.war` files are packaged as JAR files with `.ear` (enterprise archive) extensions and deployed into a container

Probability indicator:👍👍

What is JSP?

JavaServer Pages (**JSP**) is a technology that helps create dynamically generated web pages based on HTML, XML, or other types. Released in 1999 by Sun Microsystems, JSP is similar to PHP, but it uses the Java language.

Probability indicator:👍👍

What is the ACID property of a system?

ACID is an acronym commonly used to define the properties of a RDBMS; it stands for the following terms:

- **Atomicity**: This guarantees that if one part of a transaction fails, the entire transaction will fail, and the database state will be left unchanged
- **Consistency**: This ensures that any transaction will bring the database from one valid state to another

- **Isolation**: This ensures that the concurrent execution of transactions results in a system state that would be obtained if transactions were executed serially
- **Durable**: This means that once a transaction has been committed, it will remain so, even in the event of a power failure.

Probability indicator:👍 👍

What is shared nothing architecture? How does it scale?

A shared nothing architecture is a distributed approach in which each node is independent and self-reliant, and there is no single point of failure across the landscape:

- This means no resources are shared between nodes
- The nodes are able to work independently without depending on one another
- Failure on one node affects only the users of that node and other nodes continue to work without disruption

This approach is highly scalable since it avoids the existence of bottlenecks. Shared nothing is popular for web development due to its linear scalability. Google has been leveraging it for a long time. A shared nothing architecture can scale almost infinitely by adding nodes in the form of inexpensive machines.

Probability indicator:👍 👍

How do you update a heavy traffic site that is live with minimum or zero downtime?

Deploying a newer version of a live website can be a challenging task when a website has heavy traffic. Any small downtime is going to affect the end users. There are a few best practices that we can follow.

Before deploying on production:

- Thoroughly test the fixes and ensure they are working in a test environment (identical to the production environment).
- Perform automation of test cases as much as possible and one can leverage selenium functional testing.
- Create an automated sanity testing script/smoke test that can be run on production. These are typically the read-only type of test cases and ensure they can run quickly by keeping them short.
- Create scripts for all manual tasks, avoiding any mistakes during the deployment day.
- Test these script to make sure they work in a non-production environment.
- Build artifacts should be ready which includes application deployment files, database scripts, config files, and so on.
- Deploy in a non-production environment first and with production data. Please note the time for tasks so you can plan accordingly.

When deploying on a production environment, keep these things in mind:

- Keep a backup of current data in case of rollback.
- Use sanity test cases before doing a lot of in-depth testing.

Probability indicator:

What are the important competencies and soft skills of architects?

The core competencies of architects are illustrated in the following diagram:

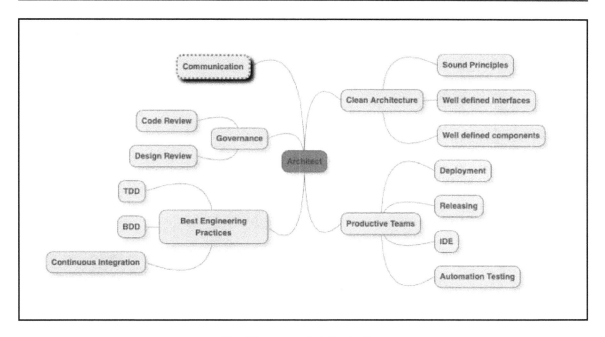

Figure 5: Competencies and soft skills of architects

- Creating a simple architecture basis, sound principles, and covering all non-functional requirements
- The framework should having good governance and review processes in place for SDLC
- Ensuring teams' productivity and empowering them with the correct frameworks and tools
- Ensuring teams are following the industry standards, frameworks, and practices
- Ensuring crisp and clear communication

The following diagram illustrates the key soft qualities of architects:

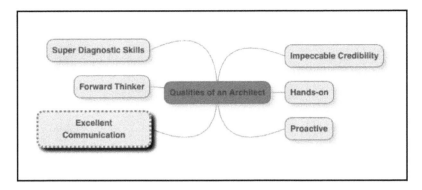

Figure 6: Key soft qualities of architects

- Impeccable credibility, to which the team looks up to and aspires to
- Excellent diagnostic ability to deep dive on a challenging issue
- Futuristic thinker, proactive, and identifies opportunities to add value to work
- Great communication in the widest sense. Communicating every aspect to the stakeholders, management, software engineers, and testers

What are the modern practices an architect should be aware of?

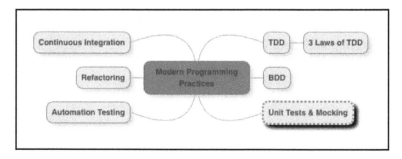

Figure 7: Modern programming practices

Probability indicator: 👍 👍

How do you ensure code quality?

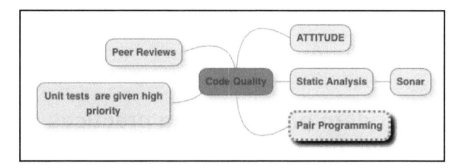

Figure 8: Code quality

Code quality is an attitude to refactor things that are wrong. The attitude to be a boy scout. An architect has to encourage an environment where such an attitude is appreciated. There are bad sheep, who take the code quality to such a level that it is not fun anymore. Have a good static analysis tool which is part of continuous integration. Understand the limits of static analysis. Results from static analysis are a signal and help to decide where to look during architect reviews. Every user story has to be reviewed. Put focus on peer reviews when there is a new developer or there is a new change being done and make the best use of pair programming.

Probability indicator: 👍 👍

How do Agile and architecture go hand in hand?

Agile and architecture do go hand in hand. Agile brings in the need to separate architecture and design and the architecture is about things which are difficult to change, such as technology, frameworks, communication, and so on. It a best practice if a big chunk of architectural decisions is done before the team starts. There will be things that are uncertain. Inputs to these can come from spikes as part of the scrum team but it is better to plan ahead.

Architecture choices should be well thought out. It's good to spend time thinking before you make an architectural choice. Change is continuous only when the team is sure nothing is broken. And automation test suites play a great role in providing immediate feedback. Important principles are tested early, fail fast, and automate.

Probability indicator: 👍 👍

What are modern programming practices leading to good applications?

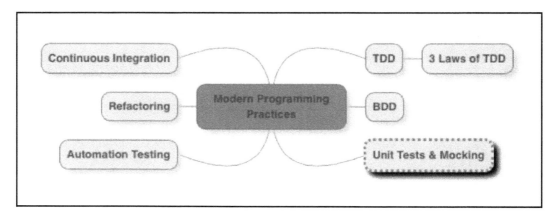

Figure 7: Modern programming practices

- **FUnit testing**: This is the age of continuous integration and delivery, and the thing that enables this is having a set of unit tests in place. Understand the concept of Mocking and JUnit.
- **Automated tests**: An automated integration test is the second important factor enabling continuous delivery. For example, Fitnesse, Cucumber, and Protractor.

- **TDD**: This a software development methodology that relies on the repetition of very short development sprints: requirements are turned into specific test cases, then the software is improved to pass these tests
- **Continuous integration**: Every project today has continuous integration. Compilations, unit tests, code quality gate, integration, and chain tests. But make sure the build does not take long. Immediate feedback is important. If needed, create a separate build scheduled less frequently for slower tests. Jenkins is the most popular continuous integration tool today.
- **BDD**: Business-driven development is a methodology for developing solutions that directly satisfy business requirements. This is achieved by adopting a model-driven approach that starts with the business strategy, requirements, and goals and then transforms them into a solution.

Probability indicator: 👍👍

What are the things that need to be considered when designing the web tier?

- Let's look into this stepwise: Do we want a modern JavaScript framework?
- Should we leverage an MVC framework such as Spring MVC or Struts, or should we use a Java-based framework like Wicket?
- What should be the view technology? JSP, JSF, or template-based?
- Do you need AJAX functionality?
- How do you map a view to business objects? Do you want to have a View and business assemblers?
- What kind of data is put in the user session? Do we need additional control mechanisms to ensure small session sizes?
- How do we authenticate and authorize? Do we need to integrate external frameworks like Spring security?
- Do we need to expose web services?

Probability indicator: 👍👍

What are the typical things you would need to consider while designing the business layer of a Java EE web application?

The following lis are the important considerations:

- Should there be a service layer as a facade to the business layer?
- How do we implement transaction management? JTA or Spring transactions or container managed transactions?
- Can we separate business logic into separate components?
- Do we use a domain object model?
- Do we need caching and at what level?
- Does the service layer or web layer need to handle all exceptions?
- Is there any specific logging or auditing needed?
- Do we need to validate the data that is coming into the business layer? Or is the validation done by the web layer?

Probability indicator:

What are the things that you would need to consider when designing the access layer (data layer) of the web application?

- Listed below are essentials things that are needed: Do we leverage a JPA based object mapping framework, such as Hibernate, or a query based mapping framework, such asiBatis or simple DO?
- How do we communicate with external systems? Web services or JMS? How do we handle XML mapping: JAXB or XMLBeans?
- How do you handle connections to a database? These days, it's an easy answer: leave it to the application server configuration of the data source.
- What are the kinds of exceptions that you want to throw to the business layer? Should they be checked or unchecked exceptions?

- Ensure that performance and scalability is taken care of in all the decisions.

Probability indicator: 👍👍

How do traditional web applications work?

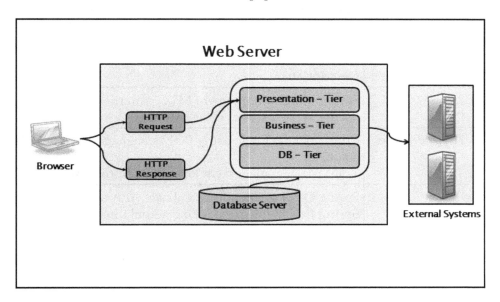

Figure 9: Traditional web applications

Web applications are based on HTTP requests and responses. Following are the steps:

- When the user initiates an action in the browser, an HTTP request is created by the browser.
- The web server creates an `HTTPServletRequest` based on the content of the HTTP request.
- The web application (based on the framework used) handles the `HTTPServletRequest`. Controllers, the business layer, the database, and interfaces)
- `HTTPServletResponse` is returned and is converted to an HTTP response.
- The HTTP response is rendered by the browser.

Probability indicator:👍 👍

Explain a web application implemented using Spring?

Various layers of web applications can be implemented using different Spring modules. The beauty of the Spring framework is that Spring provides great integration support with other non-Spring open source frameworks.

Layer	Description
Web layer	Spring MVC to implement MVC pattern. Spring WS to expose web services
Service and business layers	Core Business Logic using POJOs, managed by Spring's container Transaction management leveraging Spring AOP
Integration layer	Spring ORM to integrate databases (JPA and iBatis). Spring JMS to integrate with external interfaces using JMS Spring WS to consume web services.

Table 3: Spring Capabilities

Probability indicator:👍 👍

What is a design pattern?

A design pattern is a reusable solution to a commonly occurring problem within a context in software design. A design pattern is not a finalized design that can be transformed into a machine code. It is a template for solving a problem that can be leveraged in different situations. Patterns are best practices that can be used to solve common problems when designing an application. Object-oriented patterns typically show interactions between objects, without specifying the final application classes that are involved. Patterns that imply object-orientation or a more generally mutable state are not as applicable in functional programming languages.

Benefits of design patterns

Please refer the table for a detailed description:

Benefit	Description
Enhances code readability	Design patterns help to speed up development by providing tested development paradigms. Reusable design patterns help correct subtle problems and enhance code readability.
Robust	Besides improving readability, design patterns allow us to communicate clearly with well-defined names enhancing interaction.
Solutions to specific problems	Often, people know to use specific software tools to solve certain problems. Although design patterns offer solutions to aid in the implementation process, few techniques may be tailored to suit specific needs.
Simplify the coding process	Since it is difficult to understand code without prior knowledge of web development and object oriented design, you need to familiarize yourself with basic design patterns.
Enhances software development	A design pattern is a main component in software development. And a better understanding of design patterns will help enhance software development.

Table 4: Benefits of design patterns

Probability indicator:👍 👍

What is a MVC design pattern?

MVC stands for model, view, and controller and is a software architectural pattern for implementing UIs:

- **Controller**: Controls the flow, sends commands to the model to update the state, and sends commands to the view to change the presentation of the model
- **Model**: Represents the state of the application, notifies associated views and controllers if there is a change in the state
- **View**: Visual representation of the model for the end user

Probability indicator:👍 👍

Can you list the advantages of the Spring MVC framework?

- In Spring web MVC, any POJO can be leveraged as a command or form-backing object.
- Highly flexible data binding: If there is a mismatch, it is shown as a validation error. Business POJOs can directly be leveraged as form-backing objects.
- Flexible view resolution: Controller can either select a view name and prepare a model map for it or write directly to the response stream.
- Supports JSP, Velocity, and Freemarker view technologies.
- Can directly generate XML, JSON, Atom, and many other types of content.
- Highly convenient tag library.

Probability indicator:

What is JPA? How is Hibernate related to JPA?

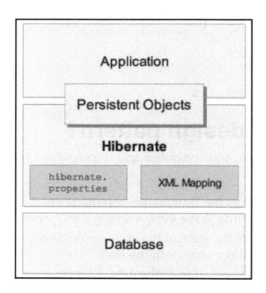

Figure 10: Hibernate best practices

Java Persistence API (JPA) is a specification of how the object-relational mapping should be done. Java is an object-oriented language. Data from Java objects need to be stored in relational SQL tables. JPA defines the interface of how mapping should be done. JPA is a specification with no implementation. Hibernate is an implementation of JPA. All annotations specified in JPA are implemented in Hibernate. The main benefit of using JPA is that at a later point in time, you can switch to another implementation of JPA. If I directly leverage Hibernate annotations, I'm locked into Hibernate. I cannot easily switch to other ORM frameworks.

Probability indicator:👍👍

Which are the three main categories of design patterns?

There are three basic classifications of patterns: creational, structural, and behavioral.

Creational patterns include:

- **Abstract factory**: Creates an instance of several families of classes
- **Builder**: Separates object construction from its representation
- **Factory method**: Creates an instance of several derived classes
- **Prototype**: A fully initialized instance to be copied or cloned
- **Singleton**: A class in which only a single instance can exist

 The best way to remember creational patterns is by remembering **Abraham Became First President of States (ABFPS)**.

Structural patterns include:

- **Adapter**: Matches interfaces of different classes
- **Bridge**: Separates an object's abstraction from its implementation
- **Composite**: A tree structure of simple and composite objects
- **Decorator**: Adds responsibilities to objects dynamically
- **Facade**: A single class that represents an entire subsystem
- **Flyweight**: A fine-grained instance used for efficient sharing
- **Proxy**: An object is representing another object

Behavioral patterns include:

- **Mediator**: Defines simplified communication between classes
- **Memento**: Captures and restores an object's internal state
- **Interpreter**: A way to include language elements in a program
- **Iterator**: Sequentially accesses the elements of a collection
- **Chain of Resp**: A way of passing a request between a chain of objects
- **Command**: Encapsulates a command request as an object.
- **State**: Alters an object's behavior when its state changes
- **Strategy**: Encapsulates an algorithm inside a class
- **Observer**: A way of notifying a change to a number of classes
- **Template method**: Defers the exact steps of an algorithm to a subclass
- **Visitor**: Defines a new operation to a class without change

Probability indicator: 👍 👍

How do you maintain your skills and stay current with IT trends?

There are various avenues to keep abreast with the technology and domain which are:

- Attending seminar, webinar, and industry events that are organized by organizations and bodies
- Reading white papers, knowledge papers, and thought papers based on your domain/competencies
- Writing white papers gives you an opportunity to do a market scan and research on various topics
- Reading books relevant for your domain/competencies
- Reading analyst reports (Gartner/Forrester/IDC) that provide data on the key players in the industry and is a crucial piece of information
- Following the recent trends in the business and technology landscape (for example, SMAC)
- Participation in forums based on your area of expertise and competencies

- Planning for certifications based on your area of expertise and competencies
- Attending training and discussions from various product vendors, standards bodies, and so on.

Probability indicator:

Solution architecture – scenario Q and A

You are creating a website to sell fine art to the rich and famous. You are only expecting to make one or two sales per week. Considering you require the system to be both secure and provide support for the transactions, which of the following describes the most appropriate architecture?

Please select from the following options:

- **A**. Use JSP/servlets for presentation, EJBs for business logic, and an enterprise database.
- **B**. Use JSP/servlets for presentation, EJBs for business logic, and a small-scale database.
- **C**. Use JSP/servlets for both presentation and business logic and JTS for the transactions.

Here is an explanation of the answers:

Choice **C** is the correct answer.

Although the scenario states that the application must be both secure and provide support for transactions, due to the low number of sales expected there is no justification for using an application server. Instead, it is more appropriate to use JTS (for the transactions) and servlets (for the business logic).

If a three-tier architecture was adopted, a Stateful Session Bean can be used to represent the shopping basket, and a Stateless Session Bean can be used to coordinate between the application and the credit card authorization system.

The correct answer is: use JSP/servlets for both presentation and business logic and JTS for the transactions.

Probability indicator:

What are the advantageous of a JSF component over traditional JSP and ServLets?

Select three choices among the following:

- **A**. No drag and drop components onto a page by adding component tags
- **B**. Wire component-generated events to server-side application code
- **C**. Bind Ul components on a page to server-side data
- **D**. No provision to construct a UI with reusable and extensible components
- **E**. Save and restore Ul state beyond the life of server requests

Here is an explanation of the answers:

Correct answers are options **B**, **C**, and **E**.

Servlets and JSP are best suited for applications where there is a need for processing dynamic requests from HTTP clients. In Model2 architectures &# 44; servlets are used as controllers and are responsible for processing incoming requests &# 44; and dispatching them to appropriate handlers. There is no component based tags available using regular JSP and ServLets. The developer has to write a lot of code to generate any Ul component code. As compared to a ServLet, JSF provides a managed bean which is a regular POJO to provide the actions for the form submissions and handling validations in an easy way.

JSP is used as a view to combine static templates with dynamic data to form HTML or XML output. Thus, options B, C and E are correct. In JSP, all the code has to be written using scripts and it's difficult to maintain and is tightly coupled with the view and data models. **Java Server Faces (JSF)** technology is a server-side user interface component framework for Java technology-based web applications.

The main components of JSF technology are as follows.

An API for representing Ul components and managing their state; handling events, server-side validation, and data conversion; defining page navigation; supporting internationalization and accessibility; and providing extensibility for all these features Custom tag libraries for expressing Ul components within a JSP page and for wiring components to server-side objects. In addition, JSF provides the following features.

- **A**. Drop components onto a page by adding component tags
- **B**. Wire component-generated events to server-side application code
- **C**. Bind Ul components on a page to server-side data
- **D**. Construct a Ul with reusable and extensible components
- **E**. Save and restore Ul state beyond the life of the server requests

The correct answer is **B**, **C**, and **E**: Wire component-generated events to server-side application code, Bind UI components on a page to server-side data, Save and restore the UI state beyond the life of server requests

Probability indicator: 👍 👍

An external system invokes a web service from your application and produces XML. You need to extract the data elements from the produced XML and create object mapping to save data into your database tables. The extract must be portable across all the Java EE servers. What would you choose from the given options based on Java EE5 technology stack?

Please select the following:

- **A.** JAXB
- **B.** JAXP
- **C.** JAXR
- **D.** JAX-WS

Here is an explanation of the answers:

Option **A** is the correct answer.

JAXP AP/ for XML processing.

JAXR API for accessing XML registries.

JAX-WS is Java API for XML web services. JAX-WS is a technology for building web services and clients that communicate using XML.JAX-WS and allows you to write message-oriented as well as RPC-oriented web services.

In JAX-WS, a web service operation invocation is represented by an XML-based protocol such as SOAP. The SOAP specification defines the envelope structure, encoding rules, and conventions for representing web service invocations and responses. These calls and responses are transmitted as SOAP messages (XML files) over HTTP.

The Java architecture for XML binding (JAXB) provides a fast and convenient way to bind between XML schemas and Java representations, making it easy for Java developers to incorporate XML data and processing functions in Java applications. As part of this process, JAXB provides methods for unmarshalling XML instance documents into Java content trees, and then marshalling Java content trees back into XML instance documents. JAXB also provides a way to generate XML schema from Java objects.

JAXB provides the following features:

- Support for all W3C XML schema features
- Support for binding Java-to-XML, with the addition of the `javax.xmLbind.annotation` package to control this binding. (JAXB 1.0 specified the mapping of XML schema-to-Java, but not Java-to-XML schema.)
- A significant reduction in the number of generated schema-derived classes
- Additional validation capabilities through the JAXP 1.3 validation APIs
- Smaller runtime libraries

The correct answer is: JAXB

Probability indicator: 👍 👍

Which of the following statements are true about RESTful web services?

Select two options among the following:

- **A**. You cannot access REST-based web services through a browser.
- **B**. REST-based web services provide regular POJO support and can be implemented as a resource.
- **C**. REST-based web services cannot be consumed with help of AJAX.
- **D**. REST-based web services provide `GET`, `POST`, `PUT` and `DELETE` operations on a given resource.

Here is an explanation of the answers:

Correct answers are option **B** and **D**.

Java API for RESTful web services (JAX-RS) is the Java EE standard for creating RESTful web services. The API offers declarative annotations that allow you to:

- Identify components of the application
- Route requests to an appropriate method in a selected class
- Extract data from a request into the arguments of a method

Provide metadata used in responses

In addition to the declarative method of extracting request data just described , JAX-RS provides a set of interfaces that may be queried dynamically:

- The application provides access to the application subclass created by the JAX-RS runtime
- The request provides methods for working with preconditions and dynamic content negotiation
- HTTP headers provide methods for working with the content of HTTP request headers

Providers support lookup of provider instances. This capability is useful in cases where one provider wants to re-use the functionality of another; for example, an entity provider that supports some kind of composite entity might use other entity providers to read/write individual parts of the whole

The correct answer is: REST-based web services provide regular POJO support and can be implemented as a resource; REST- based web services provide GET, POST, PUT, and DELETE operations on a given resource.

Probability indicator:

You have recently joined ABC Company as a J2EE architect. The business has mentioned to you that they would like to enhance the current sales application to provide different views (for customers, sales personnel managers, and so on.) of sales data, but the application maintenance team always mentioned it was difficult to provide such a wide range of views.

What is the most likely reason and what could solve the problem?

Please select from the following options:

- **A**. HTML tags are replicated in many pages. Re-factor the styling information into css. X
- **B**. Database connectivity is unreliable. Expand the number of connections in the connection pool
- **C**. Business logic is embedded in the JSPs. Refactor the code to use the business object design pattern
- **D**. Network connections are slow. Re-factor the code using the transfer object pattern

Here is an explanation of the answers:

Option **C** is the correct answer.

Option A is incorrect because it does not solve the problem. Option B is incorrect because it is unrelated to the extensibility problem. Option D is incorrect because it is unrelated to the extensibility problem.

The correct answer is: Business logic is embedded in the JSPs. Refactor the code to use the business object design pattern.

Probability indicator: 👍 👍

You have deployed a J2EE application on a single server. With the originally planned users, it was working well. But with increased roll-out users, you see that CPU and memory of the server is reaching optimum levels.

What relatively quick and cost-effective changes can you recommend to improve the system performance?

Please select from the following options:

- **A**. Switch to high-availability servers.
- **B**. Re-factor to use design patterns.
- **C**. Vertical scaling of the system.
- **D**. Horizontal scaling of the system

Here is an explanation of the answers:

Option **C** is correct.

Option A is incorrect because purchasing new servers is costly. Option B is incorrect because there is no mention of problems with code. Option D is incorrect because purchasing new infrastructure (servers and so on) may be costly and time-consuming.

The correct answer is: Vertical scaling of the system.

Probability indicator: 👍 👍

Every unit in the system needs to have a clearly defined responsibility and functionality. Units that combine multiple concerns must be split into smaller pieces. What is this concept?

Please select from the following options:

- **A**. Encapsulation.
- **B**. Delegation.
- **C**. Separation of concerns.
- **D**. Polymorphism.

Here is an explanation of the answers:

Option **C** is correct. The statement describes the separation of concerns principle.

Encapsulation (also information hiding) consists of separating the external aspects of an object, which are accessible to other objects, from the internal implementation details of the object, which are hidden from other objects. Polymorphism is a characteristic of being able to assign a different behavior or value in a subclass to something that was declared in a parent class. For example, a method can be declared in a parent class, but each subclass can have a different implementation of that method.

Delegation is the implementation of objects that forwards certain method calls to another object, a delegate. The separation of concerns principle states that every unit in the system needs to have a clearly defined responsibility and functionality. This applies to all levels of the system, from EARS to methods.

The correct answer is: Separation of concerns.

Probability indicator:

Your application throws application specific exceptions and you would like to make them immutable. Which of the following facilitates your decision?

Please select from the following options:

- **A**. Use the separation of concerns concept.
- **B**. Use the polymorphism concept.
- **C**. Use the encapsulation concept.
- **D**. Use the inheritance concept.

Here is an explanation of the answers:

Option **C** is correct. You can encapsulate the error information in private variables of the class and provide only getter methods to print the error information. Encapsulation (also information hiding) consists of separating the external aspects of an object which are accessible to other objects, from the internal implementation details of the object, which are hidden from other objects. Polymorphism is a characteristic of being able to assign a different behavior or value in a subclass, to something that was declared in a parent class.

For example, a method can be declared in a parent class, but each subclass can have a different implementation of that method. Delegation is the implementation of objects that forward certain method calls to another object, a delegate.

The separation of concerns principle states that every unit in the system needs to have a clearly defined responsibility and functionality. This applies to all levels of the system, from EARS to methods.

The correct answer is **C**, Use the encapsulation concept.

Probability indicator:

Which of the following statements is true about Model View Controller design?

Please select the following:

- **A**. Examples of the model are EJB, controller is servlet, and view is JSP
- **B**. Examples of model are servlets, controller is JSP, and view is expression language
- **C**. Examples of model are servlets, controller is JSP, and view is swing
- **D**. Examples of model are servlets, controller is JSP, and view is flash files.

Here is an explanation of the answers:

Option **A** is correct.

Option B is incorrect as EL is a language but not a component. Swing cannot be used along with servlets/JSP, so option C is incorrect. Flash files are static content, so option D is incorrect.

The correct answer is: Examples of model are EJB, controller is servlet, and view is JSP

Probability indicator:

ABC Company has a web-based labor claiming system. With the acquisition of a new company, the employee number has doubled. You have advised to host the application at a new office with one web server and two application servers.

What is the negative impact of your decision?

Please select the following:

- A. This will increase performance.
- B. This will decrease security.
- C. This will increase availability.
- D. This will decrease reliability.

Here is an explanation of the answers:

Option **B** is correct.

Additional security measures need to be taken due to the addition of new servers. Adding new servers increases performance, availability, and reliability. The correct answer is: This will decrease security.

Probability indicator:

ABC Company has recently deployed a web application. Once the application is started, after a few requests they observe that the server has stopped sending responses and requests are timing out. As a consultant, you have observed that the developers have used vendor-specific driver API to connect to the database.

Which of the following would you recommend?

Please select from the following options:

- **A**. Use the data source
- **B**. Modify timeout values for database connection
- **C**. Increase the current connection pool size
- **D**. Use web services instead of the database

Here is an explanation of the answers:

Option **A** is correct.

Java EE provides the data source which is attached to connection pools. These connection pools ensure optimum usage of physical connections. Option D is an invalid option as the application is interacting with the database. Options B and C are applicable only when a connection pool is already configured.

The correct answer is Use the data source

Probability indicator:

You are designing an application which must have high scalability and availability. You have decided to build your reusable services as BBs and deploy the application on three application servers. It means that BB services are available on three application servers. You want the web code to intelligently route requests to one of these services based on local/remote interfaces, availability of service, and so on.

Which of the following would you consider?

Please select from the following options:

- **A**. Write routing logic in the business delegate, thus making it transparent to the application.
- **B**. Use high-availability servers. They handle this logic automatically.
- **C**. Explore clustering facilities with the application servers.
- **D**. This is not achievable.

Here is an explanation of the answers:

Option **C** is correct.

Options B and D are incorrect statements. Option A could be an option but is not needed if the application server itself provides such features.

The correct answer is: Explore clustering facilities with the application servers.

Probability indicator:

What statement(s) are true among the following?

Please select from the following options:

- **A**. Unlike session beans, message driven beans are not accessed through interfaces.
- **B**. Instance variables of message driven beans can keep states across the handling of client messages.
- **C**. MOBS can also be invoked directly X
- **D**. MOBS cannot be transaction aware.

Here is an explanation of the answers:

Choices **A** and **B** are correct. Choice A is correct because MOB beans are accessed indirectly via topics/queues. Choice B is correct because MOBS can have instance variables in which the state is retained across all method calls during request processing.

Choice C is incorrect. MOBS are accessed via topics/queues. Choice D is incorrect. MOBS can be transaction aware.

The correct answer is: Unlike session beans, message driven beans are not accessed through interfaces, Instance variables of message driven beans can keep the state across the handling of client messages

Probability indicator:

In a software project of a banking domain, a large numbers of domain objects are in play. The challenges are to easily navigate complex object relationships and achieve optimal performance. What, in your opinion, will be the best way to implement this?

Please select from the following options:

- **A**. Use JDBC with Data Access Objects.
- **B**. Use stored procedures to accomplish multiple tasks on the database server for better performance.
- **C**. JPA is the best solution here.
- **D**. Create your own framework because this problem is specific to the project.

Here is an explanation of the answers:

Choice **C** is correct.

JPA will allow easy navigation through objects and can retrieve them on call for optimal performance (lazy loading).

Choice A is incorrect. With JDBC, code to create new objects, filling them and putting them into relationships, will have to be written. Custom code to implement lazy loading will have to be written. Choice B is incorrect. It will require a lot of code to map stored procedure outputs to domain objects and vice versa. Choice D is incorrect. Navigating complex object relationships while maintaining good performance are standard problems across multiple projects. JPA is a standard API that aims at solving these problems.

The correct answer is: JPA is the best solution

Probability indicator: 👍 👍

Which of the following is true about CMP and the Java Persistence API?

Please select from the following options:

- **A**. It is possible to use both CMP and JPA in one application.
- **B**. It is not possible to use both CMP and JPA in one application.
- **C**. BB CMP entity beans API is simpler and provides more features than the Java Persistence API.
- **D**. You have to migrate CMP beans to use JPA as Java EE mandates it.

Here is an explanation of the answers:

It is possible to use both CMP and JPA in one application. So, option **A** is correct and option B is incorrect. Option C is incorrect because Java Persistence API is simpler and provides more features. Option D is incorrect because there is no such requirement.

The correct answer is: It is possible to use both CMP and JPA in one application.

Probability indicator: 👍 👍

ABC Credit Card Company has been using IMS transactions for new credit card applications for past 10 years. Current/MS transactions fetch data from multiple databases, filesystems, and other systems and also have business logic. Due to constant demand for its credit cards and new employees, it decided to web-enable the application. Existing ! MS transactions will also co-exist with web applications and there should not be any duplication of logic and data. You, as a consulting architect, are asked to provide a design for the same. Which of the following would you choose for the persistence strategy?

Please select:

- **A**. Java Persistence API
- **B**. CMP
- **C**. BMP
- **D**. None of the above.

Here is an explanation of the answers:

It states current! MS transactions fetch data from multiple databases, filesystems, and other systems and also has business logic. To avoid duplication, a singular persistence layer has to be developed which can be accessed both by /MS transactions and also Java systems. Such a framework should be accessible through Cobol and Java. So option D is correct.

The correct answer is: None of the above.

Probability indicator:

In a credit card processing application developed by Java enterprise technology, the customer needs assurance about the secure access of processes such as "update account balance". How will you make sure only authorized access is allowed to invoke these parts of the application?

Please select from the following options:

- **A**. Check within each important method if the user accessing the application has permissions to invoke it.
- **B**. Run the application server behind firewall.
- **C**. This is not required as a user who is togged on to the application can access the features provided.
- **D**. Use a role based security feature available for BBS, so that users falling within a role can access methods allowed for that role only.

Here is an explanation of the answers:

Choice D is correct. Use a role based security feature of EJB's permits to define roles, add users under that role, and tie those roles to BB methods.

Choice A is incorrect. With a custom solution it is hard and unnecessary to write and maintain that much code. Choice B is incorrect; protecting the application server behind the firewall will not reduce the risk of unauthorized invocation of processes by logged in Choice C is incorrect; every user allowed to login to the system may not have permission to invoke any method.

The correct answer is: Use a role based security feature available for EJBs, so that users falling within a role can access methods allowed for that role entry.

Probability indicator:

The system under development has a module to update the status of each transaction across multiple servers and send e-mails to parties related to a given transaction. Every transaction processing can take few seconds to a few minutes depending on the network speed and how long the transaction queue is. What will be the best way to implement such a module?

Please select from the following options:

- **A**. Stateless session bean
- **B**. Stateful session bean
- **C**. Message driven bean
- **D**. JavaMail API

Here is an explanation of the answers:

Choice **C** is correct. Message driven beans are best to implement asynchronous processes that cannot be done in real time.

Choice A is incorrect because session beans cannot act asynchronously. Choice B is incorrect because session beans cannot act asynchronously. Choice D is incorrect. Message driven bean can utilize JavaMail packages to send e-mails, but for asynchronous processing, JavaMail is not sufficient by itself.

The correct answer is: Message driven beans.

Probability indicator:

Which of the following is FALSE about EJB 3.0?

Please select from the following options:

- **A.** Specification of Java language metadata annotations and XML deployment descriptor elements for the object relational mapping of persistent entities.
- **B.** A query language for Java Persistence
- **C.** Specification of programmatic defaults, including for metadata, reducing the need for the developer to specify common, expected behaviors and requirements on the BB container.
- **D.** Elimination of home interfaces for session beans.
- **E.** None of the above.

Here is an explanation of the answers:

Option **E** is correct. All of the above are true statements.

The correct answer is: None of the above.

Probability indicator:

Which of the following are benefits of EJB 3.0?

Please select from the following options:

- A. Reduction of code.
- B. Entity beans are simplified and now called.
- C. Full-support for SQL.
- D. Support for Hibernate.

The following is the explanation.

Option **A** is correct.

Using dependency injection, JNDI lookup code need not be written in the application. Options B and C are incorrect statements. JPA entities are different than entity beans. 083.0 introduced a new query language which is similar to SQL but does not provide full support for SQL.

Java EE does not mention support for any ORM frameworks such as Hibernate. So, options C and D are incorrect. The correct answer is: Reduction of code

Probability indicator:

You are gathering non-functional requirements for a fat client application that needs to be migrated onto a Java EE environment. What is true about Fat client non-functional requirements?

Select three choices from the following:

- **A**. Raw data transferred to client for processing that causes heavy network traffic
- **B**. Each client requires a connection, no connection pooling technique available
- **C**. Extensibility is easy due to presentation, and business logic are tightly coupled
- **D**. Poor maintenance because of complex client maintenance and deployment
- **E**. Easy to scale fat client applications

Here is an explanation of the answers:

Choices A, B, and D are the correct answers.

The problem statement clearly states that the current application is the fat client, which means it's a two-tier application. The following statements are true about two-tier application non-functional requirements.

Each client requires a connection, with no connection pooling technique available, and results in poor performance. Raw data transferred to the client for processing that causes heavy network traffic also results in poor performance. Extensibility is difficult due to presentation and business logic is tightly coupled. Manageability is difficult due to complex client maintenance and deployment. As each client is connected to the DB, it's very difficult to scale the two-tier applications.

C and E are incorrect, as already explained .

The correct answer is: Raw data transferred to client for processing that causes heavy network traffic, Each Client requires a connection, no connection pooling technique available, Poor maintenance because of complex client maintenance and deployment

Probability indicator:

You are given a problem statement saying that all the TV monitors are connected to a single server without separate CPUs to display online movies to the users. The most notable weaknesses of this system are that they are said to have poor _____ and _____ .

Please select from the following options:

- **A**. Availability X
- **B**. Extensibility
- **C**. Maintainability
- **D**. Manageability
- **E**. Reliability X
- **F**. Scalability
- **G**. Security

Here is an explanation of the answers:

Choices **B**, **C**, and **F** are the correct answers.

All the monitors are connected to a single server, which means the system is designed as a single tier system.

The biggest weaknesses of one-tier systems are their maintainability and scalability. They may only be scaled vertically by adding extra CPUs or increasing the amount of RAM. Additional machines may not be added and the reason that they are so hard to maintain is due to tight coupling between the presentation, business logic, and data.

Changes to any of these layers will have a direct effect on the adjacent layers. The other main weakness of one-tier systems is that they are not extensible (due to tight coupling between tiers; they are not designed to be extended). The performance of a one-tier system should (under small loads) be better than a three-tier system because there will be no network delay. It's arguable that under heavy loads the performance will deteriorate but that is really referring to scalability.

There is no reason why a one-tier system would be more unreliable than a two- or three-tier system, so choice E is incorrect.

Security and manageability are generally easier with smarter systems such as one-tier solutions, so choices D and G are incorrect.

The system is in one place, so manageability should be simple as opposed to having to administer multiple web servers, application servers, and databases. One could argue that the availability of a one-tier system is not as good as a two/three/N-tier solution (which it is not) but it is not one of the three most notable weaknesses of a one-tier system.

The correct answer is: Extensibility, Maintainability, and Scalability.

Probability indicator: 👍 👍

Your company has released the next generation of its sales system. You have several very powerful servers and a few basic servers at your disposal. A network expert has suggested that you use reverse proxy load balancing to get the best possible performance out of these machines.

What is reverse proxy load balancing?

Please select from the following options:

- **A.** Splitting requests evenly amongst all back end servers.
- **B.** The proxy sits behind the backend servers monitoring the performance of each one. When it notices one is being used too much it will automatically forward requests to a different server.
- **C.** Splitting requests amongst all backend servers depending on the amount of spare CPU time each server has available.
- **D.** A technique used to target certain requests to certain backend servers, for example AU servlet requests from one server. All static HTML from another.
- **E.** A way of filtering out certain requests. It is used to protect against denial of service attacks.

Explanation:

Choice D is correct.

Reverse proxy load balancing is generality used when you have servers with varied CPU power and memory. You may use more powerful servers for SSL sessions and others to handle static HTML Such deployment will maximize your application's performance.

Choice A is a description of a round-robin load distribution and hence is incorrect. Choice B does not describe any particular method of load balancing and hence is incorrect. Choice C is an inaccurate description of reverse-proxy load balancing and you would need access to the mainframes source code to do this. Choice E is a cross between a firewall and a standard proxy server; this does not perform any load balancing.

The correct answer is: A technique used to target certain requests to certain backend servers, for example all servlet requests from one server. All static HTML from another.

Probability indicator:

Which of the following are benefits of server clustering? Select three choices.

Please select from the following options:

- **A**. Replication.
- **B**. High security.
- **C**. Easy manageability.
- **D**. Load balancing.
- **E**. Fault tolerance.

Here is an explanation of the answers:

Choices A, D, and E are correct.

Using replicas, server clusters increase the reliability and availability of a system. They provide a fault tolerance mechanism with load distribution and load balancing capabilities. Hence, choices A, D, and E are correct. J2EE applications offer security features through identification, authentication, and authorization mechanisms. In addition, they also provide API's that allow secure communication, encryption of messages, and so on. This is not a feature of server clusters though. Thus, choice B is incorrect

Managing multiple servers is always harder than managing just one server. Hence, easy manageability may not always be true with distributed platforms. With J2EE, due to clear roles and responsibilities of tiers and layers, applications may be relatively easier to manage than other distributed systems. However, manageability is not the best asset of distributed systems. Thus, choice C is incorrect.

The correct answer is: Replication, Load Balancing, and Fault Tolerance

Probability indicator:

The current application is designed to serve 500 users based on the available system resources using one application server. Due to the new product line release, an additional 1,000 users need to be added to the existing three-tier system. You have been asked to improve the availability of this system due to the increase in the user base. How do you achieve this goal?

Please select from the following options:

- **A**. Add two web servers in front of the application server to route all the user requests to increase the availability of the system.
- **B**. Current system setup will handle the increase in load due to the addition of the user base.
- **C**. Create all the objects in the request scope rather than putting them in the session scope in the presentation tier.
- **D**. Monitor network traffic between tiers to improve availability.

Here is an explanation of the answers:

Choice **A** is correct.

The current application is running on a single application server, which means the requests from users are directly hitting the application servers. Due to the increase in load, the system will not respond to handle more requests at a certain point of time. In order to make this application available, to meet the increased user base, introduce two additional web servers in front of the application server to route the requests using a proxy plugin. The proxy plugin is configured in such a way that at any point of time two web servers will not go down. The proxy plugin will route the requests to the application server.

Choice B is incorrect. The current system will fail due to a direct hit of the application server (no load distribution) for each user request due to the increase in the load to handle the additional users. Choice C is incorrect. Creating all object in the request scope rather than the session scope will reduce the memory footprint. It will not help in achieving high availability of the system. Choice D is incorrect. Monitoring network traffic will be used to trace out the slowness and performance problems associated with an application.

The correct answer is: Add two web servers in front of the application server to route all the user requests to increase the availability of the system

Probability indicator: 👍 👍

Which of the following are NOT true about N-tier systems? Select three choices.

Please select from the following options:

- **A**. N-tier systems are distributed over many systems and hence, always present a maintenance problem.
- **B**. N-Tier systems are generally component-based and are, therefore, quite easy to maintain.
- **C**. Since N-tier systems do not use database-stored procedures or triggers for business logic processing, they are generally very slow.
- **D**. Since N-tier systems are container-based, many N-tier systems can be easily scaled (both vertically and horizontally).
- **E**. N-tier systems suffer from only one drawback over client/server systems – they do not take advantage of resource sharing techniques such as connection pooling.
- **F**. N-tier systems can use various techniques for identification, authentication, and authorization and are therefore quite secure.

Here is an explanation of the answers:

Choices A, C, and E are correct as their statements are NOT true for N-tier applications.

Though N-tier systems are distributed over many systems, they do not present any maintenance problems when architectured and designed well. This is because they are highly modular (component-container based) and it is relatively easy to correct problems in one tier without impacting other tiers. Therefore, statement A is not true and choice A is a correct choice.

N-tier systems can also yield high performance. They can be highly optimized at each tier. Server clusters can be used where bottlenecks are encountered, connection pools can be used by applications to acquire and release connections (a process more effective than the creation and destruction of connections), and so on. Hence, statement C is not true and choice C is a correct choice.

Though not relevant to the discussion, it should be noted that putting all business rules in the database tier reduces database portability and also violates tier encapsulation. Hence, it is not considered a J2EE best practice to use stored procedures and triggers extensively for business logic processing. As opposed to client/server systems, N-tier systems generally make extensive use of resource sharing capabilities. Bean pools and connection pools are good examples. Hence, statement E is not true and choice E is a correct choice.

The statement of choices B, D, and F are good examples of other capabilities of N-tier systems. Hence, choices B, D, and F are incorrect. The correct answer is: N-tier systems are distributed over many systems and hence, always present a maintenance problem, Since N-tier systems do not use database-stored procedures or triggers for business logic processing, they are generally very slow, N-Tier systems suffer from only one drawback over client/server systems, they do not take advantage of resource sharing techniques such as connection pooling.

Probability indicator: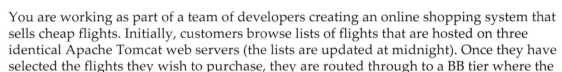

You are working as part of a team of developers creating an online shopping system that sells cheap flights. Initially, customers browse lists of flights that are hosted on three identical Apache Tomcat web servers (the lists are updated at midnight). Once they have selected the flights they wish to purchase, they are routed through to a BB tier where the booking takes place.

Which name and description describe the type of load balancing/distribution that should be used to initially direct users to the web servers?

Please select from the following options:

- **A**. Round-robin load distribution. Requests are stored in a central pool where a web server will select a request.
- **B**. Round-robin load distribution. As requests are received at the load balancer, they are forwarded on to the next web server in the list of available web servers.
- **C**. Round-robin load distribution. As requests are received, they are routed to the web server that has the freest resources, that is, the most idle CPU time.
- **D**. Load balancing/distribution would not be required as there are only three web servers.

Here is an explanation of the answers:

Choice **B** is the correct answer.

Round-robin load distribution is the simplest technique to route requests to servers. Requests are routed without any regard for the load an individual server is experiencing.

Consider the following example.

A solution consists of three web servers. Requests: Rl, R2, R3, R4, and R5 are received in this order at the load balancer. Rl will be forwarded to web server 1, R2 to web server 2, R3 to web server 3, R4 to web server 1, and R5 to web server 2. Requests are routed irrespective of whether a web server is up and running.

The description in choice A is inappropriate because there would be no guarantee that a request would be serviced if a pool was created. Also there aren't any web servers that support this type of scenario (extra code would have to be written). Targeting servers based upon their current status could be implemented via reverse proxy load balancing (there are other methods for achieving the same result – targeting particular servers).

The correct answer is: Round-robin load distribution. As requests are received at the load balancer, they are forwarded on to the next web server in the list of available web servers.

Probability indicator:

You have been assigned a task to study a Visual Basic application for future migration onto the Java EE platform. You need to create a document about various advantages of this application when compared to browser-based applications.

Select three choices.

Please select from the following options:

- **A**. Installation is very easy.
- **B**. Ul changes get reflected on the client machine automatically.
- **C**. Rich GUI features.
- **D**. Provides very good client security.
- **E**. Potentially easier deployment and configuration management.

Here is an explanation of the answers:

Options **C**, **D,** and **E** are correct.

The Visual Basic application means that it falls under the thick-client category. VB provides rich GUI features and creating the same rich Ul look and feel using browser based applications are more difficult. Thick-client based solutions have rich GUI features and also provide better security than browser based applications.

Options A and B are disadvantages of thick clients.

The correct answer is: Rich GUI features, Provides very good client security. Potentially easier deployment and configuration management issues

Probability indicator:

Which of the following statements are true about new feature resource injection usage in the Java EE platform?

Please select from the following options:

- **A**. The resource injection feature is not part of the Java EE environment.
- **B**. The container will not inject the resource when the application is initialized, instead you need to load it explicitly.
- **C**. Resource injection is not allowed at the field level.
- **D**. Resource injection is allowed at all class, method, and field levels.

Here is an explanation of the answers:

Option **D** is correct.

JAX-WS supports resource injection of Java EE 5 to shift the burden of creating and initializing common resources in a Java runtime environment at field, method, and class levels.

Option A is incorrect. Resource injection is a feature provided in the Java EE environment. Option B is incorrect. The container will initialize the resource using resource injection technique. Option C is incorrect. Resource injection is allowed at field level also.

The correct answer is: Resource injection is allowed at all class, method, and field levels

Probability indicator:

You are catting a third-party web service to retrieve the credit details of a person based on key input parameters. The issue is that the third-party server takes time to respond to the requests received from the clients. Your lead advised that you should configure a parameter which will wait for those many minutes to receive the response, otherwise the system should raise an error message saying that it did not process the request.

What features are available to handle this scenario using JAX-WS in Java EE environment?

Select two choices from the following list:

- **A**. Potting
- **B**. Dispatch handler
- **C**. Callback handler
- **D**. Using a Java thread

Here is an explanation of the answers:

Options **A** and **C** are correct.

With JAX-WS, web services can be catted both synchronously and asynchronously. JAX-WS adds support for both a polling and callback mechanism when calling web services asynchronously. Using a polling model, a client can issue a request and get a response object back, which is polled to determine if the server has responded. When the server responds, the actual response is retrieved. Using the callback model, the client provides a callback handler to accept and process the inbound response object.

Option B is incorrect. There is no dispatch handler available to handle the potting mechanism in the JAX-WS implementation.

Option D is incorrect. From the problem statement, the features from JAX-WS need to be used to provide a solution. Of course, you can handle them using the regular Java thread by configuring certain steep time using the configuration parameter specified in the problem context.

The correct answer is: Potting, Callback Handler

Probability indicator: 👍 👍

You need to communicate with a legacy banking system that has a CORBA server written in Cobol. The system is used to process transactions that are sent via the CORBA server. What is the best way to communicate with this system?

Please select from the following options:

- **A**. You will have to use JNI and RMI because it is not possible to create a CORBA client in Java.

- **B**. You will have to use JNI together with Java IDL to help create a CORBA client in Java. This will then allow you to talk directly with the CORBA server.
- **C**. Use Java IDL to create a CORBA client and then talk directly with the CORBA server.
- **D**. Add messaging capabilities to the legacy system and then communicate via JMS.
- **E**. It is not possible to communicate with this system using Java.

Here is an explanation of the answers:

Choice **C** is the correct answer.

Java Interface Definition Language (Java IDL) allows Java programmers to write both **Common Object Request Broker Architecture (CORBA)** servers and clients. (CORBA uses IIOP). Therefore, choices A and B are incorrect.

Choice D is incorrect because there is no need to add messaging capabilities if there is already the opportunity to communicate via CORBA.

Java Native Interface (JNI) allows Java to talk to code written using other programming languages (popular in legacy connectivity).

The correct answer is: Use Java IDL to create a CORBA client and then talk directly with the CORBA server.

Probability indicator: 👍 👍

You need to upgrade a legacy system. The system is used to process transactions that are sent via the CORBA server. Currently, a custom socket is created and the transaction details are sent over. Due to the unreliability of the socket connection you wish to replace it. What is the best approach you can take?

Please select from the following options:

- **A**. Add JMS capabilities to the legacy application and send XML documents containing the transaction details.
- **B**. Use JNI and expose the application via RMI and send XML documents containing the transaction details.
- **C**. Use a screen scraper.
- **D**. Use object mapping.
- **E**. None of the above.

Here is an explanation of the answers:

Choice **A** is the correct answer.

JMS is particularly suited for sending XML documents. You would typically use JNI and RMI over JMS when you try to add/manipulate the business logic. Synchronous messaging is the most appropriate type of messaging to be used in this scenario. This is due to the instant response requirement when a purchase is made. When interfacing with external payment systems, a Stateless Session Bean is typically used. This bean would handle the payment authorization request/response. Stateless Session Beans are "service" beans.

The characteristics of synchronous messaging are: Blocks until message is processed, Suitable for transaction processing, can be implemented using BBS.

The characteristics of asynchronous messaging are: Loose coupling between the sender and receiver. The network is not required to be available. Cannot be implemented using EJBs. Suitable for publish-subscribe messaging. JMS supports both point-to-point and publish-subscribe messaging.

The correct answer is: Add JMS capabilities to the legacy application and send XML documents containing the transaction details.

Probability indicator:

Which of the following is NOT an improvement of JAX-WS over JAX-RPC?

Please select from the following options:

- **A**. Reduces deployment descriptors X
- **B**. Supports WS-I Basic Profile 1.1 for improved web services interoperability.
- **C**. Supports SOAP 1.2, as well as SOAP 1.1.
- **D**. Increases the complexity of developing handlers.

Here is an explanation of the answers:

Options A, B, and C are incorrect.

Option A is incorrect because JAX-WS introduces support for annotating Java classes with metadata to indicate that the Java class is a web service. Using annotations within the Java source and within the Java class simplifies the development of web services. Options B and C are incorrect as JAX-WS supports WS-I basic profile 1.1 and SOAP 1.2 (as well as SOAP 1.1). Option **D** is correct because it simplifies the development of handlers.

The correct answer is: Increases the complexity of developing handlers.

Probability indicator:

When do you choose to design a dynamic web service client using JAX-WS Dispatch API from the given options?

Please select from the following options:

- **A**. The web service you are going to invoke has a well-published WSDL and does not change often.
- **B**. When you want to send attachments along with a SOAP message.
- **C**. To invoke a web service by using a data binding other than JAXB.
- **D**. To invoke a web service with SOAP binding.

Here is an explanation of the answers:

Option A is incorrect; the right approach here is to use the Dynamic Proxy Client. Option B is incorrect because it is a use case for SAAJ. Option C is correct. JAX-WS uses JAXB as data binding technology and if you wish to use any other technology, you must use Dispatch API. Option D is incorrect. You must use Dispatch API when you want to use XML/HTTP binding. SOAP binding is available by default.

The correct answer is: To invoke a web service by using a data binding other than JAXB.

Probability indicator:

Which of the following statements are true?

- Application clients, Enterprise JavaBeans (EJB) components, and not web components can send or synchronously receive a JMS message.
- Message-driven beans, which are a kind of enterprise bean, enable the asynchronous consumption of messages.
- Message send and receive operations can participate in distributed transactions, which allow JMS operations and database accesses to take place within a single transaction.

Please select the following:

- **A**: Statement 1 is true, Statement 2 is false, Statement 3 is true.

- **B**: Statement 1 is false, Statement 2 is true, Statement 3 is false.

- **C**: Statement 1 is false, Statement 2 is true, Statement 3 is true.

- **D**: Statement 1 is false, Statement 2 is false, Statement 3 is true.

Here is an explanation of the answers:

Choice C is correct. JMS provides the following features in the Java EE platform.

The **Java Message Service** (**JMS**) is a specification for messaging middleware. JMS provides an API for services such as persistence; transactions; and verification. Application clients, Enterprise JavaBeans (BB) components, and web components can send or synchronously receive a JMS message.

Application clients can in addition receive JMS messages asynchronously. (Applets, however, are not required to support the JMS API.)

Message-driven beans, which are a kind of enterprise bean, enable the asynchronous consumption of messages. A JMS provider can optionally implement concurrent processing of messages by message-driven beans.

Message send and receive operations can participate in distributed transactions, which allow JMS operations and database accesses to take place within a single transaction

The correct answer is: Statement 1 is false, Statement 2 is true, Statement 3 is true

Probability indicator:

Which of the following statements are true about a JMS implementation in the Java EE platform?

Select three choices from the following list:

- **A.** The provider wants the components not to depend on information about other component interfaces, so that components can be easily replaced.
- **B.** The provider wants the application to run whether or not all components are up and running simultaneously.
- **C.** The application business model allows a component to send information to another and to continue to operate without receiving an immediate response.

- **D**. The provider does not want the application to run whether or not all the components are up and running simultaneously.
- **E**. The provider wants the components to depend on information about other component interfaces, so that components can be easily replaced

Here is an explanation of the answers:

Choices **A**, **B**, and **C** are correct.

The following scenarios will demand the need for messaging implementation using JMS techniques.

The provider wants the components not to depend on information about other components interfaces, so that components can be easily replaced.

The provider wants the application to run whether or not all components are up and running simultaneously. The application business model allows a component to send information to another and to continue to operate without receiving an immediate response.

Choices E and D are incorrect.

The correct answer is: The provider wants the components not to depend on information about other components' interfaces, so that components can be easily replaced.

The provider wants the application to run whether or not all components are up and running simultaneously., The application business model allows a component to send information to another and to continue to operate without receiving an immediate response.

Probability indicator: ♦♦

You want to create template-based and separate programming logic from the view to facilitate the division of labor between software developers and web page designers. What design pattern would you use based on the given scenario?

Please select one of the following options:

- **A**. Composite entity.
- **B**. View helper.
- **C**. Dispatcher view.

- **D**. Service to worker.
- **E**. Composite view.

The following is the explanation.

Option **B** is correct.

Use views to encapsulate formatting code and helpers to encapsulate view-processing logic. A view delegates its processing responsibilities to its helper classes, implemented as POJOs, custom tags, or tag files. Helpers serve as adapters between the view and the model, and perform processing related to formatting logic, such as generating an HTML table. You want to use template-based views, such as JSP. You want to avoid embedding program logic in the view. You want to separate programming logic from the view to facilitate division of labor between software developers and web page designers.

Option A is incorrect because that deals with the model. Option C is incorrect because it does not address the requirements. Option D is incorrect because it does not address the requirements. Option E is incorrect because it does not deal with processing in the views, which is the question.

The correct answer is: View helper

Probability indicator: 👍 👍

What pattern is an example of using an Object-Relational Framework such as JDO?

Please select one the following options:

- **A**. Composite entity
- **B**. Domain store
- **C**. Data Access Object X
- **D**. Business object

Here is an explanation of the answers:

Option **B** is correct.

The composite entity implements a business object using local entity beans and POJOs. When implemented with bean-managed persistence, a composite entity uses data access objects to facilitate persistence.

The domain store provides a powerful mechanism to implement transparent persistence for your object model. It combines and links several other patterns including data access objects.

Data access object enable loose coupling between the business and resource tiers. Data access object encapsulate all the data access logic to create, retrieve, delete, and update data from a persistent store. Data access objects use transfer objects to send and receive data.

Business object implement your conceptual domain model using an object model. Business objects separate business data and logic into a separate layer in your application. Business objects typically represent persistent objects and can be transparently persisted using the domain store.

The correct answer is: Domain store

Probability indicator: ♙ ♙

You need to interface with an existing application. You have full access to the source code and UML diagrams from the existing application. Part of the requirements imply that you will need to connect unrelated objects together. You want to know whether the bridge pattern or the adapter pattern will be suitable.

Which of the following are true about the bridge and adapter patterns? Select two choices.

Please select from the following options:

- **A**. The adapter pattern implements an interface known to its clients and provides an instance of a class not known to its clients.
- **B**. The bridge pattern implements an interface known to its clients and provides an instance of a class not known to its clients.
- **C**. The adapter pattern creates a separation between abstractions and classes that implement those abstractions.
- **D**. The bridge pattern creates a separation between abstractions and classes that implement those abstractions.

Here is an explanation of the answers:

Choices A and D are correct.

As the answers state, the adapter pattern implements an interface known to its clients and provides an instance of a class not known to its clients. And the bridge pattern creates a separation between abstractions and classes that implement those abstractions.

Choices B and C are incorrect because the descriptions are the other way around.

The correct answer is: The Adapter pattern implements an interface known to its clients and provides an instance of a class not known to its clients, The Bridge pattern creates a separation between abstractions and classes that implement those abstractions.

Probability indicator:

Since Stateful Session Beans are not pooled as their Stateless counterparts, the container uses passivation and activation techniques for better resource management.

What design pattern is close to the concept of passivation, as described here?

Please select from the following options:

- **A**. Composite
- **B**. Flyweight X
- **C**. Template method
- **D**. Command
- **E**. Memento
- **F**. Chain of responsibility

Here is an explanation of the answers:

Choice **E** is correct.

Memento (GOF 283): Without violating encapsulation, capture and externalize an object's internal state so that the object can be restored to this state later. With Stateful Session Beans, the container externalizes the state of the bean via passivation for better memory management. When required, a bean in the passive state can be brought back to the method ready state via activation. Hence, choice E is correct.

Composite (GOF 163): Compose objects into tree structures to represent part-whole hierarchies. Composite lets clients treat individual objects and composites of objects uniformly. Choice A is irrelevant here and therefore incorrect.

Flyweight (GOF 195): Use sharing to support large numbers of fine-grained objects efficiently. Choice B is therefore incorrect.

Template method (GOF 325): Define a skeleton of an algorithm in an operation, deferring some steps to subclasses. The template method lets subclasses redefine certain steps of an algorithm without changing the algorithm's structure. *Choice C is therefore incorrect.*

Command (GOF 233): Encapsulate a request as an object, thereby letting you parameterize clients with different requests, queue, or log requests, and support undoable operations. *Choice D is therefore incorrect.*

Chain of Responsibility (GOF 223): Avoid coupling the sender of a request to its receiver by giving more than one object a chance to handle the request. Chain the receiving objects and pass the request along the chain until an object handles it. *Choice F is therefore incorrect.*

The correct answer is: Memento

Probability indicator:

What are the benefits of using the mediator design pattern? Select two choices.

Please select from the following options:

- **A**. Increases decoupling between objects
- **B**. Promotes decentralized control
- **C**. Promotes centralized control
- **D**. Reduces the number of low-level objects within a system
- **E**. Provides a placeholder object to control access to an object
- **F**. Provides a way to broadcast messages

Here is an explanation of the answers:

Choices A and C are the correct answers.

The mediator pattern controls how a set of objects interact (the objects refer to each other through one object).

Choice D describes a benefit of using the flyweight pattern. Choice E describes a benefit of the proxy pattern. Choice F describes a benefit of the observer pattern.

The mediator defines an object that encapsulates how a set of objects interact. The mediator promotes loose coupling by keeping objects from referring to each other explicitly, and it lets you vary their interaction independently.

The correct answer is: Increases decoupling between objects, Promotes centralized control

Probability indicator:

Which of the following statements describe the facade pattern and the benefits of using it? Select two choices from the following list:

- **A**. Changes the interface of a class to a different interface
- **B**. Shields the client from complexity
- **C**. You need to add additional responsibilities to an object dynamically
- **D**. Decouple an abstraction and implementation
- **E**. Promotes loose coupling between subsystems and clients

Here is an explanation of the answers:

Choices **B** and **E** are the correct answers.

The facade pattern hides complexity by providing a simple interface for the client to use. The facade also promotes loose coupling between subsystems and clients.

Choice A describes features of the adapter pattern. Choice C describes features of the decorator pattern. Choice D describes features of the bridge pattern.

Facade provides a unified interface to a set of interfaces in a subsystem. Facade defines a higher-level interface that makes the subsystem easier to use.

The correct answer is: Shields the client from complexity, Promotes loose coupling between subsystems and clients

Probability indicator:

Which of the following is a benefit of using the composite view pattern?

Please select the following:

- **A**. Caches results and references to remote business services.
- **B**. Facilitates division of labor between Java developers and page designers.
- **C**. Avoids unnecessary invocation of remote services.
- **D**. Handles exceptions from the business services.
- **E**. You want to avoid duplicating subviews.

Here is an explanation of the answers:

Choice **E** is correct because it describes an advantage of the composite view design pattern.

This pattern uses composite views that are composed of multiple subviews. Each component of the template may be included dynamically into the whole and the layout of the page may be managed independently of the content. This allows easy and error free modification of the layout and reuse of subviews. Since duplication of subviews are avoided, choice E is a benefit of this pattern.

Options A, C, and D describe the benefit of the business delegate pattern.

Option B is incorrect because it describes the benefit of the view helper design pattern.

The correct answer is: You want to avoid duplicating subviews.

Probability indicator:

Which of the following is a benefit of the FrontController pattern? Select two choices.

Please select from the following options:

- **A**. You want to intercept and manipulate a request and a response before and after.
- **B**. You want to apply common logic to multiple requests.
- **C**. You want to centralize controlled access points into your system.
- **D**. You want to centralize and modularize action and view management.

Here is an explanation of the answers:

Option A describes the benefit of the intercepting filter pattern.

Options B and C describe the benefits of the front controller pattern.

Option D describes the benefit of the application controller pattern.

The correct answer is: You want to apply common logic to multiple requests, You want to centralize controlled access points into your system

Probability indicator:

Which of the following design patterns can be used to create family of dependent objects?

Please select one the following options:

- **A**. Factory method
- **B**. Prototype
- **C**. Builder
- **D**. Abstract factory
- **E**. Singleton

Here is an explanation of the answers:

Choice **D** is correct.

The abstract factory (GOF 87) provides an interface for creating families of related or dependent objects without specifying their concrete classes. Hence, choice D is correct.

The factory method (GOF 107) defines an interface for creating an object, but lets subclasses decide which class to instantiate. The factory method lets a class defer instantiation to subclasses. Hence, choice A is incorrect.

Prototype (GOF 117) specifies the kinds of objects to create using a prototypical instance, and create new objects by copying this prototype. Hence, choice B is incorrect.

Builder (GOF 97) separates the construction of a complex object from its representation so that the same construction process can create different representations. Hence, choice C is incorrect.

Singleton (GOF 127) ensures that a class only has one instance, and provides a global point of access to it. Hence, choice E is incorrect.

The correct answer is: Abstract factory

Probability indicator:

Pensacola, a Florida based soda company has just started operations in Dallas, TX, to counter competition from Dr. Pepper. Pensacola believes that using a J2EE based application will put them ahead of the competition. Their new architect is suggesting that session beans should be used to provide a unified interface to the entity beans in the system. The use of session beans here illustrates the use of what design pattern?

Please select from the following options:

- **A**. Flyweight
- **B**. Proxy

- **C.** Facade
- **D.** Decorator
- **E.** Adapter
- **F.** Bridge

Here is an explanation of the answers:

Choice **C** is correct.

Facade (GOF 185) provides a unified interface to a set of interfaces in a subsystem.

Use a session bean as a facade to encapsulate the complexity of interactions between the business objects participating in a workflow. The session facade manages the business objects, and provides a uniform coarse-grained service access layer to clients. Hence, choice C is Flyweight (GOF 195). Use sharing to support large numbers of fine-grained objects efficiently. Hence, choice A is incorrect.

Proxy (GOF 207) provides a surrogate or placeholder for another object to control access to it. Hence, choice B is incorrect.

Decorator (GOF 175) attaches additional responsibilities to an object dynamically. Decorators provide a flexible alternative to subclassing for extending functionality. Hence, choice D is incorrect.

Adapter (GOF 139) converts the interface of a class into another interface that clients expect. The adapter lets classes work together that couldn't otherwise because of incompatible interfaces. Hence, choice E is incorrect.

Bridge (GOF 151) decouples an abstraction from its implementation so that the two can vary independently. Hence, choice F is incorrect.

The correct answer is: Facade

Probability indicator: 👍 👍

You can traverse through the elements of many Java collection objects because they provide a way to access their elements sequentially. What design pattern is used here?

Please select from the following options:

- **A.** Visitor
- **B.** Observer
- **C.** Builder

- **D.** Iterator
- **E.** Proxy
- **F.** Decorator

Here is an explanation of the answers:

Choice **D** is correct.

The iterator (GOF 257) provides a way to access the elements of an aggregate object sequentially without exposing its underlying representation. Hence, choice D is correct.

The visitor (GOF 331) represents an operation to be performed on the elements of an object structure. The visitor lets you define a new operation without changing the classes of the elements on which it operates. Hence, choice A is incorrect.

The observer (GOF 293) defines a one-to-many dependency between objects so that when one object changes state, all its dependents are notified and updated automatically. Hence, choice B is incorrect.

The builder (GOF 97) separates the construction of a complex object from its representation so that the same construction process can create different representations. Hence, choice C is incorrect.

The proxy (GOF 207) provides a surrogate or placeholder for another object to control access to it. Hence, choice E is incorrect.

The decorator (GOF 175) attaches additional responsibilities to an object dynamically. Decorators provide a flexible alternative to subclassing for extending functionality. Hence, choice F is incorrect.

The correct answer is: Iterator

Probability indicator:

Compact Computers is a small computer assembly company. Its customers currently have the following choices for a PC: 800 MHz processor, 40 GB HOD, 128 MB RAM GHz processor, 60 GB HOD, 256 MB RAM, 1.2 GHz processor, 80 GB HOD, 512 MB RAM. The use of what design pattern would ensure that only the legal combinations could be sold?

Please select from the following options:

- **A.** Factory method X
- **B.** Builder

- **C**. Prototype
- **D**. Abstract factory
- **E**. Singleton

Here is an explanation of the answers:

Choice **D** is correct.

This question requires that you apply your knowledge of design patterns. We are dealing with families of related objects.

The abstract factory (GOF 87) provides an interface for creating families of related or dependent objects without specifying their concrete classes.

The applicability section of the abstract factory (GOF 88) indicates that this pattern is to be used when:

- A system should be configured with one of a multiple family of products
- A family of related product objects is to be used together and the constraint needs to be enforced

Hence, the abstract factory is the right pattern for this problem. Choice D is therefore correct. The factory method (GOF 107) defines an interface for creating an object, but lets subclasses decide which class to instantiate. The factory method lets a class defer instantiation to subclasses. Hence, choice A is incorrect.

The builder (GOF 97) separates the construction of a complex object from its representation so that the same construction process can create different representations. Hence, choice B is incorrect.

The prototype (GOF 117) specifes the kinds of objects to create using a prototypical instance, and creates new objects by copying this prototype.

Hence, choice **C** is incorrect.

Probability indicator:

If you run an unsigned applet from the command line, will that applet be able to access and update a system property?

Please select one of the following options:

- **A**. Yes X
- **B**. No

Here is an explanation of the answers:

Choice **B** is the correct answer.

When running applets from the command line, a different security manager will be used (assuming a typically configured JRE) than when an applet is invoked in a web browser. However, system properties can never be modified. An applet may or may not be able to read system properties. Some system properties will require an applet to be signed but others can be read without this requirement.

Applets are permitted to make network connections back to the host that they were downloaded from. They aren't however allowed to connect to arbitrary hosts because this would provide a mechanism for denial of service attacks. Also if a firewall or server filters packets by IP address, then it would be possible for a downloaded applet to be trusted automatically by the firewall/server (a downloaded applet sending requests from your machine would be sending them with your trusted IP address).

It is not possible to change the priority of the thread that was created by the browser for the applet to run in (to do this would require an O/S call). It is possible for an applet to create new threads and manipulate the threads in the thread group that the browser created for the applet. The security manager does not monitor the memory CPU or network bandwidth usage of an applet. (It is assumed that the operating system will guard against an applet using an excessive amount of resources.) When an applet runs out of memory, a `java.Lang.OutOfMemoryError` will be thrown. Generally, operating systems will allocate a certain amount of memory for processes to use but this is not fixed (an applet can ask for more and, if available, the O/S may assign it).

The correct answer is: No

Probability indicator:

An advertising company, FancyApplets Ltd, wishes to use applets on it's website to demonstrate sample products. In order to keep track of the number of people downloading the applets, FancyApplets created a callback mechanism in the applet. (Once downloaded, the applet makes a network connection back to the FancyApplets website.)

Which of the following statements regarding this scenario are correct?

Please select from the following options:

- **A**. This will work as expected.
- **B**. This cannot be carried out by an applet.
- **C**. This will only work if the applet is signed.
- **D**. This may work, but it depends on the configuration of the user's browser.

Here is an explanation of the answers:

Choice **A** is the correct answer.

Applets are permitted to make network connections back to the host that they were downloaded from. They aren't however allowed to connect to arbitrary hosts because this would provide a mechanism for denial of service attacks. Also, if a firewall or server filters packets by IP address, then it would be possible for a downloaded applet to be trusted automatically by the firewall/server (a downloaded applet sending requests from your machine would be sending them with your trusted IP address).

Choice B is incorrect because, as just stated , it is possible for an applet to make connections back to the host. Choices C and D are incorrect because an applet is not required to be signed for this to work.

The correct answer is: This will work as expected.

Probability indicator:

You are working on a new application that will help your company co-ordinate sales data across different departments. The aim is that everyone has the same sales data at the same time. This project needs to be finished as soon as possible. You have therefore bought some third-party code to speed up the development process. The code has been signed and is packaged in a `.jar` file. To test the signature, the vendor of the software has e-mailed you the public key.

What do you know about it?

Please select from the following options:

- **A**. The code is fully tested and performs the task it was designed for.
- **B**. The JAR file contains no malicious code.
- **C**. The code could not have been modified after it was signed.
- **D**. If the public key doesn't validate the signature then you know all the code is malicious. x

- **E.** If the public key validates the signature then you know all the code is safe.
- **F.** None of the above.

Here is an explanation of the answers:

Choice **F** is correct.

There are two key aspects to this question. Firstly, this is a question about digital signatures, not digital certificates. Secondly, you were e-mailed the public key to validate the signature. You have not been passed the public key in a secure fashion. Hence, you would not know whether someone has not altered the code, signed it, and then intercepted the key that you were going to use to validate the signature.

Digital certificates solve this problem and validate that a public key belongs to its real owner. Just because the code is signed, it does not mean that it is fully tested and does what it is supposed to do.

Thus, choice A is incorrect. Choices B, C, D, and E are incorrect because you do not know if you have the real public key to validate the signature.

The correct answer is: None of the above.

Probability indicator:

You are working on a new application that will help your company co-ordinate sales data across different departments. The aim is to have everyone access the same sales data at all times. This project needs to be finished as soon as possible and you have bought some third-party code to speed up the development process. The code has been signed using a digital certificate and packaged in a JAR file.

Which of the following describes what you definitely know about the third-party code? Note: digital certificates have been signed by a trusted certificate authority.

Select two choices from the following list:

- **A.** The JAR file contains no malicious code.
- **B.** The JAR file may be signed by the third-party vendor or someone who stole his private key.
- **C.** The JAR file contents may contain malicious code.
- **D.** The code is fully tested and performs the task it was designed for.
- **E.** The JAR file is signed by the third-party vendor himself.

Here is an explanation of the answers:

Choices **B** and **C** are correct.

All you definitely know is that the code has been signed using the third-party vendor's private key. You do not know whether it was actually signed by the third-party vendor or an impersonator who stole the private key. So choice E is incorrect, while B is correct.

Just because the code is signed, it does not mean that the JAR file does not contain malicious code. Therefore, choice A is incorrect and choice C is correct.

Just because the code is signed, it does not mean it is fully tested and does what it is supposed to do. Choice D is therefore incorrect.

The correct answer is: The JAR file may be signed by the third-party vendor or someone who stole his private key, The JAR file contents may contain malicious code.

Probability indicator:

You have designed a new web service which returns credit card account statements as XML over HTTP for a particular customer. This service is available for only authenticated and authorized clients. In spite of implementing the above security features, you came to know that the data has been compromised and details are being read by unauthorized people. Which of the following best describes the above situation?

Please select from the following options :

- A. Denial of Service attack
- B. Man-in-the-Middle attack
- C. SQL Injection
- D. Phishing

Here is an explanation of the answers:

Option **B** is correct.

Since XML is not sent over HTTPS, hackers can read the details of the message. This is an example of a Man-in-the-Middle attack

The correct answer is: Man-in-the-Middle attack

Probability indicator:

What are the appropriate places for mitigating Cross-Site Scripting threat?

Please select from the following options:

- A. Requiring SSL in the deployment descriptor transport guarantee.
- B. Custom JavaScript in your JSP pages.
- C. Add an intercepting validation filter to your system.
- D. Put a disclaimer on the site advising users to disable JavaScript.
- E. Use security roles in the deployment descriptor.

Here is an explanation of the answers:

Option **C** is correct.

Filtering special characters will prevent the threat. **Cross-Site Scripting (XSS)** is a type of computer security exploit where information from one context, where it is not trusted, can be inserted into another context, where it actually is trusted. From the trusted context, attacks can be launched.

Cross-Site Scripting (also known as XSS) occurs when a web application gathers malicious data from a user. The data is usually gathered in the form of a hyperlink which contains malicious content within it. The user will most likely click on this link from another website, instant message, or simply just by reading a web board or e-mail message. Usually the attacker will encode the malicious portion of the link to the site in HEX (or other encoding methods) so the request is less suspicious looking to the user when clicked on. After the data is collected by the web application, it creates an output page for the user containing the malicious data that was originally sent to it, but in a manner which makes it appear as valid content from the website. Some of the measures to prevent it are: encode the data on the generated pages, escape user input (special characters, tags), validate user input (maximum length) using frameworks such as Struts Validator. Users can disable JavaScript and avoid using Frames/IFrames.

The correct answer is: Add an intercepting validation filter to your system.

Probability indicator: 👍👍

Which of the following is true about JAAS?

Select two choices from the following:

- A. It provides a framework for authentication.
- B. It provides a framework for authorization.

- C. It provides a framework for transport level security for communication between server and user registries such as LDAP.
- D. It provides algorithms for encrypting/decrypting passwords.

Here is an explanation of the answers:

Options **A** and **B** are correct.

Options C and D are incorrect statements.

The **Java Authentication and Authorization Service (JAAS)** can be used for two purposes:

- For authentication of users, to reliably and securely determine who is currently executing Java code, regardless of whether the code is running as an application, an applet, a bean, or a servlet.
- For authorization of users to ensure they have the access control rights (permissions) required to do the actions performed.

JAAS implements a Java version of the standard **Pluggable Authentication Module** (PAM) framework. The correct answer is: It provides a framework for authentication, It provides a framework for authorization.

Probability indicator: 👍👍

You have decided that you will use the Java Authentication and Authorization Service for security. What is the security benefit of using JAAS?

Please select from the following options:

- **A**. It provides pluggable authentication modules.
- **B**. It provides JSAPI support.
- **C**. It provides secure Internet connections via sockets.
- **D**. It provides a framework for SOA governance.

Here is an explanation of the answers:

Option **A** is correct.

Option B is incorrect because JSAPI is the Java Speech API. Option C is incorrect because that is the Java Secure Socket Extension. Option D is incorrect because it is not related to JAAS.

The correct answer is: It provides pluggable authentication modules.

Probability indicator:

You are designing a multilingual web application to support five different languages. Which of the following would you consider?

Please select from the following options:

- **A**. Java EE annotations.
- **B**. BB.
- **C**. JSF.
- **D**. Expression language.

Here is an explanation of the answers:

Option **C** is correct. JSF has inherent support for iSN through support for resource bundles.

Options A, B, and D are incorrect, as these options do not have any relation to the multilingual support features.

The correct answer is: JSF

Probability indicator:

ABC Company is building a new web application. They would like to have basic validations on user input in HTML forms and also want to have data conversion of data from view to model data. Which of the following can be used?

Please select from the following options:

- **A**. Expression language to specify validations.
- **B**. JSF.
- **C**. Write validation and conversion routines,
- **D**. JSTL.

Here is an explanation of the answers:

Option **B** is correct.

JSF provides features of validations and data conversion. Option A is incorrect as EL does not have any such feature. Option D is incorrect as JSTL does not have any validation features. Option C is incorrect as JSF already provides these features.

The correct answer is: JSF

Probability indicator: 👍 👍

You have a requirement that you want common subviews, such as headers, footers, and tables reused in multiple views, which may appear in different locations within each page layout. Which of the following patterns will you use to provide a solution?

Please select from the following options:

- **A**. Composite view pattern.
- **B**. Front controller pattern.
- **C**. Dispatcher view pattern.

Here is an explanation of the answers:

Option B is correct. The composite view pattern handles the common subviews, such as headers, footers, and tables reused in multiple views, which may appear in different locations within each page layout. In addition, it will avoid directly embedding and duplicating subviews in multiple views which make layout changes difficult to manage and maintain.

Option A is incorrect. The MVC design pattern isolates the application logic from the user interface and permits the individual development, testing, and maintenance for each component. Option C is incorrect. The front controller is the initial point of contact for handling all related requests. The front controller centralizes control logic that might otherwise be duplicated, and manages the key request handling activities. Option D is incorrect. The use dispatcher view with views as the initial access point for a request. Business processing, if necessary in limited form, is managed by the views

The correct answer is: Composite view pattern

Probability indicator: 👍 👍

An existing application has lot of redundant formatting logic (Java code) in JSP. The development team has a few weeks before the production release and requested you if they could do any minor improvements.

Which of the following can be suggested to developers? Select two choices.

Please select from the following options:

- **A**. Refactor code into simple tag files.
- **B**. Use expression language.
- **C**. Use JSF.
- **D**. Move the redundant code into static methods of Java classes.

Here is an explanation of the answers:

Options **A** and **B** are correct.

Option D is not a clean approach. It would be better to develop custom tag libraries. Option C may not be feasible due to time constraints. Within the time constraints, modifying JSP to use EL and refactoring code in JSP to tag files is feasible.

The correct answer is: Refactor code into simple tag files, Use expression language

Probability indicator:

Which of the following is FALSE about managed beans?

Please select from the following options:

- **A**. They are managed by JSF.
- **B**. They should define getter/setter methods for properties.
- **C**. They cannot use annotations.
- **D**. They can have a method to perform navigation.

Here is an explanation of the answers:

Option **C** is correct.

Since they are container-managed, they can use annotations. Options A, B, and D are features of managed beans.

The correct answer is: They cannot use annotations.

Probability indicator:

Which of these three are the steps of the JSF request life cycle?

Please select from the following options:

- **A**. Process validations.
- **B**. Invoke application.
- **C**. Restore view.
- **D**. Update model values.
- **E**. Render response.
- **F**. Apply request values.

Here is an explanation of the answers:

Options **A**, **C**, and **F** are correct.

They are the stages of a JSF request life cycle. Options B, D, and E are incorrect because these are the stages of a JSF response life cycle.

The correct answer is: Process Validations, Restore view, Apply Request Values

Probability indicator:

You are designing a web application which will be used by employees to submit and track their claims. This system will be having high usage. Which of the following technologies would you choose?

Select two choices from the following:

- **A**. Web services.
- **B**. Stateless session beans with DAO for data access.
- **C**. JSF.
- **D**. Simple POJO for data access with a DAO pattern.

Here is an explanation of the answers:

Options **B** and **C** are correct.

There is no requirement for web services/exposing services, so option A is incorrect. Since usage is high, option B is correct and option D is incorrect.

The correct answer is: Stateless session beans with DAO for data access, JSF

Probability indicator:

You are designing a real-time stock broking application. Users can log in, search for stocks, and buy and sell stocks. Money will be transacted automatically through payment gateways.

Which of the following technologies would you choose? Select two choices.

Please select from the following options:

- **A**. Web services
- **B**. Enterprise service bus
- **C**. EJB
- **D**. Java EE entities

Here is an explanation of the answers:

Options A and B are incorrect as there are no requirements for web services. Since there is high usage and transactions will be used, options **C** and **D** are correct.

The correct answer is: EJB, Java EE entities

Probability indicator: 👍👍

6
Emerging Technologies

Collectively referred to as **social, mobile, analytic, and cloud** (**SMAC**), these forces have the potential to change businesses. Taken together, SMAC represents an unprecedented wave of disruption that is creating whole new business models. SMAC will be a powerful technology. The increasing pace of change is rapidly driving customers, businesses, and technology firms with disruptive technologies, blurring the boundaries that separate them. SMAC and the emerging technologies will create avenues for new ways to develop products and services, interact with customers, find new prospects, and develop partnerships with vendors and suppliers. Companies need a systematic roadmap to engage and leverage these technologies for the benefits of their businesses.

Big data

Big data defines the business processes that capture, process, archive, and analyze large, complex datasets. The term big data defines technologies that efficiently process complex and large datasets. Big data is a parallel processing mechanism for processing and storing complex and large volumes of heterogeneous datasets at high speed. Big data includes datasets with sizes beyond the ability of normal software to capture, analyze, and process within a tolerable time.

Emerging technologies such as big data, data science, and visualization are enabling organizations to ingest, transform, and visualize information far beyond the capabilities of conventional business intelligence and data warehouses. These forces are a new wave of analytics capabilities which are creating business value and innovation and improving the decision making of senior executives.

Analytics ingests social data, combining it with other organizational data sources, and enables efficient business decision making for senior executives. These decisions drive the way products and services are marketed, sold, and serviced through both conventional and mobile channels.

Probability indicator:

How huge is big data?

Big data is large and complex and pushes the limits of the standard technology stack. The capacity to capture, store, transport, and transform data has grown rapidly. The current business drivers have doubled the amount of information the average business processes and stores. Big data is usually in the petabyte or exabyte range.

Laws of big data

The laws are as follows:

- **Volume**: Big data is characterized by large volumes of data and the challenge is to derive critical insights from this for organizational decision making
- **Variety**: Big data is collated from a variety of data sources including social media, mobile, sensors, and data warehouses and is archived in different of formats
- **Velocity**: Another key difference with big data is the data velocity, in other words the speed at which data must be collated, stored, or transformed

Big data includes a huge volume, high velocity, and extensive variety of data. The data in it will be of three types:

- **Structured data**: Relational data
- **Semi-structured data**: XML data
- **Unstructured data**: Word, PDF, text, media logs

Probability indicator:

Where is big data heading?

Trends such as social media, IoT, integration, natural language processing, analytics, and visualization will drive the adoption of big data. Enterprise data is projected to double every year. The demand for data scientists and data managers will grow in the coming years. Big data spending is estimated at around $100 billion globally with an annual growth rate of over 9% a year. Real-world case studies of big data include the following:

- Google's search index increased from 11 billion to 50 billion pages by 2012
- Facebook has more than one billion active users
- Walmart handles more than one million transactions per hour, that is two petabytes of data
- Twitter handles 400 million tweets per day

[Source: www.simplicable.com]

Benefits of big data

Big data is a really critical capability for all businesses and it's emerging as one of the most important technologies of the modern world. The benefits of the big data capabilities are:

- Leveraging social media information like Facebook or Twitter, the marketing teams are able to understand the responses for their campaigns and promotions
- Leveraging this information in the social media with regards to preferences and product perception, product companies and retail organizations are planning their production
- Leveraging the information regarding previous medical history of patients, hospitals are providing better and quicker patient service

Probability indicator: 👍👍

What is Hadoop? How does it work?

Hadoop is an open-source framework for managing large datasets and running applications on commodity hardware clusters. It provides capabilities for massive storage for any kind of data, enormous processing power, and the ability to handle virtually limitless concurrent tasks. Hadoop is an Apache open source framework leveraged for processing large datasets using distributed computing and cloud computing. It is part of the Apache project sponsored by the Apache Software Foundation.

Hadoop divides huge processing tasks into smaller manageable jobs and distributes them to commodity hardware, preferably on the cloud platform. This enables large complex problems to be solved by leveraging large amounts of commodity hardware. Hadoop consists of a distributed fault tolerance mechanism that can handle big data. Hadoop processes structured (for example, XML) and unstructured data (for example, images) in parallel. Hadoop is leveraged for a variety of business and scientific problems.

As an example, The New York Times used Hadoop to create 11 million PDFs from 4 terabytes of images in 24 hours. Google uses Hadoop to build search indexes and calculate metrics from big sets of unstructured data.

[Source: www.google.com]

Probability indicator:

What is MapReduce? How does Hadoop and MapReduce work?

Hadoop is an implementation of MapReduce, a parallel processing paradigm built by Google. MapReduce tackles problems by breaking them into two steps:

- **Map**: The master node picks a problem and divides it into sub-tasks and distributes these sub-tasks to worker nodes. Worker nodes also break processes into sub-tasks to distribute them.
- **Reduce**: The master node collects sub-tasks from the worker nodes and combines them to form the answer to the problem. Worker nodes process the reduce step.

The following depicts the Hadoop and MapReduce ecosystems:

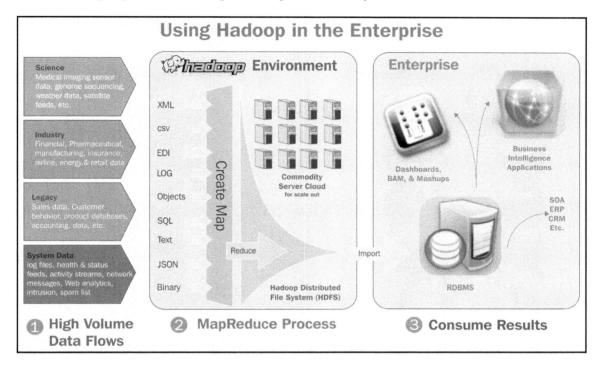

Figure1: Hadoop and MapReduce

The following explains the key components of the Hadoop ecosystem:

- **Hadoop Distributed File System (HDFS)**: HDFS is a scalable distributed filesystem that manages large files. Files are replicated to make the HDFS fault tolerant. Hadoop can also be deployed on an alternative distributed filesystem such as the Amazon S3.

- **MapReduce engine**: Hadoop's MapReduce engine leverages a tool, job tracker, to divide problems into sub-tasks which are then given to worker nodes known as Task-Trackers. Hadoop ensures that sub-problems are kept close to the data it needs for processing.

An enterprise deployment of Hadoop transfers big data from social, enterprise, legacy, and industry data sources to Hadoop nodes. When Hadoop processing is done, the results are imported into either RDBMS or BI, analytics or ERP applications.

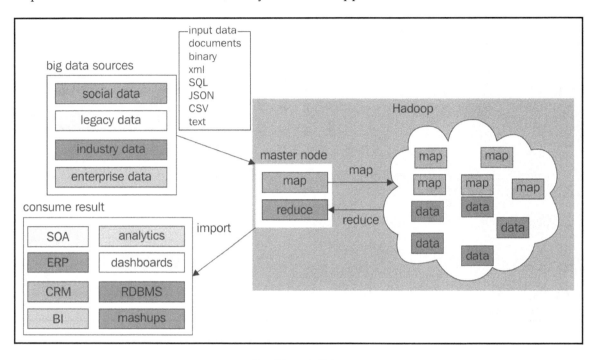

Figure 2: Leveraging Hadoop

Probability indicator:

Is Hadoop mostly batch?

MapReduce divides processing amongst several map steps and merges the results using reduce steps. This approach enables batch processing the data and importing results into RDBMS. A search index is created from billions of documents that are unstructured and input into databases to support real-time searches. Hadoop is also leveraged to process real-time transactions and decision-support applications. The overhead of dividing processing between many physical machines and merging results is a real-time applications mechanism. Real-time Hadoop platforms employ strategies to reduce the overhead such as data indexes.

Probability indicator:

What is PIG? Why do we need MapReduce during PIG programming?

PIG is a framework for analyzing large datasets. These datasets consist of a high level language for expressing data analysis programs, with infrastructure that is leveraged for evaluating these programs. PIG's infrastructure consists of a compiler producing sequence of MapReduce programs.

PIG is a high-level framework that makes Hadoop data analysis easy. The language leveraged by this platform is PIG Latin. A program written in PIG Latin is a query written in SQL and will require an execution engine to execute it. When a program is written in PIG Latin, the PIG compiler will convert the program into MapReduce jobs and MapReduce acts as the execution engine.

Probability indicator:

Why is it important to harness big data?

Typically it's not easy to capture, store, transform and analyze big data. Optimizing big data is a daunting task requiring a robust infrastructure and state-of-the-art technology to tackle security issues. But big data helps answer those questions that were lingering for a long time and helps senior executives in critical decision making with the insights it provides.

Data has never been as crucial before as it is in this modern era. This is because, for efficient decision making, it is important to analyze the right amount and type of data. We need to look beyond the concrete data stored in the databases and study the intangible data in the form of sensors, images, and social media. In fact, what sets smart organizations apart is their ability to scan data to allocate resources properly, increasing efficiency and fostering innovation.

Probability indicator:

Why big data analysis is crucial?

The following lists explains the key considerations that make big data analysis critical:

- Big data makes customer segmentation easier and visible, enabling companies to focus on more profitable and loyal customers.
- Big data is important when deciding upon the next line of products required by the customers. Thus, companies can follow a proactive approach at every stage.
- Data has become one of the critical factors of production in all the industries.
- Big data unveils crucial insights which enables the decision-making process.
- Data-driven strategies are becoming the latest trend at the senior level.
- The manner in which big data is leveraged impacts the growth and competitiveness of organizations.

Probability indicator:

Cloud

Cloud computing provides business value as an enabler of cost effective, efficient, elastic computing capacity. Cloud computing allows enterprises to pay only for the services and computing power that they need while efficiently scaling up and down in response to changing business demands. Cloud computing has enabled several "XaaS" variations such as, **Infrastructure as a Service (IaaS)**, **Platform as a Service (PaaS)** or **Software as a Service (SaaS)**. Each of the cloud-based service models provide varying degrees of technical and business capabilities and serve as enablers to various businesses.

Cloud provides efficient and elastic computing power to enable social media, mobile applications, websites, big data, and analytics.

What are the advantages of leveraging cloud computing?

The advantages of cloud computing are:

- Data backup and storage
- Powerful processing capabilities
- Software as a Service
- IT sandboxing capabilities
- Multi-fold increase in productivity
- Cost-efficiency and flexibility

Organizations get IT cost benefits via cloud computing because they don't have to revamp their infrastructure and hire IT staff for increasing productivity, ensuring that cloud-based backup will not be disruptive to the business.

Probability indicator:

What are the deployment models in cloud? What are the key considerations for the cloud platform?

Deployment models in cloud computing include:

- **Private clouds**: Organizations choose the private cloud to retain the strategic operation with them and make them more secure. It is a complete platform that is fully functional and owned, and is operated and restricted by the organization. Many enterprises have moved to private clouds due to security concerns.
- **Public clouds**: These platforms are public, which means they are open for use and deployment and focus on a few layers of cloud infrastructure such as the **IaaS**.
- **Hybrid clouds**: These are a combination of public and private clouds, offering a robust mechanism to implement cloud computing as they include the advantages of both worlds.

- **Community cloud**: A community cloud in computing is a collaborative effort in which infrastructure is shared between several organizations from a specific community with common concerns (security, compliance, jurisdiction, and so on), whether managed internally or by a third-party and hosted internally or externally.

Considerations for cloud computing include:

- Compliance
- Loss of data
- Data storage
- Business continuity
- Uptime
- Data integrity in cloud computing

Probability indicator: 👍 👍

Explaining the differences between clouds and traditional data centres

The following explain the differences between clouds and traditional data centers:

- The cost of traditional data centers is higher due to factors such as heating, hardware and software costs, and facility management.
- The cloud platform can be scaled on the basis of varying business demands. The majority of expenses are spent on the maintenance of traditional data centers. This is not the case with cloud computing.

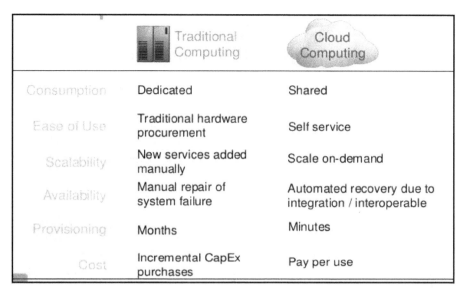

	Traditional Computing	Cloud Computing
Consumption	Dedicated	Shared
Ease of Use	Traditional hardware procurement	Self service
Scalability	New services added manually	Scale on-demand
Availability	Manual repair of system failure	Automated recovery due to integration / interoperable
Provisioning	Months	Minutes
Cost	Incremental CapEx purchases	Pay per use

Probability indicator:

Explaining the different modes of Software as a Service

The following points explain the different modes of SaaS:

- **Simple multi-tenancy**: This is an extremely efficient mode as each user has independent resources and are different from others
- **Fine grain multi-tenancy**: The resources are shared and leveraged by many, but the functionality is the same

Probability indicator:

Describe the characteristics of cloud computing. What are the characteristics that separates it from traditional ones?

The following are the characteristics of cloud computing as as follows:

- Elasticity and scalability
- Self-service provisioning and automatic de-provisioning
- Standardized interfaces
- Billing self-service based usage model

The following are the characteristics differentiating cloud and traditional architectures:

- The cloud platform provides the infrastructure as per the demands
- The cloud platform is capable of capacity scaling as per business demands
- The cloud platform is capable of handling dynamic workloads efficiently

Scalability is a cloud computing feature in which the increasing workload is handled by increasing the capacity. Elasticity is the concept of commissioning and decommissioning large amounts of resources capacity.

What do I need to do to prepare for cloud?

A cloud computing model leverages on-demand services and resources from the cloud infrastructure. The cloud architecture is a platform which provides a complete computing infrastructure and provides the resources only on demand. It is used to flexibly scale up and down the resources according to business needs.

Depending on the business needs, it could be as simple as having it outsourced to IT consultants and making the changes necessary for automatic backup. There could be more extensive preparations, such as optimizing hardware for speed or training staff in uploading to a cloud provider.

Probability indicator:

How does the cloud architecture overcome the difficulties faced by traditional architecture?

The cloud platform provides a pool of dynamic resources that can be accessed any time when there is a business requirement, which cannot be provided by traditional models. In the traditional architecture, it is not possible to dynamically scale the infrastructure with the rising business demands of services. The cloud architecture provides scalable properties to meet high business demands and provide on-demand access.

The key capabilities of cloud computing are:

- The cloud architecture provides the infrastructure according to business demands.
- The cloud architecture is capable of scaling the capacity on demand. As the demand rises, it can provide the infrastructure and the services.
- The cloud architecture handles dynamic workloads without failure.

Probability indicator:

What are the business benefits of the cloud architecture?

The cloud architecture focuses on QoS and this is a layer that manages and secures the transmission of the resources acquired on-demand. The cloud architecture provides easy to use methods and proper ways to ensure the quality of service. QoS is a cloud management platform that delivers cloud services based on the same foundation. The following lists the key benefits of cloud architectures:

- **No infrastructure investment**: A cloud architecture facilitates creating large scale architecture with machines, routers, backup, and other commodity components, thus reducing the IT cost.
- **Just-in-time infrastructure**: It is critical to scale the infrastructure as the business demand increases and this is done by taking the cloud architecture and developing the application in the cloud with dynamic capacity management.
- **More efficient resource utilization**: The cloud architecture facilitates usage of hardware and resources more efficiently.

Probability indicator:

What are the cloud service models in the cloud architecture?

There are four types of XaaS models:

- **Infrastructure as a Service**: This provides the consumer with hardware, storage, networks, and other resources to rent. Through this, the consumer can deploy and run software using dedicated software.
- **Platform as a Service**: This allows the user to deploy their software and application on the cloud infrastructure using the tools that are available with the OS.
- **Software as a Service**: This provides the ability to run an application on the cloud infrastructure with access to it from any client device.
- **Business Process as a Service**: This provides business processes that are delivered through the cloud model using the Internet and resources can be accessed through the web.

Probability indicator:

Describe virtualization and its benefits

The dynamic infrastructure is a paradigm for the design of data centers so that the underlying hardware and software can scale dynamically to changing needs of the business in a more efficient manner. The benefits of virtualization are as follows:

- Computing resources such as servers, databases, and storages, are dynamically created, expanded, or transformed on demand.
- Under-utilized servers are consolidated into a smaller number of fully-utilized nodes.
- Virtualization is a key infrastructure entity for cloud computing:
    - It provides important advantages in sharing, manageability, and isolation of computing resources.
    - It reduces costs significantly via consolidations and optimal resource utilization.
    - It provides a way for provisioning a computing resource dynamically.
- Cloud computing is a way to enable the dynamic infrastructure, specifically to optimize the IT infrastructure through virtualization.

- The dynamic infrastructure helps to virtualize all resource servers, storage, desktops, and applications and proactively handles energy management across the business. This helps to reduce the cost, resolve power and cooling issues, free up staff, and better manage and automate operations. This enables customers to dynamically adjust IT to meet changing demand needs and new business demands.

Probability indicator:

How enterprises benefit from private clouds

The following are the key benefits of a private cloud:

- A private cloud is owned by an enterprise and is exclusively leveraged by internal users.
- A private cloud is deployed internally behind the corporate's security firewall providing enhanced security.
- A private cloud is maintained by either the enterprise's IT operations or by a third-party cloud service provider which can bring the cost down through various outsourcing models.
- By totally owning a cloud computing environment, an enterprise can provide and govern computing resources (physical servers, application servers, storage space, applications, services, and so on) in an efficient, compliant, and secure manner. By leveraging a private cloud, an enterprise can also achieve significant cost savings from the infrastructure's consolidation and virtualization.

Probability indicator:

Amazon Web Services

Amazon Web Services (**AWS**) is a collection of remote computing services, also called web services, that make up a cloud computing platform by `www.amazon.com`. The most central and well-known of these services are Amazon EC2 and Amazon S3 Amazon Web Services offers reliable, scalable, and inexpensive cloud computing services.

What are the key components of AWS?

The AWS components are:

- S3 is used to retrieve datasets involved in cloud architecture and is used to store the output datasets that are the result of the computations.
- SQS is leveraged for buffering requests received by the Amazon controller. It is the component used for communication between different controllers.
- SimpleDB is used to store intermediate logs and tasks performed by the user.
- EC2 is used to run a large distributed processing on the Hadoop cluster and provides automatic parallelization and scheduling.

Probability indicator:

Why is the isolation feature needed in Amazon Web Services?

Isolation facilitates a way to hide the architecture and gives an efficient mechanism to leverage the services without hassle. When a message is passed between two controllers, a queue is maintained to store these messages. Controllers don't call each other directly. The communication happens between the controllers by storing their messages in a queue. This mechanism provides a uniform way to transfer messages between different application components. This way all the controllers are isolated from one another in the ecosystem.

Probability Indicator:

What is the function of the Amazon Elastic Compute Cloud?

The Elastic Compute Cloud, also known as EC2, is an Amazon Web Service that provides scalable resources and makes computing easier. The main functions of Amazon EC2 are:

- It facilitates configurable options and allows users to configure the capacity
- It facilitates complete control of computing resources and lets users run the computing environment according to requirements

- It facilitates a fast way to run the instances and quickly book the system, thus reducing the time
- It facilitates scalability to resources and changes its environment according to requirements
- It facilitates a variety of tools to build failure resilient applications

Probability indicator:

What are the different types of instances used in Amazon EC2?

The instances that can be used in Amazon EC2 are:

- Standard instances provide small, large, and extra large instances that give various configuration options from a low to very high range of computing power, memory, processors, and so on
- Micro instances provide small consistent resources such as CPU, memory, and computing units, and provide resources to applications that consume a lesser amount of computing units
- High memory instances provide large memory sizes for high-end applications, and include memory caching applications as well

Probability indicator:

What are the provisions provided by the Amazon virtual private cloud?

The following list explains the capabilities of the **virtual private cloud (VPC)**:

- The Amazon private cloud provides a provision to create a private networking infrastructure
- Virtual network topologies define the traditional data center approach to control and manage the files from a single location
- It provides complete control over the IP range, the creation of subnets, and the configuration of network gateways and router tables

- It provides easy to customize network configuration such as the creation of public subnets to access the Internet
- It allows for the creation of multiple security layers and provides network control lists by which you can control the access to Amazon EC2 instances

Probability indicator:

What is Amazon EC2 service? What are the features of EC2?

Amazon EC2 is a web service that provides scalable computing capacity in the cloud. You can use Amazon EC2 to launch as many virtual servers as are required. With Amazon EC2, you can configure security and networking, and manage storage.

Amazon EC2 provides the following features:

- A virtual computing environment with instances
- Pre-configured templates for instances, such as Amazon Machine Images
- Amazon EC2 provides various configurations of CPU, memory, storage, and networking capacity
- Secure login information for instances using key pairs
- Storage volumes for temporary data that's deleted when you stop or terminate your instance
- Amazon EC2 provides persistent storage volumes with the Amazon Elastic Block Store
- Static IP addresses for dynamic cloud computing with Elastic IP
- Amazon EC2 provides virtual networks that are logically isolated from the rest of the AWS cloud through virtual private clouds

Probability indicator:

What is an Amazon Machine Image and what is the relation between an instance and AMI?

An **Amazon Machine Image (AMI)** is a template that contains software configurations (for example, an OS, application server, and applications). An AMI can launch an instance, which is a copy of the AMI running as a virtual server in the cloud.

AWS provides several ways to access Amazon EC2, such as a web-based interface, AWS **Command Line Interface (CLI),** and Amazon tools for Windows Powershell. The requests are HTTP or HTTPS requests that use the HTTP verbs GET or POST and a Query parameter named Action.

One can launch different instance types from a single AMI. An instance type essentially determines the hardware of the host computer. After an instance is launched, it looks like a traditional host, and we can interact with it as we would any computer. We have complete control of our instances; we can use sudo to run commands that require root privileges.

Probability indicator:

How the cloud users utilize services from a public cloud in an economical way

Approaches to leveraging services from a public cloud platform include:

- Leveraging a public cloud computing platform is easy and inexpensive as hardware, applications and network costs are covered by the cloud provider and are charged on a usage basis.
- Computing resources in a public cloud can be scaled to meet the needs of the cloud consumers.
- A public cloud leverages flexible pricing models. No resources are wasted because the cloud users pay for the consumption on an on-demand basis, without the need to invest in additional infrastructures.
- A public cloud helps businesses shift the costs from capital expenditures and IT infrastructure investment to a utility operating expense model. A public cloud helps segregate the end users from the complexity of IT operations management.

Probability indicator:

Explain the key concepts of SaaS

The key concepts of SaaS are:

- Tenancy in the same environment can be shared among many customers
- The payment method in SaaS is normally modeled as pay-as-you-go, which is different from traditional licenses
- The SaaS provider is responsible for managing the computing environment
- The SaaS provider can upgrade the application or release new features seamlessly, in contrast to the traditional and costly software upgrade

The following are the examples of SaaS:

- Google Docs
- LotusLive
- Salesforce.com

Probability indicator:

Explain the difference between grid and cloud computing

Grid computing is a type of distributed architecture that enables sharing, selection, and aggregation of geographically distributed **autonomous** resources dynamically at runtime depending on their availability, capability, performance, cost, and users' quality-of-service requirements.

Grid computing involves distributed computing and parallel computing, whereby a cluster of networked, loosely-coupled nodes act in concert to perform very large tasks. The goal of grid computing is to divide a single and large task among many loosely-coupled computers. Grid computing may run in a cloud computing environment. The main difference is that grid computing is comprised of many nodes working together to achieve one goal, and cloud computing is aimed at providing computing resources for various tasks.

Probability indicator: 👍 👍

Analytics

Emerging technologies such as big data, data science, and advanced visualization are allowing companies to ingest, process, and visualize information beyond the capabilities of conventional business intelligence and data warehouse environments. These forces are behind a new level of analytics which in turn create business value and innovation through improved decision making.

Analytics take social data, combine it with other data sources, and enable improved business decision making. These decisions affect the way products and services are marketed, sold, and provided to end users through both traditional and mobile channels.

Can you outline various steps in an analytics project?

The following are the various steps in an analytics project:

1. **Problem definition**: The first step is to, articulate the business and technical requirements. The step requires understanding the business problem and then converting the business problem into the analytics problem. It is necessary to establish what needs to be predicted with the model.

2. **Data exploration**: Once the problem is defined, the next step is to explore the data and become more familiar with it. This is important while dealing with a completely new large dataset.

3. **Data preparation**: Once there is a good understanding of the data, one will need to prepare it for data modeling, identify and treat missing values, detect outliers, transform variables, and create binary variables. This stage is influenced by modeling techniques that will be leveraged in the next stage.

4. **Modeling**: Once the data is prepared, one can begin modeling. This is an iterative process to run a model, evaluating the results, tweaking the methodology, running another model, evaluating the results, and re-tweaking. This is done until one comes up with a model that is the best possible result with the current data.

5. **Validation**: The final stage is the validation process. In this process, one tests the model using a completely new dataset. This process ensures that the model is good in general and not just good for the specific dataset

6. **Implementation and tracking**: Then start implementing the model and tracking the results. One will need to track the results and analyze the performance of the model.

Probability indicator:

What do you do in data preparation?

In data preparation, one prepares the data for the data modeling stage. It is influenced by the choice of mechanism one will use in the next stage. Identifying missing values, identifying outlier values, transforming variables, and creating binary variables. This is the stage where you will partition the data as well, that is, create training data and validation.

Data preparation is leveraged to harmonize, enrich, or standardize datasets in scenarios where multiple values are leveraged in a dataset to represent the same value. A data preparation tool could be leveraged in this scenario to identify an incorrect number of unique values. These values would then need to be standardized to leverage only abbreviations or only full spellings in rows. Data preparation is most often used when:

- Handling messy, inconsistent, or unstandardized datasets
- Trying to consolidate data from multiple data sources
- Reporting on data that was entered manually
- Dealing with data that was scraped from an unstructured source such as PDF documents

The process of data preparation typically involves:

- **Data analysis**: The data is audited for errors, issues, and anomalies to be corrected. For large datasets, data preparation applications prove helpful in producing metadata and uncovering problems.
- **Creating a workflow**: An intuitive workflow consisting of a sequence of data preparation operations for addressing the data errors is then established.
- **Validation**: The correctness of the workflow is validated next against a representative dataset. This process may need tuning to the workflow as previously undetected errors are uncovered.

- **Transformation**: Once the effectiveness is established for the workflow, transformation may be initiated, and the actual data prep process takes place.
- **Backflow of cleaned data**: Finally, steps must be undertaken to replace the original dirty data sources with the clean datasets.

Probability indicator:

What is streaming?

Streaming is a feature in the Hadoop framework that facilitates programming using MapReduce and leveraging any programming language which can accept standard input and can produce standard output. It could be Perl, Python, Ruby, and not necessarily be Java. However, customization in MapReduce can only be done using Java and not any other programming language.

Probability indicator:

Social media

Social media allows people to connect and interact while leaving a trail of data on preferences and relationships. Every time you "like" something you are generating data that someone, somewhere, might be interested in knowing. The interaction benefits the user by allowing them to have access to feedback and commentary from other participants in the social network. This data trail benefits the consumer of the data and can be harnessed to provide insight into products, trends, and the sentiments of participants to identify social value.

Social media is used to market products and services while simultaneously collecting a social trail of data about customers' perceived value of products and services. Social networks are both standalone and integrated and are used across both mobile and traditional websites and applications.

How do you use social media as a tool for customer service?

Social media is an efficient tool for customer service since one can converse with customers directly, leverage analytics to know how they're responding, and find influencers to chat with and bring over to the network. Some of these influencers might even be customers. Most social media employers stress the power of conversation so as to have examples of how you've reached out to customers. Social media is a good indicator of an organization's overall vitality.

Probability indicator:

How do you measure social return on investment?

You can leverage tools such as the conversion measurement tool on Facebook and the optimized **Cost per Mile (CPM).** The website will often have analytics leveraged to measure social media ROI. Lastly, some of the platforms themselves such as LinkedIn have their own analytics. The fundamental measures are the same as in other areas of marketing: clicks, likes, shares, purchases, and changes in attitude.

Probability indicator:

What are the benefits of a LinkedIn group against a LinkedIn page?

A group of writers started a discussion based on this question. It can function almost like an exclusive version of Quora or Reddit. Groups tend to have a better reach and it is therefore a worthy place for sharing. They also offer an excellent space for engaging with customers and other businesses, and increasing interest in your organization. A LinkedIn page is where people go when they are already interested in the company. Thus, it should be informative above all else. Pages also function as a feed for putting out content and have at least a bit of SEO value.

Probability indicator:

How could you leverage YouTube in order to promote our brand and increase engagement?

People love to see original video content that is fun and shareable. It shouldn't be so obviously promotional from the start. People should want to share it simply because it is amazing! This video content ultimately connects to all the other social media platforms you are working with and benefits strategy and marketing as a whole. It might even go viral. Dollar Shave Club is a great example of video content that went viral thanks to excellent social media marketing!

Probability indicator:

What are the two most important social marketing metrics a dealer should monitor regularly?

The two key social marketing metrics are as follows:

- The first metric is engagement. With Facebook, Twitter, and YouTube, there needs to be a measurable conversation around the brand. Content drives social marketing success so if the content stinks; one won't see people engaging. Candidates should be well versed in writing and curating content for the audience.
- The second is leads. Once the organization runs a social campaign this will generate leads. Very often, leads from social media may look different than the ones you are already aware of. Listening and responding timely to social marketing leads is crucial.

Probability indicator:

Which social media channels do you recommend for the business?

Make sure you study the business, think about the target audience, the industry, and possible strategies to follow and then compare them to each social network offering. You'll have no problem in tackling this question if you have done the homework and informed yourself about the business/brand beforehand.

Probability indicator:

How can social media help create value for SEO?

SEO competencies are key to have when you are working with social media. Talk about the SEO strategies, tools, and the way you measure and analyze the results. Google Analytics is a must here.

It's important to understand one or more social media management platforms such as, HootSuite, Sprout Social, or TweetDeck.

Probability indicator:

Explain the difference between SEO and SEM

Search engine optimization (SEO) is the mechanism of affecting the placement of a website in natural, unpaid search engine results. **Search engine marketing (SEM)** is a form of Internet marketing that affects the placement of a website in the search engine page through a combination of SEO and paid advertising.

Probability indicator:

What is Facebook EdgeRank? Why is it so important to understand?

Facebook Edgerank is the algorithm used to determine where your posts show up in the newsfeed of your page and your followers' pages. Affinity, weight, and time decay are the three factors measured in Edgerank. Facebook looks at the connection between you and the users, how engaging the post is with content, images, links or videos, and how old the post is, namely the time decay. This relationship is important to understand as it impacts how well your strategy will be implemented on the company Facebook page.

Probability indicator:

What is your definition of social media marketing and digital marketing? How does that relate to our company?

Social media marketing is the process of generating awareness, website traffic, or new business through the use of social media sites. Digital marketing is a marketing process that brings leads and new business to a company through the use of digital channels such as e-mail, social networks, and smartphones. After conducting basic research about your company, I can form an idea of how social media marketing and digital marketing could play a role and what the return might be. However, I'd like to conduct a full assessment before I tell you what role that will be.

Social media has become all about engagement. We should be looking to sites such as, Vine, Instagram, Pinterest, and the new MySpace. Constantly be looking at newer things with Google, as their new products and features could benefit B2C companies. Of course, all of this should be consistent with the goals and approaches set out in our strategy.

Probability indicator:

What is the first thing that you would do for the company in this position if we hire you?

The first thing one should do is to meet the team and determine the goals organizations want to set for social media and digital marketing. One would conduct an assessment of the company and competitors to gauge where they are in the social media and digital marketing domain.

These questions might differ depending on the nature of business and the types of positions. No matter the end goal for hiring social media or digital marketing professionals, the principles remain the same for the social media approach. Understand the position and how it will work within the organization. Interview candidates using a tough, but fair questionnaire that includes various social media and digital marketing expertise.

Probability indicator: 👍 👍

Enterprise mobility

The mobile web is bringing users closer and closer to businesses and giving businesses the opportunity to interact with their customers in much more engaging ways. The mobile web is made possible by wireless data networks, smartphones, and tablets, but truly excels when businesses take advantage of the user's context (who, what when, where, and how) to deliver robust, context-aware business services. High context interactions lead to higher customer engagement and satisfaction in using the service.

Mobile enables users to connect to social networks from anywhere at any time, which enables them to provide social feedback more frequently increasing the volume of their data trail. Mobile also provides a significant data trail from a machine-to-machine perspective.

What is enterprise mobility? Why enterprise mobility?

Enterprise mobility provides flexibility in the way people work anywhere. It means more employees do business tasks out-of-the-office using mobile devices. In the last few years, a greater number of employees have bought smartphones and tablet computing devices It is essential to evolve your business into the next generation of technology. Enterprise mobility brings with it the convenience of size from a hand-held device as well as the savings in cost.

A road map depicting the enterprise mobility stages is illustrated in the following figure:

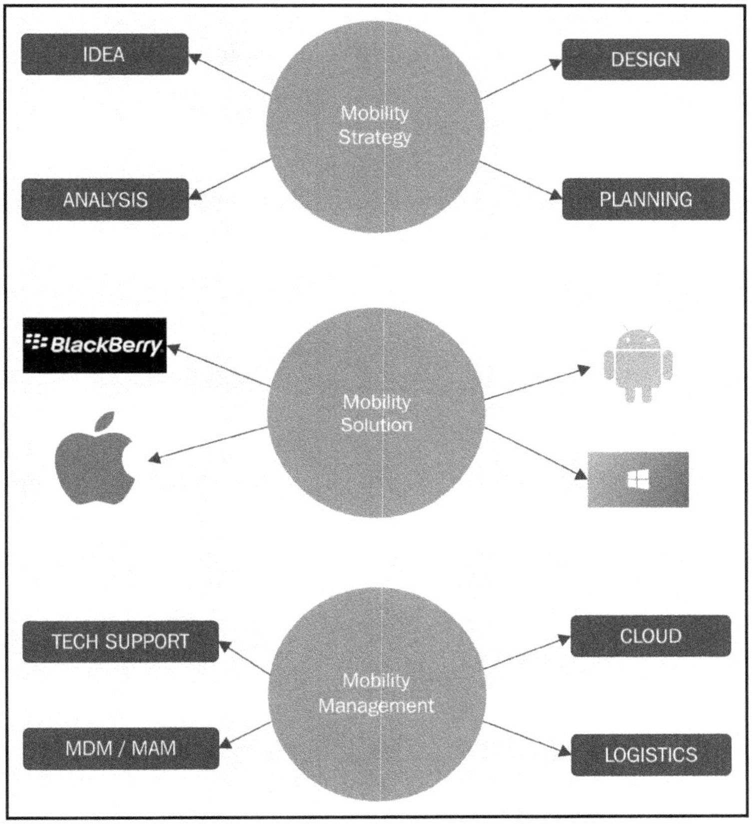

Figure 3: Enterprise mobility

There are three main stages for enterprise mobility:

- **Mobility strategy**: This is the first part of enterprise mobility management:
    - Mind your business objective for mobility
    - Start with the end in mind and define your business goals
    - Be sure to take control with the end-to-end security strategy
    - Analyze working styles of the organization's employees to determine where you can allocate your mobility investments most effectively
    - Identify the resources and processes necessary to mobilize these roles

- **Mobility solution**: Study the mobile strategy aligned with their business due to complexities that are arising from multiple platforms, devices, and delivery channels:
    - Compatibility supporting new platforms and operating systems.
    - Manage all OSs including iOS, Android, Windows 8, and BB operating systems.
    - Create apps in various operating systems.
    - Once you create an app, then implement an update. Its impact is to identify opportunities for improvement or change.
- **Mobility management**: Mobility management is one of the major functions of enterprise mobility:
- **Mobile device management**: MDM is leveraged in the administrative area. In this area, you can deploy, secure, manage, integrate and monitor such devices as smartphones, tablets, and laptops, in the workplace. MDM can reduce support costs and business risks.
- **Deployment options**: A cloud deployment option is very important for every business. One can change the deployment option to match your business requirements.
- **Mobile operations management**: In mobile operations management, you can improve service delivery and delight customers with your mobile app.

The following are the benefits of enterprise mobility:

- **Portability**: Leverage the device anytime and anywhere
- **Availability**: Leverage the device anytime
- **Sharing**: Share data and screens with others easily
- **Capture data in real time**: Improved accuracy of data through process improvement and BI in real time
- **Personal ownership of devices**: Enabling access to corporate systems through an employee's own mobile device(s)

Probability indicator: 👍 👍

Summary

The rapid technology changes in SMAC and the overall complexity involved in implementing an integrated SMAC solution can be challenging and demonstrating business value on investment can be difficult. A systematic approach to creating SMAC capability to create business value includes:

- Define business objectives, assess the as-is state and identify a set of initiatives and goals
- Define manageable projects to build capabilities with each of the SMAC domains and understand benefits it provides to the organizations
- Pursue an architecture-focused approach leveraging modern best practices and standards to integrate SMAC tack
- Build on early successes to generate momentum and demonstrate early value to the business
- Leverage technology partners to manage the risk of the evolving SMAC environment

This chapter covered the Q&As for emerging technologies which includes big data, clouds, AWS, analytics, social media, and enterprise mobility.

The next chapter will cover the Q&As for frameworks and the non-functional requirements domain. An architecture framework provides principles and practices for creating and using the architecture description of a system. It structures architects' thinking by dividing the architecture description into domains, layers, or views, and offers models – typically metrics and diagrams – for documenting each view.

This next chapter will also cover the solutioning of NFRs, providing insights into how they will be addressed in the solutioning phase. The chapter will cover key NFRs that are most critical for any project and for each NFR provide the various alternatives pertaining to the solution, the design principle that needs to be applied to achieve the desired outcome for, for example, high availability or scalability or reliability as covered.

7
Methodologies, Frameworks, and NFRs

This section covers the Q&A for the frameworks and nonfunctional requirements domain. An architecture framework provides principles and practices for creating and using the architecture description of a system. It structures architects' thinking by dividing the architecture description into domains, layers or views, and offers models–typically metrics and diagrams–to document each view.

This section also covers the solutioning of NFRs, providing insights into how they will be addressed in the solutioning phase. This section covers the key NFRs that are most critical for any project. For each NFR, it provides the various alternatives pertaining to the solution and the design principle that needs to be applied to achieve the desired outcome, for example, high availability, scalability, or reliability.

Methodologies and frameworks

Enterprise architecture frameworks drive the creation and governance of enterprise architecture. A framework is a collation of best practices, principles, and practices for creating the architecture definitions. It structures the thinking of architects by segregating the architecture into domains, layers or views, tiers, and models. The components of a framework provide guidance in three main areas:

- Descriptions of architecture deal with documenting the enterprise from various viewpoints. Each view describes one aspect of the architecture; it includes entities and relationships that address specific concerns of the key stakeholders.
- Methods for designing the architecture deal with processes that the SMEs adapt. The EA methodology is composed of different domains, and deep-dives into lower-level processes consisting of fine-grained tasks. A process is defined by objectives, inputs, activities, and outputs. This would be complemented via approaches, tools, principles, and practices.
- Organization of architects is the guidance around the team structure consisting of governance, skills, experience, and training and enablement.

What is the TOGAF framework?

The Open Group Architecture Framework (TOGAF) is an enterprise architecture framework that defines a comprehensive approach to planning, architecting, implementation, and governance of enterprise architectures.

TOGAF defines the enterprise as four architecture domains: business, application, technology, and data. It consists of a methodology for defining an architecture in terms of building blocks and is an iterative process. It also contains a set of tools, vocabulary, standards, principles, and compliance tools. TOGAF contains an iterative methodology for defining enterprise architecture, called **Architecture Development Method (ADM)**. TOGAF needs to be tailored before adopting it for an organization, and this is a one-time activity:

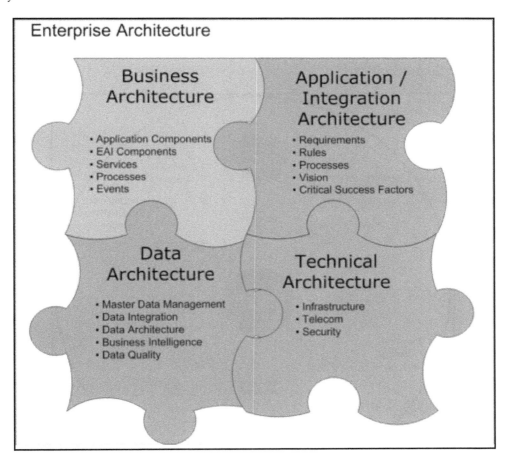

Figure 1: Four architectural domains

Probability indicator: ♻♻♻

What do you understand by the TOGAF Architecture Development Method?

The ADM is the core entity of the TOGAF framework. This is the methodology for defining organization-specific enterprise architectures. ADM is a framework that provides repeatable processes for defining and implementing organization-specific enterprise architectures. ADM establishes the architecture framework, developing and governing the architecture content. These activities are carried out in an iterative cycle, facilitating the transformation of their enterprises in response to business goals. The ADM is described as a number of phases within a process of change, illustrated by an ADM cycle graphic. Phases within the ADM are as follows:

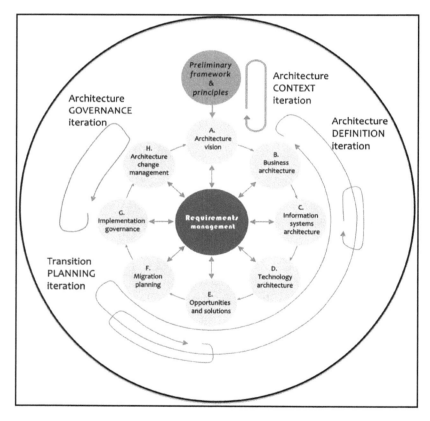

Figure 2: TOGAF ADM

Probability indicator:

What are the four TOGAF architecture domains?

TOGAF consists of the following four architecture domains:

Domain	Description
Business architecture	The business strategy, business processes, governance, and organization.
Data architecture	The logical and physical data assets, and data management resources and tools.
Application architecture	A blueprint of application systems, interactions, and relationships with the business processes.
Technology architecture	The infrastructure's capabilities to support the deployment of business, data, and application services. This includes IT infrastructure, middleware, networks, and communications.

Table 1: TOGAF Domains

Probability indicator:

What is the TOGAF enterprise continuum?

Enterprise continuum is a framework for structuring the organization's architecture assets and provides guidelines and methods for classifying architecture assets, also describing how they can be leveraged. This is based on assets such as models, standards, frameworks, and patterns that exist in the enterprise and in the industry at large, and also which the enterprise has created while developing the architectures. The architecture repository is a structure of a physical instance of enterprise continuum.

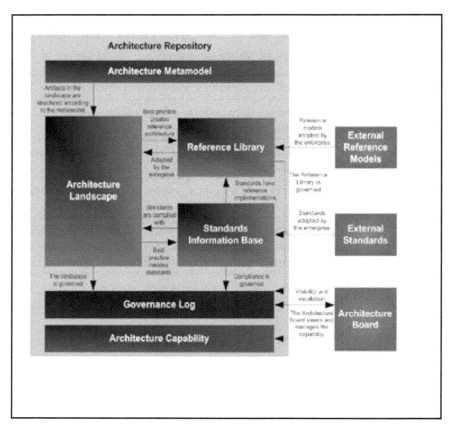

Figure 3: TOGAF architecture repository

Probability indicator:

What are the different TOGAF certified tools?

The following is the list of TOGAF certified tools:

Tools	Description
Troux platform	The Troux platform defines a best-in-class tool in each critical capability area, delivering the information capabilities required to understand the relationships between IT and business and answer key business questions.

ARIS	This is a modeling tool for business process analysis and management. It supports different modeling standards such as **Business Process Model and Notation (BPMN)**, **Event-driven Process Chains (EPC)**, organizational charts, and process landscapes.
iServer	iServer is a unified software platform that provides an easy-to-use, collaborative modeling tool that extends Microsoft Office and Visio. Core components include a Microsoft Visio interface, a powerful repository for architecture, process and governance models; and a range of tools for presentation, analysis, and decision making.
System architect	IBM rational architect is an EA tool leveraged to model businesses and IT applications and databases that support them. System architect is leveraged to build architectures using various frameworks, including TOGAF and Zachman.
ABACUS	ABACUS is a tool used for enterprise architecture and process modeling, and supports key frameworks. ABACUS includes multiple architecture alternatives and runs calculations for each alternative metric such as cost, agility, performance, and reliability.

Table 2: TOGAF tools

Probability indicator:

What is the Zachman framework?

The Zachman framework is an EA framework that provides a methodology for defining an enterprise according to a 6 x 6 architecture matrix. This framework was initially developed at IBM by John Zachman. The columns of this framework consist of questions like why, how, what, who, where, and when. The rows consist of questions such as contextual, conceptual, logical, physical, and detailed.

Zachman framework provides views for various roles, including planners, owners, designers, builders, and contractors. This creates a holistic view that enables different stakeholders to view the enterprise from different perspectives:

Abstraction/ Perspective	Data - *What*	Function - *How*	Network - *Where*	People - *Who*	Time - *When*	Motivation - *Why*
Scope *Contextual*	List of Things	List of Processes	List of Locations	List of Organizations	List of Events	List of Business Goals & Drivers
Enterprise Model *Conceptual*	Semantic Model	Business Process Model	Logistic Network	Workflow Model	Master Schedule	Business Plan
System Model *Logical*	Logical Data Model	Application Architecture	Distributed Systems Architecture	Human Interface Architecture	Processing Structure	Business Rule Model
Technology Model *Physical*	Physical Data Model	System Design	Technical Architecture	Presentation Architecture	Control Structure	Rule Design
Detailed Representation *Sub-Contractor/Out of Context*	Data Definition	Program	Network Architecture	Security Architecture	Timing Definition	Rule Specification
Functioning Enterprise	Data	Function	Network	Organization	Scheudle	Strategy

Figure 4: Zachman framework

Probability indicator: 👍

What is the difference between traditional methodology and Agile?

Agile is a methodology for organizations to produce IT solutions and products by ensuring that they bundle their solutions and products by business-driven factors, which we know as requirements, features, enhancements, and fixes. Agile is a way of building solutions and products by leveraging optimized increments that resemble the iterative and incremental methodology. The key to the Agile methodology is that it ensures that risks are at bay. The older methodologies have galvanized into Agile, and Agile is a derivative of its predecessor's best practices.

One sprint of agile includes analysis, design, build, testing, and deployment. There would be multiple such sprints across the entire project life cycle. The following diagram depicts a comparison:

Agile	Traditional
Incremental value and risk management	Phased approach with an attempt to know everything at the start
Embracing change	Change prevention
Delivery early, fail early	Delivers value at the end; also fails at the end
Transparency	Detailed planning and stagnant control
Inspect and adapt	Meta Solution with tightly controlled procedures and answers
Self-managed	Command and control
Continual learning	Learning is secondary

Table 3: Agile versus Traditional

Agile leverages light-weight methodologies such as SCRUM, **Extreme Programming** (**XP**), and **Rapid Application Development** (**RAD**). These methodologies focus on the development of solutions in an iterative manner. Scrum is also one of the agile methods, used to develop information systems iteratively. In this technique, a small team typically works on the assigned tasks for a time period of 30 days.

Probability indicator: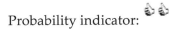

How did you prioritize the requirements for a large program?

Requirement prioritization is leveraged to identify requirements for a given release. The requirements prioritized ensure that the risk is minimized, so high-risk requirements are implemented first. There are a number of possible business considerations, including value, cost, risk, difficulty in implementation, likelihood of success, stakeholder agreement, and urgency, each of which is described in more detail here:

- **Value**: This approach focuses on the business value of the requirement. The requirements that will create the greatest business value are given the highest priority. This helps to ensure quick wins for the organization.
- **Cost**: Implementing the least expensive requirements first or implementing requirements with the greatest **return on investment** (**ROI**), and the alternatives for this option.
- **Risk**: This is basically the risk associated with the requirement's implementations and will be prioritized from low to high risks.
- **Dependencies**: This is typically the relationship between requirements and will require the completion of another requirement first before it can be taken up.
- **Regulatory compliance**: These are the requirements that must be implemented to meet the regulatory policies.

There are numerous prioritization techniques that are leveraged today; we have listed some of the more frequently used techniques here:

- **Cost-value approach**: The principle is to determine for an identified requirement the implementation cost and the business value it provides. The key is, for the identified requirements, we assess the value or cost comparing them.
- **Numerical assignment grouping**: This method is based on grouping requirements into different priority groups with each group representing value for stakeholders. For example, requirements can be grouped into critical, moderate, and optional priorities. Stakeholders may also classify requirements as compulsory, very important, rather important, and not important in order to describe their importance. To prevent stakeholders from putting all requirements in one category, the percentage of requirements that can be put in each group should be restricted.

- **MoScoW technique**: Instead of numbers, this method uses four priority groups: MUST have, SHOULD have, COULD have, and WON'T have. With this technique, stakeholders can prioritize requirements in a collaborative fashion. The acronym represents the following:
  - **MUST**: Mandatory
  - **SHOULD**: high priority
  - **COULD**: Preferred but not mandatory
  - **WOULD**: Can be postponed and suggested for the future
- **Timeboxing**: Timeboxing or budgeting is leveraged when there are fixed timelines and budgets for the project. It is leveraged in projects where the delivery of the project is as important as the project being delivered on time and developed within budget. This technique is based on the paradigm that it is important to release the product with the basic product features on time rather than building all features and launching the product at a later date.
- **Voting**: When there are many requirements that need to be categorized, voting is one of the best ways to sort out the prioritization of requirements. Typically the requirement with the highest points will be chosen for implementation in the initial iterations.

Probability indicator:

What is a project charter? What essential elements should be captured in a project charter?

A project charter artifact outlines the existing project and provides **project manager** (**PM**) with the confirmation to initiate the work proceedings for the project. The artifact helps the PM to communicate the stakeholders, goals, objective, IT roadmap, cost, resources, risks, and how successful completion will help the enterprise. Based on organizational culture, the charter serves a similar purpose as a business case. In large enterprises, the charter is a multi-page document written by the mid-level management after a business case has been finalized. In small organizations the charter is a few paragraphs with bulleted items and is signed by the company's senior executive. A project charter includes the following:

- Organizational goal–the drive for undertaking the initiative
- Stakeholders involved in the project and their roles and responsibilities
- Business and functional requirements of the organization to be fulfilled
- Potential risks and roadblocks

- Important milestones including the start date and end date
- Protocol leveraged by the PM to communicate with stakeholders
- Deliverables, assets, artifacts, products, processes, or services the project produces upon completion

Probability indicator:

What is reference architecture?

Reference architecture is a template, methodology, practice, and standards based on a set of successful solutions in the past. These are generalized solutions depicting logical and physical architecture views, and are based on harvesting a set of patterns, standards and best practices in successful solutions in the past. This is a critical reference asset for the architecture engagements which the enterprise can implement to solve business problems. It provides multiple views to different stakeholders and is the starting point or the point of comparisons for business entities. Major artifacts of the reference architecture are methodologies, standards, metadata, documents, and patterns. Examples of reference architecture are:

- TAM
- SID
- Integration frameworks
- eTOM business processes

Probability indicator:

What is benchmarking?

Benchmarking is about measuring the performance of an organization to compete in the industry. It is a strategic tool for portfolio analysis and strategic management. In this process, a company measures its policies, performance, rules, and other critical KPIs and metrics.

Benchmarking involves examining how others achieve their performance levels and understanding the processes they have leveraged. When lessons learned from a benchmarking exercise are applied appropriately, they facilitate improved performance in critical functions or in key business areas.

The application of benchmarking involves these key steps:

1. Understand the existing business processes
2. Analyze the business processes of the competitor, including industry standards and best practices
3. Compare the current business performance with these industry standards, reference business processes frameworks, and competitors
4. Identify gaps, issues, and challenges on the basis of the deep dive analysis of the earlier steps
5. Plan a road map to implement the steps necessary to close the performance gap

To be effective, the benchmarking mechanism must become an integral part of an ongoing process; the goal is to stay abreast of industry best practice and trends.

There are two primary types of benchmarking:

- **Internal benchmarking** is a comparison of practices and performance between teams, SMEs, or groups within the same organization
- **External benchmarking** is a comparison of organizational performance with its industry peers or across industries

These can be further segregated as follows:

- **Process benchmarking**: This demonstrates how top-performing organizations accomplish a specific business process. This benchmarking data is collected via research, surveys, and interviews. By understanding how the peer performs for the same functional task or objective, organizations provides critical insight. Such information affirms and supports decision-making by SMEs.
- **Performance metrics**: Performance metrics give numerical standards, which are nothing but best practices against which an organization's own processes can be compared. These metrics are usually determined via a detailed survey and interviews. Organizations can identify performance gaps and issues and then conduct follow-on analyses to determine methods of improvement.

- **Strategic benchmarking**: This means identifying the winning strategies that have enabled high performing organizations to be successful in their market. Strategic benchmarking examines how organizations compete and is ideal for corporations with a long-term goal in mind.

DIFFERENT BENCHMARKS YIELD DIFFERENT INSIGHTS

✓ Strategy ✓ Structure ✓ Leadership	✓ Cost ✓ Investment ✓ Business Economics	✓ Staffing ✓ Skills ✓ Talent	✓ Services ✓ Activities ✓ Impact Analysis
✓ Technology ✓ Innovation ✓ Future Trends	✓ Quality ✓ Cycle Times Yields ✓ Productivity	✓ Best Practice Insights ✓ Process Excellence	✓ Analogs ✓ Launch ✓ Planning ✓ Lifecycle Insights

Figure 5: Benchmarking

Probability indicator:

What is the business value assessment technique?

The technique to assess business value consists of defining a matrix based on a business value and a risk on the XY axis. The value index includes parameters such as compliance, financials, strategic alignment, and market position. The risk index includes parameters such as size, complexity, technology, capacity, and impact of failure. Each parameter is then assigned an appropriate weight. The index, criteria, and weights are approved by the senior management and this establishes the decision-making criteria.

This is the approach leveraged for finding the business value of user stories:

- We first decide what values (or benefits) we want to achieve before launching a project or product.
- Then we find and improve the business processes that deliver that value.
- Then we find and improve the supporting business processes that make the value delivering processes possible.
- When the team needs user stories, we take the processes with the highest value and break them down into user stories at the right level of granularity for the team's needs. The team pulls the stories, so we only generate a minimal set of user stories.

The following is the approach for business value modeling:

- Identify all the relevant stakeholders
- Define their objectives and goals for the organization's initiatives
- Establish a mechanism to measure the achievement of the organizational goals
- Identify the most important measurements and tests–Value Drivers
- Define the relationship between the different Value Drivers

- Leverage the Value Drivers to focus on and prioritize the initiatives for the organization's road map

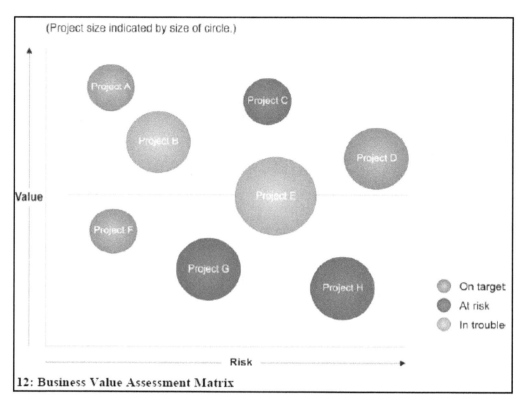

Figure6: Business Value Analysis

Probability indicator:

What is Continuous Integration? Why is Continuous Integration important?

Continuous Integration (**CI**), is creating software and testing it multiple times with every iteration. Different tools that support this methodology are Hudson, Jenkins, and Bamboo where Jenkins is the most popular one. They are integrated with version control systems and IDE. Deploying tools for Continuous Integration is very easy, but leveraging and establishing best practices for Continuous Integration methodology is complex.

Key considerations for CI:

- How often is code committed? If the code is committed once a day or week, the CI setup is underutilized and may defeat the purpose of CI.
- How is a failure handled and is immediate action taken? Do failures promote fun in the team?
- What are the steps in continuous integration?
    - Compilation
    - Unit testing
    - Code quality check point
    - Integration testing
    - Deployment
    - Chain testing
- Additional steps in continuous integration may take more time but result in a more stable application.
- How much time does Continuous Integration take? One option is to reduce the time and ensure that we have immediate feedback is to split the long-running tests into a separate build that runs less often.

The following are the benefits of continuous integration:

- **Defects found early will cost less**: When defects are found early during or after coding, it takes 10 times less to fix it compared to finding the defect at a later stage of the SDLC.
- **Reduced Time to Market**: Software is always tested, so it is always ready to move to the next environment.

Probability indicator:

What is dependency injection?

Dependency injection is a software design pattern providing inversion of control for resolving dependencies. A dependency is an object that is injected by passing this dependency to a client and is made part of the state of the client's. Passing the object to the client, rather than building or the service, is the fundamental essence of this pattern.

Dependency injection allows a program to leverage the dependency inversion pattern by delegating to external code the responsibility of providing its dependencies. It is the injecting code that constructs the object and calls the client to inject themselves and the client is not allowed to call the injector function. The client code does not need to know the injecting code, construction mechanism and the services it is using. The client only needs to know the interfaces of the services because these define the use of services. Following are the benefits of Continuous Integration:

- Reduced dependencies
- Reduced dependency carrying
- More reusable code
- More testable code
- More readable code

What is ITIL?

Information Technology Infrastructure Library (ITIL) is a set of best practices and standards for service management, development and operations. ITIL defines a number of important concepts including checklists, tasks, and procedures that can be tailored for specific organizations ITIL goals. In the service domain, ITIL includes support desk, incident, problem, change, release and configuration management. In the service delivery domain, it includes service-level management, capacity management, and service continuity management.

The ITIL framework includes:

- Service support
- Service delivery
- ICT infrastructure management
- Security management
- Application management
- Software asset management

The benefits of ITIL:

- Develops a long term relationships with the customers by delivering efficient services that meets the business demands
- Establishes cost-efficient framework for managing demand for these the services
- Manages business change while ensuring a stable service environment
- Enables stronger alignment between business and IT
- Enhances IT service delivery and customer engagement
- Produces greater visibility of IT costs, organizational assets, and transparency
- Provide better management of organizational risk and service disruption and failure
- Enables a stable service environment to support constant business change

The barriers for ITIL:

- Little short-run payback as benefits accrue slowly over time
- Implementation is a long process requiring extensive training
- Imposing changes on the organization can be disruptive
- The predictive approach may lack flexibility
- Sustained efforts are easily disrupted by short-term needs

The capabilities of the ITIL framework are as follows:

Strategy (Portfolio)	Design (Product Management)	Transition (Development)	Operation (Support)	Continual Improvement (Quality)
Portfolio Strategy	Capacity Management	Transition Planning & Support	Service Desk	The 7- Step Improvement Process
Financial Management	Availability Management	Service Assets & Configuration Management	Incident Management	Quality Management System
Service Portfolio Management	Security Management	Change Management	Event management	Business Questions For CSI
Release management	Continuity Management	Service Validation & Testing	Request Fulfilment	ROI For CSI
	Demand Management	Knowledge Management	Problem Management	Service Management
	Service Catalogue Management	Deployment Management	Access Management	Service Reporting
		Evaluation	Application Management	
			IT Operation Management	
			Technical Management	

Figure 7: Information Technology Infrastructure Library (ITIL)

Probability indicator: ♻♻♻

Non-functional requirements

Maintaining software is hard and therefore expensive; and IT departments are often under-funded. However, if they are in a *Just do it* mode, then non-functional requirements are easy to be forgotten. The consequences of leaving these NFRs lead directly to the aforementioned maintenance problems and increased technical debt.

NFRs are necessary to finishing the IT applications journey. While one might consider two or three important NFRs (such as performance and security), one will probably not cover the others extensively, or you might miss out on them all together. And if one does allocate time to deal with them, when the schedule slips, the NFRs may be the first thing to get dropped. So, whether you plan for NFRs or not, chances are high you won't cover them 100%. One should try to avoid adding technical debt and maintenance nightmares to the application portfolio.

What are the best practices to ensure good performance in an application?

Performance is defined as the responsiveness of the application to perform specific tasks in a given span of time. It is scored in terms of throughput or latency. Throughput is the number of events in a given span of time while Latency is the time it takes to respond to an incident. An application's performance directly impacts software scalability. Enhancing application's performance often enhances scalability by virtue of reducing shared resource contention. Following is a list of design principles:

- Load balancing is a key technique used to spread the load evenly between various nodes. Load balancing or distribution through the DNS Round Robin algorithm will facilitate superior performance.
- Lowering traffic on the wire and only sending what is required and only retrieving what is necessary.
- Reduce the number of transitions between boundaries, and reduce the amount of data transferred over the wire. Choose batch mode to minimize calls over the network channel.
- When communications tier boundaries are crossed, leverage coarse-grained interfaces requiring a reduce number of calls for a specific process, and consider using an asynchronous model of communication.
- Design effective locking, transactions, queuing, and threading mechanisms. Leverage optimum queries for superior performance, and avoid bulk fetching of data when only a subset is required for the operation. Leverage asynchronous APIs, message queuing, or one-way calls to minimize blocking while making calls across tier boundaries.
- Application, database, and server tuning also improve system performance.
- Architect efficient communication methodology and protocols between tiers to ensure entities securely interact with no performance degradation.
- Leverage the container's built-in features such as distributed transaction and authentication that will improve robustness and simplify the architecture.

- Largely granular interfaces require multiple invocations to perform a task and are the best solution alternatives when located on the same physical node.
- Interfaces that make only one call to accomplish each task provide outstanding performance when the components are distributed across physical boundaries.

Separate long-running critical processes that might fail by using a separate physical cluster. For example, a web server provides superior processing capacity and memory but may not have robust storage that can be swapped rapidly in the event of a hardware failure.

The following is a list of the typical units of measurement:

- **Throughput**: The ability of the system to execute a specified number of transactions in a given span of time
- **Response times**: The allowable distribution of time which the system takes to respond to the request
- **Time**: The time it takes to complete a transaction

Probability indicator: ♟♟♟

What are the best practices to ensure scalability?

Scalability is the capability of the application to handle an increase in workload without performance degradion, or the ability to quickly enlarge. Scalability is the ability to enlarge the architecture to accommodate users, processes, transactions, and additional nodes and services as the business system evolves to meet the needs of the future. The existing systems are extended as far as possible without replacing them. Scalability directly affects the architecture as well as the selection of hardware and system software components. Following is a list of design principles:

- There are two architecture choices for achieving scalability. One is vertically, by adding memory, processors, or disks. The other is horizontally, by adding more machines to the system.

 Vertical scalability is easier to achieve than horizontal scalability.

- Handling more customer requests requires the system to be scaled by deploying additional web servers.

- Design layers and tiers for scalability, namely to scale out or scale up a web, application, or database tier.
- The key scalability patterns include distributed computing, parallel computing, SOA, event-driven architecture, a push-and-pull data model, optimal load sharing, enterprise portals, and a message model.
- Clustering allows the ability to add processing capability by simply adding nodes to the cluster.
- Using connection pooling for database and resource pooling improves the scalability of applications. Resource pooling, such as database connection pools, is also maintaining multiple logical connections over fewer physical connections and they reusing the connections, bringing in more scalable efficiencies.
- Supplementary application or database servers can be added (horizontal scaling) to improve the scalability of the application.
- Partitioning data across multiple database servers to improve scalability and allowing flexible location for datasets.
- Design logical layers on the same physical tier to reduce the number of physical nodes while also increasing load sharing and failover capabilities.
- Leverage design that uses alternative systems when it detects a spike in traffic or increase in user load for an existing system.
- Architect store and forward technique to allow the request to be stored when the target is offline, and send it when it's back online.
- Stateless nature of transactions and requests makes the application more scalable. Design applications using stateless session beans improve the scalability.
- Business logic needs be loosely coupled with the web tier, hence deploying the application components on the separate node is easier. SOA provides scalability at the integration layer through the loose coupling.

The following is a list of typical units of measurement:

- Throughput–how many transactions per hour the system needs to be able to handle
- Year-on-year growth requirements
- Storage–the amount of data the system requires to archive

Probability indicator: 👍👍👍

What are the best practices to ensure high availability?

- Availability is defined as the time span the application is normally functional. It is scored as the percentage of total application downtime over a specified period. Availability is affected by faults and exceptions, hardware issues, malicious attacks, and maintenance and upgrades. Availability is the span of time the system is operational and available for its end users. Availability is established as few applications are architected with expected downtime for activities like database upgrades and backups. Following is a list of design principles.

- The application is designed with a hot standby configuration for high availability. In case the primary servers go down the load balancer will be able to route the request to secondary/hot standby nodes. Make the system more available so if one node is down, another node can take over the work.

- The load balancer is configured to route traffic to hot standby if the primary reaches its threshold. The load balancer policies should be optimized to distribute the burden and fail over to standby instances in the event of issues with the primary node.

- Transaction Manager component increases availability and reliability by ensuring the application is always in a consistent state and through a strategy for handling certain classes of failures.

- The design should be stateless so that when a stateless server fails, its work can be routed to a different server without implications for state management.

- The ability to prevent application failures in the event of service/s failures, is commonly architected via redundancy. This can be achieved through fault tolerance techniques such as active and passive replication.

- A robust monitoring infrastructure set up to frequently do a health check of all internal systems such as the web server, application server, and database servers. Develop an internal and external monitoring and alerting infrastructure. This serves as an early warning indicator and helps the operations team to respond quickly in case of issues. Continuous real-time monitoring of internal and external systems is essential to identify and fix production issues

- Ensure that a **disaster recovery** (**DR**) site is present, and should have a mirror replica of the code and data from the main site. The load balancer is configured to route the requests to the DR site during peak traffic. A geographically separate site is a redundant site to fail over in the case of natural disasters such as hurricanes or floods.

- Recommended high availability: HA configurations for the database can be set up and configured. This includes clusters, data replication, and all other configuration proposed by the product vendor.
- Avoiding chatty conversations with upstream services to minimize data transfer.
- An open source caching framework, Memcached, can be leveraged to cache the database records and search results. Additionally, a distributed and cluster cache can be implemented for handling large data.

The following are the typical units of measurement:

- **Availability:** Application availability considering weekends, holidays, and maintenance times and failures.
- **Geographic location**: Connection requirements and the restrictions of a local network prevail.
- **Offline requirement**: Time available for offline operations including batch processing and system maintenance. Length of time between failures.
- **Recoverability:** This is the time needed to be able to resume operation in the event of fault or exceptions.
- **Resilience:** The reliability characteristics of the system and sub-components.

Probability indicator: 👍👍👍

What are the best practices to ensure reliability in your application?

Reliability is the characteristic of an application to continue functioning in an expected manner over time. Reliability is scored as the probability that the application will not fail and that it will keep function for a defined time span. Reliability is the ability of the application to maintain its performance over a specific time span. Unreliable software fails frequently, and specific tasks are more prone to failure because they cannot be restarted or resumed. The following are the design principles:

- Establish an alternative to detect exceptions and automatically initiate a system fail over, or redirect the request to a standby system. Implement code that leverages alternate nodes when a failed request is detected from an existing application.

- Design for instrumentation, such as events or performance counters, that is unavailable, and detects performance problems or external systems failures and expose information through standard interfaces like **Windows Management Interface** (**WMI**), Trace files, event Log. Log performance, errors, exceptions and auditing information about calls made to other systems and services.
- Establish alternatives to manage unreliable application, failed APIs, and failed transactions. Identify queuing pending requests if the application goes offline.
- Design store and forward or cached mechanism that allows requests to be stored when the target application is unavailable, and to be forwarded when the target is online.
- Design the solution by leveraging queuing to provide a reliable alternative for asynchronous APIs.
- Solution capability of recovering from error or exception on the basis of the defined error and exception strategy.
- The primary node serves the entire request, but a backup server is added to route traffic if the primary goes down or is made offline for upgrades.
- Data Integrity is established with security controls/mechanisms preventing a third party from making any unauthorized access and/or changes to data.
- Database transactions ensure data integrity as it will be a full commit or a rollback based on the success/failure status.

The following are the typical units of measurement:

- The capability of application to perform required functions under stated conditions for a specific time period.
- Mean Time Between Failures is the acceptable threshold for downtime
- Mean Time To Recovery: Is the time available to get the application back online.
- Data integrity is the referential integrity in databases
- Application Integrity and Information Integrity – during transactions
- Fault trapping (I/O): Handling failures and recovery

Probability indicator:

What are the best practices to ensure maintainability?

Maintainability is the quality of the application to go through changes with a fair degree of effortlessness. This attribute is the flexibility with which the application can be modified, for fixing issues or to add new functionality with a degree of ease. These changes could impact components, services, functionality, and interfaces when modifying for fixing issues, or to meet demands of the future. Maintainability has a direct baring on the time it takes to restore the application to a normal status following a failure or an upgrade. An enlightening maintainability attribute will enhance availability and reduce run-time defects. Following is a list of design principles:

- The logical separation of the application into different tiers (client, presentation, business logic, integration, and **Enterprise Integration System** (**EIS**) tier) allows a system to be flexible and easily maintained. When there are any changes in the presentation, they will be done at the presentation tier, and it will not affect the other tiers. If there are any business logic changes, only the EJB component's business logic gets changed; it will not affect other tiers and vice versa.

- The MVC pattern leverages the command pattern at the web tier (JSF Backing Bean classes) for handling web events. Therefore, when new functionalities are added to the system, it will not affect the existing system. We can easily create a new web action by developing new Backing Bean class and configuring it in the `faces-config.xml` file. Even modifying the existing functionality becomes easy by changing the respective Backing Bean classes.

- Object orientation like encapsulation, inheritance, low coupling and high cohesion are leveraged in application design. Any changes to subsystems will have less impact on systems which are using it as long as the interfaces remain the same.

- Independence of the interface from the implementation permits substituting of different implementations for the same functionality.

- Design applications consisting of layers, or areas of concern; that clearly demarcate the UI, business processes, and data access layers.

- Design cross-layer dependencies by using abstractions instead of concrete classes, and minimize dependencies between tiers, layers, and components.

- Define and establish proper communication protocols, models, and formats.

- Design pluggable architecture that facilitates easy maintenance, and improves testing processes.

- Architect interfaces to provide plug-in architecture to maximize flexibility and extensibility.

- Leverage built-in container and platform functions and features wherever possible instead of custom application.
- Architecture to have high cohesion and have low coupling in order to maximize flexibility and facilitate reusability.
- Establish methodology to manage dynamic business processes and dynamic business rules, by using workflow engine for dynamic business processes.

Following are the typical units of measurement:

- Conformance to design standards, coding standards, best practices, reference architectures, and frameworks
- Flexibility: The degree to which the system is intended to support change
- Release support: The way in which the system will support the introduction of initial release, phased rollouts and future releases
- Up-to-date and consistent documentation

Probability indicator: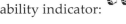

What are the best practices to ensure extensibility?

Extensibility is a characteristic where-in the architecture, design, and implementation actively caters to future business needs.

Extensible applications have excellent endurance, which prevents the expensive processes of procuring large inflexible applications and retiring them due to changes in business needs. Extensibility enables organizations to take advantage of opportunities and respond to risks. but While there is an significant difference extensibility is often tangled with modifiability quality. Following is a list of design principles:

- The logical separation of the application into various tiers (that is, client, presentation, business logic, integration, and EIS tier) allows a system to be flexible and easily maintained. When there are any changes in presentation, it will be done at presentation tier, and it will not affect the other tiers. If there are any changes to the business logic, only the EJB component's business logic is changed; it will not affect other tiers, and vice versa.

- The MVC architecture leverages the command pattern at the web tier (JSF Backing Bean classes) for handling web events. Therefore, when new functionalities are added to the system, it will not affect the existing system. We can easily create a new web action by developing a new `BackingBean` class and configuring it in the `faces-config.xml` file. Modifying the existing functionality becomes easy by changing the respective `BackingBean` classes.
- Object orientations such as, encapsulation, inheritance, high cohesion and low coupling are leveraged in application design. So the subsystem's changes will have less impact on applications that are using it as long as the interfaces remain the same.
- Independence of the interface from the implementation permits substituting different implementations for the same functionality.
- Design systems and layers that demarcate the system's UI, processes, and data access functionality.
- Design cross-layer inter dependencies by leveraging abstractions rather than concrete implementations, and minimize dependencies between layers and components.
- Design a plug-and-play architecture that facilitates easy maintenance and upgrades, and improves QA processes by solutioning APIs, enabling plug-n-play modules or components to maximize flexibility and extensibility.
- Leverage the built-in platform's features wherever available instead of a custom implementation.
- Design modules to have high cohesion and low coupling to enhance flexibility and provide reusability and replacement.
- Establish a method to manage dynamic processes and dynamic rules, by leveraging the workflow engine if the business process tends to change.
- Solution business components to implement the rules if the rule values are dynamic, or a component such as rules engine if the business decision rules are dynamic.
- Provide artifacts that explain the overall structure of the application. Good documentation of the application consists of architecture diagrams, interfaces, class diagrams, sequence diagrams, coding guidelines are the key criterion for maintainable IT systems.
- Identify areas of concern and consolidating them into the logical depiction, business, data, and service layers as appropriate.
- Establishing a development model with tools and frameworks to provide workflow and collaboration.

- Establishing guidelines for architecture, design and coding standards, and incorporating reviews into your SDLC process to ensure guidelines are diligently implemented.
- Establish a migration roadmap from legacy applications, and isolating applications from inter dependencies.
- Expose functionality from layers, subsystems, and modules through APIs that other systems and layers can invoke.

Typical units of measurement:

- Handles new information types
- Manages new or changed business entities
- Consumes or provides new feeds

Probability indicator:

What are the best practices to ensure high security?

Security is the ability to avoid the malicious events and incidences of the designed system usage, and prevent loss of information. Establishing proper security enhances the reliability of system by reducing the likelihood of an attack succeeding and disrupting critical functions. Securing protects assets and prevents unauthorized access to sensitive data. The factors affecting security are integrity and confidentiality. The features used to secure applications are authorization, authentication, logging, auditing and encryption. Following is a list of design principles.

- Leverage authorization and authentication to prevent spoofing of identity and identify trust boundaries.
- Design various controls to prevent access to sensitive data or system.
- Establish monitoring and instrumentation to analyze user interaction for critical operations.
- Protect against damages by ensuring that you validate all inputs for type, range, length, and sanitized principles.
- Partition users into anonymous, identified, and authenticated and leverage monitoring and instrumentation for audit instrumentation, logging, and root cause analysis.
- Leverage encryption, sign sensitive data, and use secured transport channels.

- Reduce session timeouts and implement solutions to detect and mitigate against attacks.
- Security will be provided through the DMZ using an inner and outer firewall. Application and database servers will be behind the inner firewall, and the web server will be behind an outer firewall in the DMZ.
- The architecture uses Form Based authentication for the web tier, and the security logic is implemented in are usable business component in the application tier.
- SSL will provide the desired security for sending sensitive information to critical systems like Merchant Bank and Market Place.
- Leverage message-level encryption, digital signatures, and transport-layer security (SSL).
- The application will use LDAP for authentication at the web tier and will use role-based security at the web and business tier for authorization.
- Authorization is control access to information in the application once a user is identified and authenticated.
- Authentication: Identification of the end user in the system and validating that the user is telling the veracity.
- Auditing: Instrumentation and monitoring of security.
- Integrity: Protection against improper modification of information in transit or storage.
- Confidentiality: Protection against inappropriate disclosure of data during transit and storage.

The following are the typical units of measurement:

- **Authentication:** Correct Identification of parties attempting to access systems and protection of systems from unauthorized parties
- **Authorization:** Mechanism required to authorize users to perform different functions within the systems
- **Encryption (data in flight and at rest)**: All external communications between the application data server and clients to be encrypted
- **Data confidentiality**: All data must be proactively established, secured, and archived
- **Compliance:** The process to confirm systems compliance with the organization's security standards and policies

Probability indicator:

How is a session failover handled?

The requirement for session failover enables that the data specific to user sessions needs to be available across all cluster nodes. This mechanism is required to be made invisible to the end users. Session replication is leveraged in application server to achieve session failover namely a session is replicated to other machines, every time the session changes. If a node fails, the load balancer routes in-coming requests to another server in the cluster since all machines in a cluster have a copy of the session. Session replication allows session failover, but it costs in terms of memory and network bandwidth.

Sharing of session data is also implemented through application-level APIs. This is enabled through the persistence layer that allows session data to be managed by other nodes when a failure occurs. Sessions stored in cookies are often cryptographically signed, but the data is not unencrypted. Session data stored in cookies should not contain any sensitive information like credit card data or other personal data. The session data can also be stored in a database or in Memcached component.

The efficiency of session management comes with a cost. Applications that leverage a session management mechanism must maintain each user's session state, stored in memory. This greatly increases the memory footprint of the application. If the session management capability is not implemented, applications will have a smaller footprint.

Probability indicator:

How does your design handle transactions?

Java EE includes distributed transactions through two specifications:

- **Java Transaction API (JTA)**
- **Java Transaction Service (JTS)**

JTA is an protocol that is implementation-independent and allows applications to handle transactions. On the other hand, JTS specifies the implementation of transaction manager for JTA and implements the OMG or Object Transaction Service specification for Java mapping. JTS enables transactions using the **Internet Inter-ORB Protocol (IIOP)**. The transaction manager supports both JTA and JTS. The EJB container itself leverages the Java Transaction API to interact with JTS component. The transaction manager controls all EJB transactions, except for bean-managed transactions and Java Database Connectivity transactions, and allows beans to update multiple databases with a single transaction:

- The application design incorporates container-managed transaction for database transactions, which allows for simpler, more portable code.
- All transactions for one component are managed by a single workflow manager object which is typically stateless bean.
- Architecture leverages JPA Entity to manage payment transactions. The method is invoked with Requires New transaction attribute by a stateless session bean.
- Entity instance is based on rows and Entity Manager takes care of concurrency.

Transaction properties

These properties are known by the ACID acronym. Each letter stands for a property:

- **Atomicity:** This means that the operations are executed as a whole and by an "all or nothing" rule
- **Consistency**: Data must be consistent at the beginning and the end of the **transaction**
- **Isolation:** When we have concurrent access to data, operations cannot access modified data in the current transaction
- **Durability:** Once the transaction is finished, modified data must not be lost and should be the same afterward

Transaction types

The following are the types of transactions:

- **Global transactions**: These transactions are leveraged when dealing with multiple resources such as databases or message queues. In order to use global transactions, **Java Transaction API (JTA)** is leveraged and it's available in the application server environment.
- **Local transactions**: Unlike global transactions, local transactions are used to deal with a single resource for example, a JDBC connection for a single database. Normally local transactions are easier to manage than global transactions.

Probability indicator: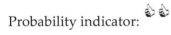

How does the design handle authentication and authorization?

Java Authentication and Authorization Service (JAAS) is leveraged to control authentication and authorization in the application. Authentication and role are stored in LDAP server. The UI framework is configured to connect with LDAP and control access according to the roles in the application. Access to the JSP page is controlled by the UI framework. Authentication is done via the HTTP form. Username is the e-mail address mostly and once the user submits the form with username and password, the application checks the details against LDAP server.

Probability indicator:

What is application instrumentation (or profiling)?

Instrumentation is the ability to measure the level of a IT system's performance, diagnose errors, and trace audit information. Instrumentation takes the form of code instructions that monitor specific components in an IT application, for example, logging information to appear on UT. When an application has instrumentation embedded, it can be managed using a management tool. Instrumentation is mandatory for reviewing the performance of an application.

Probability indicator:

What are legal and regulatory considerations?

Compliance means conforming to rules, principles, policies, standard or law. Regulatory compliance describes the goal organizations aspirations to achieve to ensure that they comply with laws and regulations. Due to the increase in regulation domains and the need for transparency, enterprises are adopting consolidated and harmonized sets of compliance controls. This approach ensures that all necessary governance policies can be met without the unnecessary duplication of effort from resources. Data retention is one part of regulatory compliance that is a challenge for many organizations. The security that comes from compliance with regulations can be contrary to maintaining user privacy. Data retention regulations requires the service providers to retain extensive logs of activities beyond the time for normal business hours.

Probability indicator:

What are Business Continuity and Recovery Considerations?

Business Continuity (**BC**) reflects an organization's capability to maintain access to IT resources after unexpected system outages or natural calamities. A comprehensive BC plan and strategy defines an instantaneous failover to redundant resources hosted on-site, off-site, or on the cloud.

Disaster Recovery (**DR**) strategy provides an organization with recovery for its applications and data within an accepted recovery time, which can translate into hours or even days in the absence of DR plan. The goal is to achieve the best **recovery time objective** (**RTO**) and minimize data loss a good **recovery point objective** (**RPO**).

Probability indicator:

How do we define and finalize NFRs for the projects or KPIs for the project?

Such a list can be drawn up and maintained by getting together the heads of IT Operations, IT Architecture and other stakeholders who have an interest in the project's outcome and the solution it will create. The organization must decide who these stakeholder groups are–operations/support and security, architecture, and business.

The following is a checklist of NFRs:

NFR	Attributes
Performance	• Throughput: The ability of the system to execute a given number of transactions within a given unit of time. • Response times: The distribution of time which the system takes to respond to the request.
Scalability	• Throughput: The number of maximum transactions your system needs to handle. Example., thousand a day or a million • Storage: The amount of data you going to need to store • Growth Requirements: Data growth in the next 3-5 years
Availability	• Availability: Application availability considering weekends, holidays, and maintenance times and failures. • Locations of operation: Geographic location, Connection requirements, and the restrictions of a local network prevail • Offline requirement: The time available for offline operations, including batch processing and system maintenance • Length of time between failures • Recoverability: The time required by the system is able to resume operation in the event of failure • Resilience: The reliability characteristics of the system and sub-components

Capacity	• Throughput: The number of peak transactions the system needs to handle • Storage: The volume of data the system will persist at run time to disk. This relates to the memory/disk • Year-on-year growth requirements (users, storage, and processing) • e-channel growth projections • Activities or transactions supported for each type of transaction, volumes on an hourly, daily, weekly, monthly,or yearly basis • Is the workload significantly higher during specific time of the day (for example, at noon), week, month or year • Transaction volumes growth expected and additional volumes you will be able to handle
Security	• Authentication: Correct identification of parties attempting to access systems and protection of systems from unauthorized parties • Authorization: Mechanism required to authorize users to perform different functions within the systems • Encryption (data in flight and at rest): The external communications between the application and clients must be encrypted • Data Confidentiality: All data must be proactively marked, stored, and protected • Compliance: The process to confirm systems compliance with the organization's security standards and policies
Maintainability	• Conformance to design standards, coding standards, best practices, reference architectures, and frameworks. • Flexibility: The degree to which the system is intended to support change • Release support: The way in which the system will support the introduction of initial release, phased rollouts and future releases • Up-to-date and consistent documentation
Manageability	• The system must maintain full traceability of transactions • Audited objects and audited database fields to be included for auditing • File characteristics such as size before and after, and structure • End user and transactional time stamps • Receive alerts, events and notices as thresholds are approached (memory, storage, processor) • Create new virtual instances at the click of a button and remotely manage systems • Rich graphical dashboard for all key applications metrics

Reliability	• The ability of an application to perform its required functions under predefined conditions for a specific span of time • Acceptable threshold for downtime (Mean Time Between Failures) • Time available to get the system back up online (Mean Time To Recovery) • Data integrity: This is the referential integrity in database tables and interfaces • Application Integrity and Information Integrity: During transactions • Fault trapping (I/O): Handling failures and recovery
Extensibility	• Handle new information types • Manage new or changed business entities • Consume or provide new feeds
Recovery	• Recovery process: **Recovery Point Objectives (RPO)** and **Recovery Time Objectives (RTO)** • RTO/Restore time: The time required to switch to the secondary site when the primary fails. • RPO/Backup time: The time taken to back up your data. • Backup frequencies: Frequency of backing up the transaction data, config data, and code
Interoperability	• Other systems it needs to integrate in the ecosystem • Other systems it has to live with amicably in the ecosystem • Different OS compatibility • Hardware platforms it needs to support – run-on
Usability	• Look and feel: layout and flow, colors, screen element density, keyboard shortcuts, and UI metaphors • Localization/Internationalization requirements: Spellings languages, paper sizes, keyboards, and so on

Table 1: NFRs KPIs

Probability indicator:

What is clustering and what are the benefits of clustering?

Clustering consists of a group of loosely connected servers or nodes that work in tandem are viewed as a single entity. The components of clusters are connected to each other through fast networks, each node running an instance of the operating system. Clustering provides superior performance and availability over single node, while being more cost-effective than single computers of comparable speed. The benefits of clustering include fault tolerance, load balancing, and replication.

Server clustering is a technique of inter-connecting a number of servers into one group, which works as a unified solution. Server clustering enables multiple servers together to form a cluster that offers higher power, strength, redundancy and scalability. The server clustering ensures high availability and performance, even if there are challenges with one of servers in the cluster solution. The main objective of clustering is to achieve greater availability. A typical server runs on a machine and it runs till there is no hardware failure or some other failure. By creating a cluster, one reduces the probability of the business service and components becoming unavailable in case of a hardware of software failure.

 Clustering is leveraged in many types of servers for high availability.

Here are the two types of clusters:

- **Application cluster**: An application server cluster is a set of machines that can run an application server and can be reliably leveraged with minimum downtime
- **Database cluster**: A database server cluster is a set of machines that run a database server can be reliably leveraged with a no downtime

The following are the benefits of clustering:

- Server clustering is designed for high availability. In case one of the servers has faults, another server from the cluster takes over and ensures high availability for the business.
- Server clustering is scalable solution and hence nodes can be added or deleted from the cluster as per the business demands.
- If a server from the cluster requires maintenance, it can be made offline while other servers handle its load, making the maintenance simpler.

These are the disadvantages of clustering:

- Server clustering requires more servers to manage and monitor. Thus it increases the infrastructure and cost of IT.
- Server clustering is not very flexible, as not all types of servers can be clustered. There are many applications that do not support clustering.
- It is not a cost-effective solution, as it needs an optimum server design, which can be expensive.

Middle tier clustering

Middle tier clustering is configured in the middle tier of an IT application. This is a common topology as many applications have a middle tier and heavy loads are serviced through the middle tier requiring high scalability and availability. Failure of middle tier causes multiple systems and components to fail. Therefore one of the approaches to do clustering is at the middle tier of an IT application. In the Java world, it is common mechanism to create EJB containers clusters that are leveraged by many clients. Applications with the business logic that needs to be shared across multiple clients can leverage middle tier clustering.

Probability indicator:

What do you understand by distributed caching?

Distributed caching, compared to in-memory caching, is one of the common caching mechanisms that deal with large and unpredictable data volumes. In an IT landscape with multiple application instances, consistency of cache and reliability in case of node failures are critical challenges. An in-memory cache resides in the memory of the application instance. So if a node goes down, its cached data is lost. This means another instance of the application has to fetch the data all the way from the database and populate its in-memory cache which is an overhead and inefficient.

Distributed cache stays outside of the application instance. Although there would be several 'cache nodes' part of this distributed cache solution (for high availability), the object is passed from the application to the cache through a single API. This preserves the state of the cache, and results in data consistency. The cache engine determines which node to get the object from, leveraging a hashing algorithm. Also, since the distributed cache isn't linked to any one node, node failures wouldn't always make a difference to the application performance.

Examples of distributed cache solutions are Memcached, Redis, and HazelCast.

Probability indicator: 👍 👍

What do you understand by the capacity planning?

Capacity planning is a technique of estimating the space, hardware, software and network infrastructure resources that will be needed by an enterprise over future time span. A capacity concern for many enterprises is whether resources will be in place to handle increasing demands on the workload as the number of users increase. The aim of planner is to plan so that new capacity is added just in time to meet the future needs but ensuring the resources do not go unused for a long period. The successful planner is one that makes the trade-offs between the present and the future and proves to be the most cost-efficient.

The planner, leverages business plans, forecasts, trends, and outlines the future needs for an organizations. Analytical modeling tools are also leveraged by planner to get answers to different scenarios and options. The planner leverages tools that are scalable, stable and predictable in terms of upgrades over the life of the product.

Probability indicator: 👍 👍

What are the different performance troubleshooting tools for Java application?

The table lists various tools that are leveraged by the SMEs for troubleshooting performance issues in Java applications:

Tool	Description
VisualVM	jconsole comes with JDK 1.5. It is Java Monitoring and Management Console -JMX compliant tool for monitoring a Java VM. It can monitor both local and remote VMs.
VisualVM	VisualVM integrates with various existing JDK softwares and provides lightweight CPU and memory profiling capabilities. This tool is designed for both production and development environments and enhances the capability of monitoring and analysis for solutions.
HeapAnalyzer	HeapAnalyzer allows finding possible heap leak area through its heuristic engine and analysis of the heap in applications. It analyzes heap dumps by parsing the heap dump, creating graphs, transforming them into trees, and executing the heuristic search engine.
PerfAnal	PerfAnal is a GUI tool for analyzing performance of applications on the Java Platform. One can leverage PerfAnal to identify performance problems in code and locate areas that need tuning.
JAMon	JAMon is a free, simple, high performance, thread safe, Java API that allows developers to easily monitor production applications.
Eclipse Memory Analyzer	Eclipse Memory Analyzer is a feature rich Java heap analyzer that helps find memory leaks and reduce memory consumption.
GCViewer	GCViewer is an open source tool used to visualize data produced by the VM options: `verbose:gc` and `-Xloggc:<file>`. It also calculates garbage-collection-related performance metrics (throughput, accumulated pauses, longest pause, and so on).
HPjmeter	HPjmeter diagnose the performance problems in applications on HP-Unix, Monitors Java applications and analyzes profiling data. HPjmeter also captures profiling data and improves garbage collection.

HPjconfig	HPjconfig is a configuration tool for tuning your HP-UX system kernel parameters to match the characteristics of application. HPjconfig provides kernel parameter recommendations tailored to your HP-UX platform. When given specific Java and HP-UX versions, HPjconfig will determine if all of the latest HP-UX patches required for Java performance and functionality are installed on the system, and highlight any missing patches.

Table 2: Performance Tools

Probability indicator:

What is load balancing? What are the different tools available for load balancing?

A load balancing mechanism is leveraged for distributing user loads across multiple nodes. The most common algorithm for a load balancing algorithm is the Round Robin algorithm. In this mechanism the request is divided in a circular format ensuring all nodes get an equal number of requests and no single node is over or under utilized. The failover mechanism switches to another nodes when one of the node fails or becomes offline. Typically a load balancer is configured to support fail over to another node when the primary node fails. To achieve least downtime, most load balancers support the feature of heart beat check which ensures that target machine is responding and is up and running. As soon as a heartbeat signal fails, load balancer stops sending the requests to that node and redirects the requests to other node of the cluster solution.

The most common load balancing techniques for applications are:

- Round-Robin load balancing
- IP address affinity
- Session affinity or sticky session load balancing

The benefits of load balancing:

Benefit	Description
Redundancy	Redundancy is a mechamisn of running two or more identical servers, providing a fail-safe behaviour in the event of one server going offline. With load balancing, the system "senses" when a server becomes unavailable and instantly reroutes traffic to other nodes in the cluster. A load-balanced architecture always includes a secondary load balancing device, guaranteeing full redundancy across every component of the network.
Scalability	Even if there is currently a modest resource requirement, scalability should always be given a consideration for the solution. In a few months, there may be a requirement to add more horse power to your cluster. The smart thing to do is to configure load balancing, which not only lets you get the most out of your current hardware, but also lets you scale your application as needed.
Resource optimization	With a load balancer in place, one can optimize the traffic distribution to the server cluster to ensure best performance. Load balancers also speed up the application by taking over time-consuming tasks such as SSL encryption and decryption.
Security	The appliction's security is improved many-fold. Load balancing exposes only one IP to the external world, that is, the Web, which greatly lowers the number of breach points for any attack. The topology of the IT network is hidden, which improves the safety of the entire setup. The servers from the cluster receive virtual IPs, which enables the load balancer to route traffic as needed without exposing the addresses to hackers.

Table 3: Benefits of LoadBalancing

Load balancing tools

There are both hardware and software load balancing solutions. Hardware load balancers are usually located in front of the web tier and sometimes in between web and application tiers. Most software clustering solutions include load balancing software that is leveraged by upstream software components. A reverse proxy, such as Squid, is used to distribute the load across multiple servers. Open source load balancing software solutions include Perlbal, Pen, and Pound. Hardware-based solutions include BigIP and ServerIron, among others.

Probability indicator:

What is the IP affinity technique for load balancing?

IP address affinity is a common mechanism for load balancing. In this method, the client IP address is associated with a server node. All requests from a client IP address are serviced by one server node. This technique is very simple to deploy since the IP address is available in the HTTP header and no additional configuration is required to be done.

This type of load balancing can be useful if the clients are likely to disable cookies. There is a flipside to this approach, however. If the users are behind a network address translation or NATed IP address, then all of them will end up routed to the same server node. This may lead to uneven load on the server. NATed IP addresses are very common; in fact, if one is browsing from an office network, it's likely that NATed IP address is leveraged.

Probability indicator: 👍 👍

Summary

Software quality attributes are a critical factor in the long-standing success of any enterprise IT. Quality attributes increase organizational efficiency and profitability, reduce maintenance cost, and achieve customer loyalty. Quality audits help ensure that the software achieves value and efficiency. It is critical to perform quality audits in a consistent and planned manner. These audits should be typically carried out throughout the SDLC to validate artifacts produced at the end of various SDLC phases. Effective audits should not only focus on process conformance but also incorporate software architecture, design, build, and test to improve software quality.

Software quality is best achieved in the early stages of the SDLC, when the cost to remediate is less than it would be during the later phases of SDLC. Hence it is advisable to find and rectify defects close to their point of origin to reduce the impact. Normally, a software development life cycle is composed of many phases, ranging from inception, requirement, architecture and design, development, testing, deployment, and operations. Exceptions and errors can occur at any point in the SDLC. Therefore, a rigorous audit program should be a continuous process run in parallel with the SDLC.

This section covered the Q&A for frameworks and NFR domains. An architecture framework provides principles and practices for defining and implementing the architecture of an enterprise. It structures the architect's thinking by dividing the architecture description into domains and layers or views. It offers models-typically metrics and diagrams-for documenting each view. This chapter also covered NFRs, providing insights into how they will be addressed in the architecture phase. We covered the key NFRs that are most critical for any project and for each NFR provides the various alternatives pertaining to the solution, the design principle that needs to be applied to achieve the desired outcome for example, high availability or scalability or reliability as covered.

The next chapter will cover the do's and don'ts during interview preparations, architects' competencies, and case studies.

8

Interview Preparation

This chapter covers guidance on architects interview preparations guidelines, dos and don'ts for interviews, architects competencies and case studies.

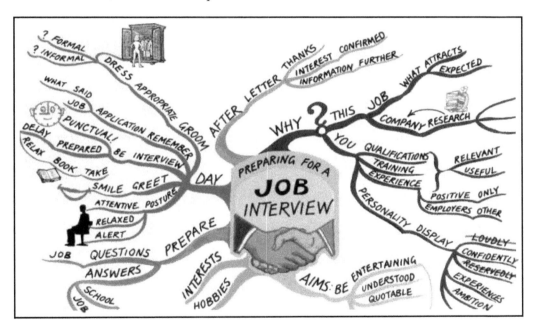

Figure 1: Architect job interview

Dos and dont's for interviews

This section describes the do's and dont's while preparing for an architect job interview:

- **Collect great examples from the past**: Consolidate the key engagement case studies you have done in the past. Articulate all details about the processes, methodologies, and frameworks required for building enterprise/solution architecture. Collate key case studies in the area of data, application, business, and infrastructure architecture, and the work done in the NFRs domain.

- **Speak the language of business**: An EA or SA needs to connect with strategic business stakeholders. Make sure the discussions don't emphasize technology jargon as the business stakeholders do interviews for these key positions and may not be able to relate to jargon. An SME in this position who fears not being at your knowledge level will be intimidated. Make sure that any questions you ask come as inquisitive and not condescending.

- **Share vision and critical decisions**: EAs have to share the vision and critical decision in an engagement with all the key stakeholders. They have to collate a prioritized list and share the key concerns during the discussions. These need to be articulated in the EA blueprints as well.

- **Be the change agent**: Enterprise architects are change agents in organizations through technology leadership. The drive the adoptions of technology strategy and roadmaps.

- **Be able to articulate architecture processes**: Leverage TOGAF, COBiT, ITIL, and all key frameworks and methodologies as they are built on best practices and standards.

Architect job descriptions

This section describes various architect profiles in terms of role description, the accountabilities and competencies.

Enterprise architect – consulting

Summary of job description is as follows:

The enterprise architect will be responsible for assessment of high-risk, high-value proposals for process compliance, competitive approach, and risk identification and mitigation. The role ensures that the risks identified during the initial phases are addressed while in execution. The role also provides technical management support to troubled delivery projects. This role requires regular direct interfacing with the C-level management, including the CEO, CFO, and CTO; and providing internal technical consultative services and evaluation reports of complex, high-risk system integration deals.

The responsibilities of this role are as follows:

- Key activities revolve around driving proposal and delivery consistency for complex deals through the entire life cycle, providing proposal and project assessment reports to C-level management, and providing feedback to the proposal or project teams with regards to risk mitigation and planning.
- Validation of identified risks and the associated mitigation plan of complex, high-risk, and high-value deals delivered to C-level management, including the CEO.
- Quality assessment for process compliance with a quarterly assessment summary provided to the management. The quarterly report includes process assessment findings, recommended process changes and measurements meeting SEI CMMI level 5 practices.
- Solution validation and competitive analysis of proposed solutions.
- Proposal team mentoring in technology, approach, and method of delivery.
- Facilitation of transition to ensure that risks in the initial stages are mitigated during the startup and governance phases.
- Reporting to the C-level and theater-level deal review board, providing approval guidance.
- Provide guidance to selected or high-risk or troubled projects.
- EA reports into executive/senior management, the role also supports creation of intellectual properties or in merger and acquisition.

The accountabilities for this role are as follows:

- Enable proposal and delivery tasks at a group level
- Collaborate with sales and engineering groups to provide guidance to proposal and artifact creation, engagement delivery plans, requirements traceability, technical solution, risk identification, and risk mitigation

- Preparation of assessment reports and presentation for the approval process including C-suite deal reviews and approval
- Be the face of the organization at media and analyst events to represent the proposal team
- Advocates for incorporation and use of reusable assets from the Unisys portfolio
- Advocates for adherence to defined Unisys standard corporate proposal and delivery standards

The competencies for this role as as follows:

- Experience of 15+ years in IT and 5+ years in software architecture, including estimation and architecture of large-scale complex engagements (> $10M).
- Technical acumen and experience in architecting large and complex solutions as a senior lead architect.
- Risk assessment and demonstrated skills regarding risk identification and risk mitigation planning. Knowledge and application of CMMI risk management.
- Demonstrated skills in process analysis, understanding of delivery processes and the technical depth to assess the quality of the technology deliverables and the proposed solution. Ability and experience in examination technical artifacts to provide staff and management with objective insights into processes and work products.
- Broad software development process expertise with demonstrated experience in requirement analysis, solution architecture, configuration management, and quality assurance.
- Broad technical knowledge in the areas of cloud computing, networking, security, application modernization, and data center with demonstrated in-depth knowledge in at least two of the areas.
- Demonstrated experience in a significant senior technical leadership position such as a chief engineer, chief technology architect, or chief technical officer.
- Large technical project experience involving high-dollar-value technical projects above $20 million USD, with delivery and performance periods exceeding two years.
- System integration lead experience using model-driven delivery methods and tools.
- Strong experience in requirements management methods and tooling.
- Experience with project management methods aligned to Prince 2 or PMI standards as required for technical leadership and project governance.

- Experience working in cross-functional and global environments, including disciplines for virtual proposal and delivery environment.
- Experience with all of the following: developing and delivering presentations to multiple levels of internal stakeholders, including C-level management, partners, and customers.
- Master's degree or bachelor of science degree or higher in computer technology or electrical engineering.
- Experience with industry standard frameworks, models, and UMLs.
- Experience in leveraging rational unified processes: RUP or Microsoft frameworks and tooling.
- Systems engineering lead experience and familiarity with the **International Council on Systems Engineering** (**INCOSE**).
- Experience with large complex systems integration projects with multi-year delivery schedules. A project would typically be over $20 million revenues.
- Intellectual property valuation experience.
- Travel: 20%-50%.

Enterprise architect – domain

Summary of the job description:

The enterprise architect leads and contributes to delivery excellence, technology adoption, IP creation and reuse, and innovation. The group provides technology leadership to various accounts and business units and helps build technical assets and solution frameworks for the banking and financial services vertical.

As part of the delivery teams, the group members lead the specification, design, and implementation of cutting-edge solutions and act as consultants to the client's teams in their respective area of expertise. The group also leads specification of a solution's architecture, design and implementation as part of the business development teams.

Play a leadership role (IT architecture and technology) for major LOBs and programs of strategic importance. In this role, the individual will be working closely with BU leadership, talent acquisition leadership, and SBU's chief architect to play a leading role in technology consulting through leadership, architecture delivery, innovation, and business development services for the customer. Additionally, the candidate will be responsible for providing leadership to one or more parts of the SBU talent acquisition team, thereby ensuring career growth, competency development, and reusable asset development.

The competencies for this role are as follows:

- An enterprise architect with 15+ years of architecture experience and 5+ years in architecture leadership roles for large and complex engagements
- Must be hands-on in terms of definition, developing, or implementing an enterprise architecture
- Experience in leadership roles as EA with the team of architects/solution designers
- Must have global exposure in terms of customers, solutions, industry, and work
- Hands-on experience in technology and architecture leadership
- Excellent leadership, communication, analytical, and decision making skills
- Ability to interconnect with customer leaderships, for example, LOB heads, CxOs, and chief architects
- Expertise in working in organizational dynamics of a large IT services firm such as SI or consulting
- Excellent articulation, documentation, specification expertise
- Broad exposure across SOA, web solutions, large-scale complex distributed systems
- Experience in pattern-oriented designs in both OO and service-oriented applications
- Experience and knowledge of one of the said domains

The responsibilities of this role are as follows:

- EA frameworks, integration, and data architecture
- SOA and technologies involved in contemporary SOA
- Expertise in BPM, business rules, workflows, and middleware technologies
- Enterprise Java and familiarity with the .NET framework
- Platform-based, framework-driven software solution development
- Architecture governance, complexity reduction, and technology selection
- NFRs, SLAs, architecture evaluation tools, and methods
- Expertise in multi-channel technologies and technology stacks on the HTML5 paradigm
- Expertise in mobile methodology and frameworks and social media tools
- Good grasp of big data and analytics, and familiarity with DW, BI, and ETL tools and platforms

The accountabilities for this role are as follows:

- Own and drive enterprise architecture, technology strategy, solution architecture, and thought leadership initiatives within the scope of the role
- Develop self- and team capabilities on emerging technology and architecture topics and deliver solutions in line with customer's IT architecture strategies, business priorities, and industry best practices
- Collaborate with client's architects, SBU leadership, client relationship management, and Cognizant's technology groups to develop and apply the applicable best practices and patterns in the context of the program/LOB
- Lead and support Cognizant's account management team in various business development activities, primarily within the SBU and help similar customer engagements with solutions, experiences, and learnings from the SBU

Enterprise architect – SI

Summary of job description is as follows:

The enterprise architect plays a leadership role (IT architecture and technology) for major LOBs and programs of strategic importance. In this role, the individual will be working closely with BU leadership, talent acquisition leadership, and SBU's chief architect to play a leading role in technology consulting through leadership, architecture delivery, innovation, and business development services for the customer. Additionally, the candidate will be responsible for providing leadership to one or more parts of the SBU – talent acquisition team, thereby ensuring career growth, competency development, and reusable asset development.

The accountabilities for this role are as follows:

- Own the technical architecture for global accounts
- Typical accounts will be $3-5M in annual revenue
- Define standards, best practices, and templates on a Microsoft platform
- Drive the standards, best practices, and templates
- Engage with CTO teams for technology evaluation/recommendation on the Microsoft platform
- Implement productivity enhancers for the account(s) that you will own
- Engage in pre-sales activities
- Define new service lines based on the Microsoft roadmap

- Build a technical ISV partner ecosystem
- Groom the next-level team like architects and designers
- Bring in rookie grooming programs

The experience required for this role is as follows:

- 9 to 15 years of IT experience.
- Excellent consulting skills, experience in influencing change, negotiating and selling.
- Experience in defining enterprise architectures on Microsoft technologies. Extensive exposure across domains such as portals, integration, SOA, web services, BI, and so on.
- Large implementation exposure (>$3-$4M in development stage) on the Microsoft technology stack.
- Experience in technology evaluation and recommendation. Awareness of industry trends and competitive strategy.
- Experience in framework development. Ability to create point solutions in key vertical areas.
- Experience leading architects and specialists from the business, application, data and infrastructure domains.
- Experience on large management (deals >$3-$5M), both on homogeneous and heterogeneous.

The competencies for this role are follows:

- Ability to analyze the current state and map the overall IT landscape using techniques such as application and technology portfolio management
- Ability to analyse enterprise mission, goals and drivers, and synthesize the IT capabilities to address business goals
- Comfortable with the grooming process
- Competent in standard engagement models such as RUP, Agile, MSF
- Architectures: Ability to present solutions to customers along with schedule and costing
- Experience in enterprise architecture methods and frameworks: TOGAF, Zachman, FEAF, Gartner EA framework, and so on
- Extensive expertise in Microsoft technology frameworks and stacks

Solution architect – domain

Summary of the job description is as follows:

The solution architect will help in the selection of technologies solutions and will be the liaison between business teams and architecture teams. Solutions architects will analyze the current architecture and define the to-be solution architecture and roadmaps. Skilled in architecting, designing, and implementing configuration changes to applications to meet both business needs.

The competencies for this role are as follows:

- Develop a solution strategy for the group unit based on an articulation of various business scenarios and motivations
- Apply a structured approach and methodology for capturing the key views of the BU and LOBs in the context of enterprise
- Develop a long-term technology roadmap for the organization
- Develop integrated view of business units, using a repeatable approach, cohesive framework, and industry standard and techniques
- Propose changes in process, policy, and standards as they relate to the architecture and design principles
- Articulate, analyze, and suggest improvements to strategic, tactical and support processes of BU to support strategic and operational goals
- Research and recommend on software products for the group
- Design and evolution of the business process design within the overall architectural framework of enterprise

The responsibilities of this role are as follows:

- Capturing tactical and strategic goals that provide traceability and are mapped to metrics to provide governance
- Articulating business, technical requirements and driving the creation of architectural assets to achieve business goals
- Creating and managing RFP and vendor evaluation for transparent software product and service provider evaluation
- Developing enterprise solutions that integrate across applications and platforms together with enterprise architecture to define and manage group architecture and compliance
- Assisting in identifying, analyzing and mitigating to project and operational risks

The accountabilities for this role are as follows:

- Collaboration with enterprise, application and infrastructure teams to produce optimal, assets
- Collaborating with business analysts in requirement gathering and process reviews

Solution architect – SI

Summary of the job description is as follows:

The solution architect will help in the selection of technologies solutions and will be the liaison between business teams and architecture teams. Solutions architects will analyze the current architecture and define the to-be solution architecture and roadmaps. Skilled in architecting, designing, and implementing configuration changes to applications to meet both business needs.

The competencies for this role are as follows:

- 5+ years of experience as solution architect.
- Expertise in architecture, designing and development as an architect.
- Expertise in unified modeling language and object oriented analysis and design.
- Participation in all phases of software development life cycle, including analysis, design, coding and testing.
- Experience in implementing design patterns such as MVP, front controller, singleton, subject-observer, composite and dispatcher-view.
- Extensive hands-on experience with JBOSS application server.
- Experience in large system development background.
- Should have worked in R and D department. Exploring and experiments with new tools/technologies.
- Experience in solution designing and development.
- Experience leading large group meetings and workshops with senior executives.

The experience required for this role is as follows:

- Expertise in Spring and Hibernate is a must
- Expertise in Java, JDBC, JSPs, and various design patterns
- Strong leadership skills-leading, mentoring, and guiding technical teams
- Able to explain/direct the teams to follow guidelines and principles

- Support complex engagements by taking a central role in the journey and incorporating best practices and standards
- Ensure integrity and completeness of all software development from conceptualization to deployment and maintenance
- Participate in regular periodic technical reviews with team and assist in solutions
- Flexible for travel 50% of the year

The accountabilities for this role are as follows:

- Collaboration with enterprise, application and infrastructure teams to produce optimal, assets
- Collaborating with business analysts in requirement gathering and process reviews

Case studies

This section lists different enterprise architecture domain case studies.

Enterprise architecture

The next paragraphs describe the enterprise architecture domain case studies. Each case study explains the background in terms of the existing business setup, the business problem or requirements and the expected output/s

Case study one

An enterprise runs a portal for its retailers spread across the world. The portal uses BEA web logic portal, Siebel **Customer Relationship Management** (**CRM**), Oracle database, Informatica ETL, and Vignette content management. The enterprise wishes to upgrade all the products to the latest versions because:

- Vendors of all products will eventually stop supporting older versions
- The enterprise would like to use the latest features provided by the new versions of all/some products
- The enterprise would like to scrap custom code for features that have now been introduced as out-of-the-box features from these products

The client wants us to define a strategy for this upgrade initiative. Provide a high-level approach towards defining this upgrade strategy:

- Inputs that must be requested from the enterprise
- Stakeholders that we would like to meet to gather information
- How the information that was gathered would be analyzed
- High-level **table of contents** for our deliverable to the customer
- Leveraging offshore consultants in combination with on-site consultants
- Rough timelines, staff strength, and consultant profiles for this engagement

In addition to all this, please provide a high-level solution architecture depiction.

Case study two

The government of a small country wishes to provide its citizens with a portal using which all citizen interaction with the government can be possible. For example:

- Apply for / renew a passport, driving license, ration card, income tax registration, or birth/marriage/death certificate
- Check income tax balances and account statements
- File income tax

The previous list is just indicative; in all, there are 40 such agencies whose backend applications would be exposed to citizens in a secure manner. It is expected that the backend applications would be on diverse technology platforms and in different stages of maturity with different levels of automation.

Assume that this is only an enterprise architecture consulting engagement, where we need to include business, application, technology, integration, and information architecture for the government. Provide a high-level approach towards defining a strategy for this portal:

- Inputs that must be requested from the enterprise
- Stakeholders that we would like to meet to gather information
- How the information gathered would be analyzed
- High-level table of contents for our deliverable to the customer
- Leveraging offshore consultants in combination with on-site consultants
- Rough timelines, staff strength, and consultant profiles for this engagement

In addition to the previous, please provide a high-level solution architecture depiction.

Case study three

An organization has 800 sales people and 40 branch offices spread over the world. The organization has decided to create an application that would be used to connect all the sales people with the head office and their respective branches. This application should provide the following features:

- Placing of orders by sales people on behalf of distributors connected to them in their zone
- Tracking of orders by salespeople
- Viewing outstanding payment details of all their connected distributors
- Viewing of invoices for all sales in their zones
- Filing a monthly expense statement
- Filling requisitions for catalogs/samples and so on
- Filing a weekly activity report

The customer has contacted us to provide a solution architecture. There are backend applications which will be interfacing with this application.

We need to include business, application, technology, integration and information architecture for this application Provide a high-level approach for this application:

- Inputs that must be requested from the enterprise
- Stakeholders that we would like to meet to gather information
- How the information gathered would be analyzed
- High-level table of contents for our deliverable to the customer
- Leveraging offshore consultants in combination with on-site consultants
- Rough timelines, staff strength, and consultant profiles for this engagement

In addition to the previous, please provide a high-level solution architecture depiction.

Case study four

A large commercial bank has grown very rapidly over the last few years and aspires to maintain its CAGR over next three to five years. The bank wants to review its systems strategy to:

- Ensure that the IT is well positioned to support the future growth plans of the bank
- Enable business innovations using IT

- Ensure quality services to customers
- Reduce costs of operations

Assume that this is a single engagement covering applications, integration, information, technology, and infrastructure architecture. Provide a high-level approach to this engagement:

- Overall approach for the engagement
- Inputs that must be requested from the enterprise
- Stakeholders that we would like to meet to gather information
- How the information gathered would be analyzed and analysis dimensions for each architecture domain
- High-level table of contents for our deliverable to the customer
- Rough timelines, staff strength, and consultant profiles for this engagement

In addition to the previous, please draw a high-level IT landscape for the bank, for example, core banking, treasury applications, support functions like HR, finance, CRM, and so on.

Solution architecture

Background:

Various industries are under constant pressure to innovate, including the oil and gas sector. Geo-political and environmental factors, and rising prices and consumption have created a complex environment, where inflexible companies are punished by free market pricing and government sanctions, but nimble and flexible companies can reap monetary rewards.

Zamco is an oil and gas company headquartered in UK, with operations in Russia and the Middle-East. The company has entered into an agreement with a oil auctioning marketplace to sell its product efficiently, improving cash flow and reducing cost. The internal business case at Zamco projects cost savings of 20 percent over the next five years and improved margin and yield management of seven percent per annum over the current steady state of the business, making this one of the most important projects currently under development at the company.

Workshop output:

You are the architect for the marketplace integration project at Zamco and are tasked by Zamco top management with the design, implementation and management of a turnkey solution. After series discovery workshops with business analysts and SMEs, you know the following facts:

- The oil auctioning marketplace publishes Java API using Java Message Service to allow companies to send messages placing oil for sale and to bid for oil with characteristics, such as reliable messaging, acknowledgment, and security.
- Zamco already runs a complex pricing system that calculates the price for each placement of oil in the auction marketplace should be basis extraction and its distance and likely transportation method to its final destination point. As a solution architect, you need to integrate the system using web services to price oil before making it available to the auction marketplace for sale.
- The final remaining external system inventory management is also accessed using web services and will allow you to see what unsold capacity remains available for auction.
- Zamco has a relationship with merchant bank to handle transactions.
- The order placement is handled manually by a team of traders who track the rise and fall of oil prices and use a combination of timing and pricing information and other systems outside the scope of this project to determine the best time to buy or sell oil placements.
- System performance (99 percent of all messages to be constructed and sent in three seconds or less to the IP address of the API server), scalability (to 400 concurrent users), availability (99.999 percent during core working hours), and security (128-bit encryption at a minimum) are all key requirements and you must explicitly address each requirement in your proposed solution.

Summary

An architect is like a pilot. He does not look busy all the time, but he leveages years of expertise to monitor the situation and take immediate action in case of out-of-the-ordinary events. The project manager performs the management chores, freeing the architect from the hassles of operational tasks. The architect is responsible for the quality of the engagement and the delivery to business.

This will be difficult to achieve without authority and requisite skills, which is key to the success of any engagement. An excellent architect should be able to spot an issue in the landscape, get the team together, and, without picking victims, explain the issues and provide an elegant resolution. It is respectable for an architect to ask for help from his team. The team should feel they are part of the journey, but the architect should orchestrate these discussions and recommend the right road map.

Index

www.ingramcontent.com/pod-product-compliance
Lightning Source LLC
Chambersburg PA
CBHW060523090326
40690CB00068BA/4365